THE CHRYSOSTOM BIBLE
A Commentary Series for Preaching and Teaching
Ezekiel: A Commentary

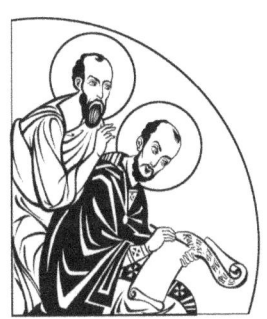

THE CHRYSOSTOM BIBLE
A Commentary Series for Preaching and Teaching

Ezekiel: A Commentary

Paul Nadim Tarazi

OCABS PRESS
ST PAUL, MINNESOTA 55124
2012

THE CHRYSOSTOM BIBLE
EZEKIEL: A COMMENTARY

Copyright © 2012 by
Paul Nadim Tarazi

ISBN 1-60191-017-7

All rights reserved.

PRINTED IN THE UNITED STATES OF AMERICA

Other Books by the Author

I Thessalonians: A Commentary

Galatians: A Commentary

The Old Testament: An Introduction
Volume 1: Historical Traditions, revised edition
Volume 2: Prophetic Traditions
Volume 3: Psalms and Wisdom

The New Testament: An Introduction
Volume 1: Paul and Mark
Volume 2: Luke and Acts
Volume 3: Johannine Writings
Volume 4: Matthew and the Canon

The Chrysostom Bible
Genesis: A Commentary
Philippians: A Commentary
Romans: A Commentary
Colossians & Philemon: A Commentary
1 Corinthians: A Commentary

Land and Covenant

The Chrysostom Bible
Ezekiel: A Commentary

Copyright © 2012 by Paul Nadim Tarazi
All rights reserved.

ISBN 1-60191-017-7

Published by OCABS Press, St. Paul, Minnesota.
Printed in the United States of America.

Books are available through OCABS Press at special discounts for bulk purchases in the United States by academic institutions, churches, and other organizations. For more information please email OCABS Press at press@ocabs.org.

Abbreviations

Books by the Author

1 Thess	*1 Thessalonians: A Commentary,* Crestwood, NY: St. Vladimir's Seminary Press, 1982
Gal	*Galatians: A Commentary,* Crestwood, NY: St. Vladimir's Seminary Press, 1994
OTI₁	*The Old Testament: An Introduction, Volume 1: Historical Traditions,* revised edition, Crestwood, NY: St. Vladimir's Seminary Press, 2003
OTI₂	*The Old Testament: An Introduction, Volume 2: Prophetic Traditions,* Crestwood, NY: St. Vladimir's Seminary Press, 1994
OTI₃	*The Old Testament: An Introduction, Volume 3: Psalms and Wisdom,* Crestwood, NY: St. Vladimir's Seminary Press, 1996
NTI₁	*The New Testament: An Introduction, Volume 1: Paul and Mark,* Crestwood, NY: St. Vladimir's Seminary Press, 1999
NTI₂	*The New Testament: An Introduction, Volume 2: Luke and Acts,* Crestwood, NY: St. Vladimir's Seminary Press, 2001
NTI₃	*The New Testament: An Introduction, Volume 3: Johannine Writings,* Crestwood, NY: St. Vladimir's Seminary Press, 2004
NTI₄	*The New Testament: An Introduction, Volume 4: Matthew and the Canon,* St. Paul, MN: OCABS Press, 2009
C-Gen	*Genesis: A Commentary.* The Chrysostom Bible. St. Paul, MN: OCABS Press, 2009
C-Phil	*Philippians: A Commentary.* The Chrysostom Bible. St. Paul, MN: OCABS Press, 2009
C-Rom	*Romans: A Commentary.* The Chrysostom Bible. St. Paul, MN: OCABS Press, 2010
C-Col	*Colossians & Philemon: A Commentary.* The Chrysostom Bible. St. Paul, MN: OCABS Press, 2010
C-1Cor	*1 Corinthians: A Commentary.* The Chrysostom Bible. St. Paul, MN: OCABS Press, 2011
LAC	*Land and Covenant,* St. Paul, MN: OCABS Press, 2009

Abbreviations

Books of the Old Testament*

Gen	Genesis	Job	Job	Hab		Habakkuk
Ex	Exodus	Ps	Psalms	Zeph		Zephaniah
Lev	Leviticus	Prov	Proverbs	Hag		Haggai
Num	Numbers	Eccl	Ecclesiastes	Zech		Zechariah
Deut	Deuteronomy	Song	Song of Solomon	Mal		Malachi
Josh	Joshua	Is	Isaiah	Tob		Tobit
Judg	Judges	Jer	Jeremiah	Jdt		Judith
Ruth	Ruth	Lam	Lamentations	Wis		Wisdom
1 Sam	1 Samuel	Ezek	Ezekiel	Sir	Sirach	(Ecclesiasticus)
2 Sam	2 Samuel	Dan	Daniel	Bar		Baruch
1 Kg	1 Kings	Hos	Hosea	1 Esd		1 Esdras
2 Kg	2 Kings	Joel	Joel	2 Esd		2 Esdras
1 Chr	1 Chronicles	Am	Amos	1 Macc		1 Maccabees
2 Chr	2 Chronicles	Ob	Obadiah	2 Macc		2 Maccabees
Ezra	Ezra	Jon	Jonah	3 Macc		3 Maccabees
Neh	Nehemiah	Mic	Micah	4 Macc		4 Maccabees
Esth	Esther	Nah	Nahum			

Books of the New Testament

Mt	Matthew	Eph	Ephesians	Heb	Hebrews
Mk	Mark	Phil	Philippians	Jas	James
Lk	Luke	Col	Colossians	1 Pet	1 Peter
Jn	John	1 Thess	1 Thessalonians	2 Pet	2 Peter
Acts	Acts	2 Thess	2 Thessalonians	1 Jn	1 John
Rom	Romans	1 Tim	1 Timothy	2 Jn	2 John
1 Cor	1 Corinthians	2 Tim	2 Timothy	3 Jn	3 John
2 Cor	2 Corinthians	Titus	Titus	Jude	Jude
Gal	Galatians	Philem	Philemon	Rev	Revelation

*Following the larger canon known as the Septuagint.

Contents

Preface	*17*
Introduction	*21*

Part I - Ezekiel's Call

1 Deconstructing the Statuesque Deity	27
2 The Commissioning of Ezekiel	45
3 God's Glory is Independent of the Temple	67

Part II - The Ezekelian Story

4 The Ezekelian Story	95
Excursus · The Divine Indictment · The Height of Arrogance	
5 Abominations Bring an End to Jerusalem	113
6 Reprise of the Ezekelian Story	119
7 God's Glory Abandons the Jerusalem Temple	135
The God of Ezekiel is the Sole Deity	
8 Witnessing the Abominations in Jerusalem	143
Ezekiel Leaves Jerusalem	
9 The False Prophets	163
10 Ezekiel's First Encounter with the Exiles	169
11 The Parabolic Stories	177
The Metaphor of the Vine · A Story of Harlotry · The Parable of the Eagles and the Vine	
12 Individual Accountability	217
13 Lamentation for the Princes of Israel	223
14 The Abominations of the Fathers while in Egypt	231
15 The Wrath of the Lord	259
16 The Parable of Oholah and Oholibah	267
17 A Review of the Story	277
18 Oracles against the Nations	283

Part III - The Restoration

19 The Offer for Repentance	293
20 God the Shepherd and his Flock	299
The Mountain of God	
21 God and Gog of Magog	311
22 The New Jerusalem	329
The Temple Building and Its Law · The Water of Life	
Further Reading	*349*

Preface

The present Bible Commentary Series is not so much in honor of John Chrysostom as it is to continue and promote his legacy as an interpreter of the biblical texts for preaching and teaching God's congregation, in order to prod its members to proceed on the way they started when they accepted God's calling. Chrysostom's virtual uniqueness is that he did not subscribe to any hermeneutic or methodology, since this would amount to introducing an extra-textual authority over the biblical texts. For him, scripture is its own interpreter. Listening to the texts time and again allowed him to realize that "call" and "read (aloud)" are not interconnected realities; rather, they are one reality since they both are renditions of the same Hebrew verb *qara'*. Given that words read aloud are words of instruction for one "to do them," the only valid reaction would be to hear, listen, obey, and abide by these words. All these connotations are subsumed in the same Hebrew verb *šama'*. On the other hand, these scriptural "words of life" are presented as readily understandable utterances of a father to his children (Isaiah 1:2-3). The recipients are never asked to engage in an intellectual debate with their divine instructor, or even among themselves, to fathom what he is saying. The Apostle to the Gentiles followed in the footsteps of the Prophets to Israel by handing down to them the Gospel, that is, the Law of God's Spirit through his Christ (Romans 8:2; Galatians 6:2) as fatherly instruction (1 Corinthians 4:15). He in turn wrote readily understandable letters to be read aloud. It is in these same footsteps that Chrysostom followed, having learned from both the Prophets and Paul that the same "words of life" carry also the sentence of death at the hand of the scriptural God, Judge of all

(Deuteronomy 28; Joshua 8:32-35; Psalm 82; Matthew 3:4-12; Romans 2:12-16; 1 Corinthians 10:1-11; Revelation 20:11-15).

While theological debates and hermeneutical theories come and go after having fed their proponents and their fans with passing human glory, the Golden Mouth's expository homilies, through the centuries, fed and still feed myriads of believers in so many traditions and countries. Virtually banned from dogmatic treatises, he survives in the hearts of "those who have ears to hear." His success is due to his commitment to exegesis rather than to futile hermeneutics. The latter behaves as someone who dictates on a living organism what it is supposed to be, whereas exegesis submits to that organism and endeavors to decipher it through trial and error. There is as much a far cry between the text and the theories about it as there is between a living organism and the theories about it. The biblical texts are the reality of God imparted through their being read aloud in the midst of the congregation, disregarding the value of the sermon that follows. The sermon, much less a theological treatise, is at best an invitation to hear and obey the text. Assessing the shape of an invitation card has no value whatsoever when it comes to the dinner itself; the guests are fed by the dinner, not by the invitation or its phrasing (Luke 14:16-24; Matthew 22:1-14).

This commentary series does not intend to promote Chrysostom's ideas as a public relation manager would do, but rather to follow in the footsteps of his approach as true children and heirs are expected to do. He used all the contemporary tools at his disposal to communicate God's written instruction to his hearers, as a doctor would with his patients, without spending unnecessary energy on peripheral debates requiring the use of professional jargon incomprehensible to the commoner. The writers of this series will try to do the same: muster to the best of their ability all necessary contemporary knowledge to communicate to the general readers the biblical message without burdening them with data unnecessary for that purpose. Whenever it will be deemed necessary or even helpful to do so, and in order to curtail burdensome and lengthy technical asides within the commentaries, specialized monographs related either to specific topics or to the scriptural background—literary, sociopolitical, or archeological—will be issued as companions to the series.

Paul Nadim Tarazi
Editor

Introduction

Among the Latter Prophets, it is only Ezekiel who is called to be God's prophet while in exile, and his mission is to prophesy to his exiled peers in Babylon. His translation to Jerusalem and his activity there as well as his parables concerning Jerusalem and Samaria in chapters 16 and 23 are aimed at bolstering his message to the exiles which, in turn, explains all the special characteristics of his message.

The most striking aspect of the prophet's message is that the exile has been willed by God not in view of exterminating the exiles, but rather as a teaching lesson. After all, the exiles survived the punishing siege during which their co-citizens perished by pestilence, sword, or fire. The exiles were thus spared rather than condemned. Put otherwise, they were punished unto instruction instead of destruction. As for the lesson, it is primarily that the scriptural God does not need a temple building as the other deities do. It is he who took the people out of Egypt, the land where they were enslaved to build cities and temples for Pharaoh. He intervened to save them and implant them in Canaan, the earth which their shepherd forefathers enjoyed, on the condition that they do his bidding. Instead, especially under Solomon and his successors, they treated Canaan as another Egypt where, this time round, they would be "masters" of their own destiny. Little did they realize that neither they nor the Pharaohs are "masters" of their fate. God alone is the Lord and master of all. Thus, it is God himself who calls upon the new "Egyptians," the Assyrians and the Babylonians, to punish Samaria and Jerusalem.

This new exile away from Canaan is not a mere repetition of the sojourn in Egypt as the leaders of the exiles thought (Ezek

20). In order to bring this point home, Ezekiel, alone among the Prophets, treats Babylon as God's beneficent client. Unlike Egypt who is treated very harshly, at no point is Babylon criticized for anything she has done, even when she destroys Jerusalem. If the long exile in Egypt was the result of a slip on the part of Jacob who, during a famine, sought bread from Egypt instead of from the Lord, Jerusalem decidedly sought the support of Egypt by appealing to it for help against the Babylonians (17:15), who were God's medium for his chastisement of the Jerusalemites. This explains the severity with which Egypt is handled in Ezekiel (chs.29-30).

Yet, the exiles should not mistake God's intermediary for God himself. They are to remember that their only King is the Lord himself who punished them at the Babylonians' hand (20:32-33). God is their King in Egypt, and in Canaan, and in Babylon as well. Actually, he is the only King and thus proprietor,[1] and any earth is his and his alone. That is why, in the new order of things which he will bring about, the Samaritan exiles will join those of Jerusalem (37:15-28), and even Egypt will be restored, though not to her former glory: "For thus says the Lord God: At the end of forty years I will gather the Egyptians from the peoples among whom they were scattered; and I will restore the fortunes of Egypt, and bring them back to the land of Pathros, the land of their origin." (29:13-14a) The combined "house of Israel" (37:15-22) will be restored into pasture land rather than a land filled with cities (chs.34 and 48), and Egypt will be restored into a "lowly kingdom" (29:14b-15). Consequently, God alone is to be praised among all the nations of the one earth he has created (Gen 1) and thus is his in its entirety (Ps 24:1-2). That is why the new "order" is not a setting that is "free for all"; rather it

---

[1] Which is the actual meaning of the Hebrew *melek* (king).

is an "order" where everyone one will have to follow God's "orders" (11:19-20; 18; 33; 36:26-27; 37:24). Only then will all who tread that path of unconditional obedience "*become* God's people and he their God" (11:20; 36:28; 37:23, 27).

Part I

Ezekiel's Call

1
Deconstructing the Statuesque Deity

In the thirtieth year, in the fourth month, on the fifth day of the month, as I was among the exiles by the river Chebar, the heavens were opened, and I saw visions of God. On the fifth day of the month (it was the fifth year of the exile of King Jehoiachin), the word of the Lord came to Ezekiel the priest, the son of Buzi, in the land of the Chaldeans by the river Chebar; and the hand of the Lord was upon him there. (Ezek 1:1-3)

The first chapter of Ezekiel is equaled in its majesty only by Genesis 1. It imposes on the hearer a new kind of God after having deconstructed the statuesque deity of the Greco-Roman and the Ancient Near East worlds in the first three verses. The entire socio-polity of those worlds was woven around the temple-palace complex of the capital or major city of a given society. The main representative of the city's deity was the monarch who, as the "son of the deity" (son of God, divine son; royal son; Ps 72:1), wielded absolute authority over the entire city and its two foci, the palace and the temple. He was de facto the high priest, as is clear from the fact that King Solomon was the one who, at the inauguration of the temple, both blessed the people (1 Kg 8:1) and prayed on and in behalf of them (vv.30-61) as well as for himself (vv.22-29). Since the administration of the palace and public life took most of his time, a monarch would appoint at will one of the priests as high priest (1 Kg 2:35b), who would be his locum tenens in the temple service. That is why whenever a city was overtaken, the conqueror would "decapitate" it by taking away its leadership consisting mainly of the residents and servers of the temple-palace complex, often leaving the general populace in place:

> And Nebuchadnezzar king of Babylon came to the city, while his servants were besieging it; and Jehoiachin the king of Judah gave himself up to the king of Babylon, himself, and his mother, and his servants, and his princes, and his palace officials. The king of Babylon took him prisoner in the eighth year of his reign, and carried off all the treasures of the house of the Lord, and the treasures of the king's house, and cut in pieces all the vessels of gold in the temple of the Lord, which Solomon king of Israel had made, as the Lord had foretold. He carried away all Jerusalem, and all the princes, and all the mighty men of valor, ten thousand captives, and all the craftsmen and the smiths; none remained, except the poorest people of the land. And he carried away Jehoiachin to Babylon; the king's mother, the king's wives, his officials, and the chief men of the land, he took into captivity from Jerusalem to Babylon. And the king of Babylon brought captive to Babylon all the men of valor, seven thousand, and the craftsmen and the smiths, one thousand, all of them strong and fit for war. And the king of Babylon made Mattaniah, Jehoiachin's uncle, king in his stead, and changed his name to Zedekiah. (2 Kg 24:11-17)

This is precisely the situation referred to in Ezekiel 1:1-3. Both "King" Jehoiachin (v.2) and Ezekiel "the priest" (v.3) were among "the exiles by the river Chebar" (v.1), which is in "the land of the Chaldeans" (v.3).

One can sense the irony used to allude to the temple of Jerusalem and its services when looking more closely at these verses. Calendar dating was essentially a priestly function which allowed the temple servers to keep the "seasons, the days, and the years" (Gen 1:14), especially the feast days that were sociopolitical as well as religious festivities. Yet, in the first three verses of Ezekiel dating is used twice to refer to the exile priest and king (Ezek 1:1 and 2) and thus to the demise of the Jerusalem palace-temple complex, bidding the hearers to realize that this would be the last time dating would be functional in Jerusalem. Henceforth, all dating would remind the Judahites, not of their feasts and celebrations, but of their exile in a foreign land.[1] This belittling of the Judahites will be an opportunity for the exaltation of the Lord over and beyond their imaginations and those of their new lords. The wordplay reflected in these few verses is masterful and its versatility is unmatched in scripture. Unlike any other prophetic book, the first reference to the deity is "God" (*'elohim*) instead of "the Lord" (*yahweh*);[2] *'elohim* is the plural of *'el,* the Zeus-Jupiter figure of the Semite pantheon. Thus, the word *of the Lord* (1:3) to Ezekiel will reveal that the Lord is actually the universal God of all nations[3] as well as the father and judge of all the deities. This is iterated in Psalm 82 where it is God (*'elohim*) who holds judgment in the divine council (v.1) and before whom even the deities function as mere humans: "I say, 'You are gods, sons of the Most High, all of you; nevertheless, you shall die like men, and fall like any prince.'" (vv.6-7) The psalmist ends by proclaiming God's universality: "Arise, O God (*'elohim*), judge the earth; for to thee belong all the nations!" (v.8). The intentional primary reference to Ezekiel's deity as "God" is further evident in the unique handling of the introduction of the prophet himself. Usually, the prophet is first introduced by name and then one starts hearing the prophetic "I." In Ezekiel, however, one immediately encounters the

---

[1] 8:1; 20:1; 24:1; 33:21; 40:1.
[2] Habakkuk 1:1 is no exception since "of God" after "The oracle" in RSV is an addition and is not found in the original.
[3] E.g., Ps 9:19-20; 22:27-28; 46:10; 47:8; 67:4.

enigmatic personal pronoun "I" and no less than twice,[4] which leaves the hearer wondering who is speaking. We do not find the classic "the word of the Lord came to Ezekiel" until verse 3. Even the name of King Jehoiachin is introduced parenthetically in verse 2, whereas the mention of the names of kings in other prophetic books is done right at the beginning in order to "date" an event.[5] The intended impression is evident: the opening of the book points exclusively to "God" who is "in the heavens." Anything and anyone else cannot even compare with such God, as will become clear in the rest of the chapter which is a detailed "description" merely of his "likeness" (v.28). At the introduction of the prophet by name (v.3), we hear the absolute dominance of God reflected in the name Ezekiel (*yeḥezqe'l*). A theophoric name linked to *'el* instead of *yahweh* is unique in the Prophets.[6] Thus Ezekiel's commissioning deity is not so much *yahweh*, the local deity of Jerusalem, as it is *'el* who resides "in the heavens" (v.1) and not in the Jerusalem temple.

The phrasing of verse 3 is, in a nutshell, the blue print of the entire book. To be sure, it is "the word of the Lord (*yahweh*)" that comes to Ezekiel, a temple priest, however, the time and the place of such communication underscore that his priesthood is non-functional, and thus the addition of "the priest" is clearly a taunt. Indeed, until chapter 40, where implementation of God's

---

[4] In the original Hebrew the second instance of the pronoun "I" before "saw" is not to be found since it is subsumed in the ending of the verbal form. However, the first instance (I [was]) appears in the original as the first person pronoun *'ani*.

[5] Is 1:1; Jer 1:2, 3; Hos 1:1; Am 1:1; Mic 1:1; Zeph 1:1; Hag 1:1; Zech 1:1. In those times, the official dating was linked to the monarch's reign period.

[6] The other prophetic names end with the suffix *yahu* which is a shortened form of *yahweh*: e.g. *yeša'yahu* (Isaiah) and *yirmeyahu* (Jeremiah). Joel is only an apparent exception since that name means "*yahweh* is *'el*," that is "the Lord is indeed God [divine]." As for Daniel, in the Hebrew canon that book is found in the third part of the Old Testament, the Writings or *ketubim*.

good order takes place, we encounter the noun "priest" only twice and both times with negative connotations. It is actually because "her [Jerusalem's] priests have done violence to my law and have profaned my holy things; they have made no distinction between the holy and the common, neither have they taught the difference between the unclean and the clean, and they have disregarded my sabbaths, so that I am profaned among them" (22:26) that God decrees: "Disaster comes upon disaster, rumor follows rumor; they seek a vision the prophet, but the law perishes from the priest, and counsel from the elders." (7:26) The non-functionality of Ezekiel's priesthood is further underscored in the name Buzi, who is identified as Ezekiel's father. The Hebrew *buzi* means "my shame, my contempt," which is the way Ezekiel often refers to God's punishment of his people, that is, by putting them to shame.[7] Actually, the original is more forceful than the usual translations which append "priest" to Ezekiel: "Ezekiel the priest, the son of Buzi." The Hebrew, however, reads "Ezekiel the son of Buzi, the priest," making of the apposition "priest" a title for either Buzi or Ezekiel; in other words, when hearing the Hebrew, one gets the impression that the name of the priest is "my shame, my contempt," and Ezekiel would be his "son." When one considers than the Semitic expression "son of" means "someone pertaining to, bound to," then the hearer of the Hebrew concludes that Ezekiel is essentially bound to the Babylonian plundering and exile and thus, de facto, he is not "son of Jerusalem and Judah,"

---

[7] The other possibility is to consider the root as *baz* meaning "spoil, plundering," which again fits the exile setting of vv.1-2. This is the noun found in Is 8:3 in reference to the Assyrian plundering: "And I went to the prophetess, and she conceived and bore a son. Then the Lord said to me, 'Call his name Mahershalalhashbaz (*maher šalal ḥaš baz*); for before the child knows how to cry 'My father' or 'My mother,' the wealth of Damascus and the spoil of Samaria will be carried away before the king of Assyria." (Is 8:3-4)

but rather is "son of the land of the Chaldeans, by the river Chebar" (v.3), the prototype of all exiles, including the king, as will be fleshed out later in the book (12:1-20).

Another aspect of Ezekiel's name is that it means "God will be (grow) strong and firm," that is to say, "God will be (grow) stronger" than anyone or anything else, "God will prevail" over anyone or anything else, "God will be greater"[8] than anyone or anything else. Such statement becomes eloquent to the hearer's ear when one remembers that Chebar in Hebrew has the connotation of "great," and thus "powerful" and "majestic." Consequently, the God who is about to intervene through his prophet in order to subdue the arrogance of Jerusalem and Judah will in turn subdue the power of Babylon in order to show his people that neither the Egypt of the majestic Nile nor the Babylon of the grandiose Euphrates can do anything against his will to bring his people out of Egypt or Babylon in order to enact his judgment against them (20:32-39). The exiles are not to dream that they could hide from God in "the wilderness of the peoples" (v.35). Indeed, their fathers tried and failed to do the same in "the wilderness of the land of Egypt" (v.36). This is confirmed in that the verb *ḥazaq* (prevail) assumes power and, in most languages including Hebrew, is metaphorically expressed as "hand" or "arm," as one would say "the city fell into the hand of the attackers." The hand that will perform God's will in vv.33 and 34 is identified from the beginning: "...the hand of the Lord was upon him *there* (in the land of the Chaldeans by the river Chebar)." (1:3)

The God who appears to Ezekiel is not to be simply equated, functionally, with *yahweh*, the local deity of the city Jerusalem,

---

[8] As one hears in the Muslim's confession *'allahu 'akbar*.

whose priest Ezekiel used to be. Neither is that same God to be viewed in terms of the Babylonian deity Bel whose "universality" is co-extensive with the Babylonian empire. Put otherwise, the God of Ezekiel is not a deity of a city-state and its surrounding area, nor is he an inflated imperial deity whose hegemony extends over an extensive area comprising many cities and their lands. The destiny of such deity would be dependent on the fate of its empire and eventually would find its end. Indeed, when Cyrus the Medo-Persian overtakes Babylon, Bel's demise is described in these terms:

> Bel bows down, Nebo stoops, their idols are on beasts and cattle; these things you carry are loaded as burdens on weary beasts. They stoop, they bow down together, they cannot save the burden, but themselves go into captivity. (Is 46:1-2)

> The word which the Lord spoke concerning Babylon, concerning the land of the Chaldeans, by Jeremiah the prophet: "Declare among the nations and proclaim, set up a banner and proclaim, conceal it not, and say: 'Babylon is taken, Bel is put to shame, Merodach is dismayed. Her images are put to shame, her idols are dismayed.' For out of the north a nation has come up against her, which shall make her land a desolation, and none shall dwell in it; both man and beast shall flee away." (Jer 50:1-3)

> How Babylon is taken, the praise of the whole earth seized! How Babylon has become a horror among the nations! The sea has come up on Babylon; she is covered with its tumultuous waves. Her cities have become a horror, a land of drought and a desert, a land in which no one dwells, and through which no son of man passes. And I will punish Bel in Babylon, and take out of his mouth what he has swallowed. The nations shall no longer flow to him; the wall of Babylon has fallen. (Jer 51:41-44)

In other words, an imperial deity is ultimately of the same "fabric" as a local one, albeit on a larger scale. In contradistinction with both, the God who appears to Ezekiel by the river Chebar is of a totally different fabric. This is clear from the unusual terminology in chapter 1, which is replete with approximations when describing that God: "as it were" (vv.4, 16, 26, 27), "likeness" (vv.5, 10, 16, 22, 26 [thrice], 28), "appearance" (5, 16 [twice], 26, 27 [four times], 28 [thrice]), "form" (vv.5, 26), "like" (vv.7 [twice], 13 [twice], 16, 22, 24 [twice], 26, 27, 28). The "vision" of Ezekiel cannot be translated into a positive painting that one could put on canvas. Ezekiel's God could not have had a statue representing him, which in turn would have required a stone temple. Yet, as we shall soon hear, that same God appeared to Ezekiel at the distant Chebar River *because* he relinquished his Jerusalem temple never to return to it. Rather than being defined by a location, God's new city will be defined by him: "And the name of the city henceforth shall be, 'The Lord is there.'" (48:35b) The "there" of that God is "the likeness of a throne, above the firmament" whence proceeds his "voice." [9]

The first item on God's agenda is destruction, namely, the destruction of his own city Jerusalem and its temple, which he is about to abandon, leaving the entire city at the mercy of the Babylonians. This is evident in that Ezekiel's first sighting is "a stormy wind (*ruaḥ*; spirit) coming out of the north" (1:4). Before proceeding, especially in view of the fact that the *ruaḥ* plays a pivotal role throughout the book, it behooves us to digress in order to understand the meaning of that noun, which is tainted in the minds of an overwhelming majority of Christians with the

---

[9] The seer John will later write that all he—and by surmise Ezekiel—"saw" was "a voice that was speaking to him" (Rev 1:12).

connotation of a divine ethereal presence. Classical English renders this as "ghost." A further complication is created by the translations. In RSV, for instance, the majority of its hearers or readers will encounter at different points "wind," "spirit," or "Spirit" when, in all three cases, the original is the same *ruaḥ*. Notice that RSV differentiates even between "spirit" and "Spirit." Those hearers not cognizant of Hebrew are actually misled by the philosophical, religious and even theological presuppositions of translators who impose the meaning of *ruaḥ* according to their own preconceptions. The result is that the common hearers or readers are not hearing Ezekiel but a caricature of him. Thus, the original is voided of its potentially compelling wordplay whereby *ruaḥ* is essentially the destructive face of the judging God which ultimately turns, by sheer grace, into a breeze that fills the human nostrils with life-giving breath (Ezek 37) as in Genesis 2:7. Ezekiel's approach is a far cry from the classic theological one whereby the "spirit" is *by definition* a goodly element. Such assumes that the scriptural God of Psalm 82, who judges even the deities as though they were mere humans, can be enslaved within the confines of philosophical preconceptions. At any rate, in this opening statement of Ezekiel 1:4, the *ruaḥ* is unmistakably threatening since the appositional noun *se'arah* that follows it means "gale, (wind)storm" and later qualifies it twice in the following context:

> Because, yea, because they have misled my people, saying, 'Peace,' when there is no peace; and because, when the people build a wall, these prophets daub it with whitewash; say to those who daub it with whitewash that it shall fall! There will be a deluge of rain, great hailstones will fall, and a stormy wind (*ruaḥ se'arot*)[10] break out; and when the wall falls, will it not be said to you, 'Where is

---

[10] *se'arot* is the plural of *se'arah*.

the daubing with which you daubed it?' Therefore thus says the Lord God: I will make a stormy wind (*ruaḥ se'arot*) break out in my wrath; and there shall be a deluge of rain in my anger, and great hailstones in wrath to destroy it. (Ezek 13:10-13)

The destructive function of that *ruaḥ* will be evident in the following chapters.

Besides its power, the wind has another formidable feature: speed. From the human perspective, it can move almost instantly from one place to another; put otherwise, it can suddenly appear whenever and wherever, totally unexpected, giving the impression that it is ubiquitous. Again, this is not to be confused with classic philosophical theology's divine ubiquity meaning that God *is* everywhere. Scripture never speaks of God *being* everywhere; rather it repeatedly tells us that God *comes*—and thus makes himself present[11]—in a sudden manner wherever he chooses and especially where he is unexpected. In this he is different than the other deities who have statues that need to be carried around in a cortège,[12] which takes time. Ezekiel projects into the mind of the hearers a God whose throne is not stationary in a temple made by the hand of man, but rather his throne is carried around by the *ruaḥ* and thus "mobile" and at the will of the one seated on it. This is an essential feature of the scriptural God that will become clear when we hear that he, through Ezekiel, will destroy the temple built for him in Jerusalem, thus reminding that city's residents that, unlike them, God is in no need of an abode of stone or otherwise (Is 66:1). This is precisely what the first chapter of Ezekiel is all about. The proof is that Ezekiel relates his description of God's appearance

---

[11] Whence the Greek *parousia* from the verb *pareimi* (be [become] present).
[12] Later Ezekiel will make fun of that aspect of the other deities, just as Isaiah does.

to him throughout the chapter as a mere "likeness" and thus, as we shall see, something impossible to fathom. Indeed, how could a chariot go in the four cardinal directions at the same time (1:17)?

In order to "construct" in the minds of his hearers the new deity that comes out of the scroll he will be made to ingest, Ezekiel has first to "deconstruct"—make irrelevant—the setting as well as the shape of the deities surrounding the hearers and thus, de facto, make them "non-existent" *as deities*, that is to say, *non-functional* when compared to the scriptural God.[13] Ezekiel's God is cast as a deity of thunder and lightning, and thus also of the rain that is essential for vegetation and animal life. Unlike the other such deities who are represented by statues of bronze or other lasting sturdy material, the presence of Ezekiel's God is only "as it were" gleaming bronze (v.4). In other words, by using common terminology linked to the deities of his time, yet at the same time distancing himself from that terminology through the device of approximation, Ezekiel was asserting in the mind of his hearers that his God is indeed a God, yet unlike the other gods that are in need of a statue and a temple.

Ezekiel pushes the imagery even further, just as Psalm 82 does, in order to underscore that his God is "above" the other deities. The closeness between Ezekiel 1 and Psalm 82 is reflected in the comparison of God to other deities who are on the level of human beings: "And this was their appearance: they had the

---

[13] Paul would write in the same vein: "Formerly, when you did not know God, you were in bondage to beings that by nature are no Gods" (Gal 4:8); "Hence, as to the eating of food offered to idols, we know that 'an idol has no real existence,' and that 'there is no God but one.' For although there may be so-called Gods in heaven or on earth—as indeed there are many 'Gods' and many 'Lords'—yet for us there is one God, the Father, from whom are all things and for whom we exist, and one Lord, Jesus Christ, through whom are all things and through whom we exist." (1 Cor 8:4-6)

form of men" (Ezek 1:5b); "I say, 'You are gods, sons of the Most High, all of you; nevertheless, you shall die like men, and fall like any prince.'" (Ps 82:6-7) This subservience of the other deities to the Ezekelian God is underscored in that they are tetra-faceted and three of their facets, besides the human one, are taken from the animal realm (Ezek 1:10), which reflects the usual pantheon deities that were associated with animals, if not outright representations of such. This is confirmed by the mention of wings, which links these creatures to the cherubim of Ezekiel (10:5, 8, 16, 19, 20, 21; 11:22) and the seraphim of Isaiah (6:2) who function as mere servants of the Lord; the thunder associated with God is produced by the movement of their wings (Ezek 1:24). Moreover, these creatures are just supporting the divine chariot in which the Ezekelian God rode (Ezek 1:15; see also Ezek 10).

More impressive than a God who has no representation is that he has no voice, at least in the way humans and the other human-like deities emit a voice through vocal chords. The "voice" of the Ezekelian God—and he does have a voice since his main activity in scripture is speaking—is communicated through his servants, the four living creatures, just as later it will resound through the mouth of Ezekiel: "And when they went, I heard the sound (*qol*) of their wings like the sound of many waters, like the thunder of the Almighty, a sound of tumult like the sound of a host; when they stood still, they let down their wings. And there came a voice (*qol*) from above the firmament over their heads; when they stood still, they let down their wings." (1:24-25) As for God himself, he is said twice to be "above the firmament" (vv.25 and 26). Since the firmament separates the divine realm from the human one (vv.22-23; see also Gen 1:7-8), in comparison with God, the four living creatures are not of the divine realm and thus, functionally, are of the human realm.

Like the wheels of the Ezekelian God's chariot (Ezek 1:14-19), they merely carry him around at the bidding of the divine *ruaḥ* (vv.20-21).

The phraseology in Ezekiel 1 is not to be understood against the non-tangible philosophical and mystical backgrounds that plague historical Christian and Jewish theologies. Rather it is to be understood against the background of Ancient Mediterranean and Middle-Eastern religions that revolved around physical temples and statues of deities. This is important because the original meaning of the "glory of God," introduced in verse 28, is often misconstrued. It has been tainted by Platonic philosophy and Plotinic religious philosophy channeled through Alexandrian Christian as well as Jewish thoughts. The Hebrew *kabod* and its LXX equivalent the Greek *doxa* reflect a tangible reality and not a divine or mysterious attribute. The choice of the Greek *doxa* in the LXX is more intentional than fortuitous since it has the connotation of "brightness, radiance, splendor" and, consequently, "fame, renown, honor, prestige"; in both instances, it applies to the "value" of a senior when compared to a junior.[14]

The Hebrew *kabod* means "heaviness, weightiness" and refers to the impressive stature of a deity's statue; the larger and thus heavier the statue, the more valued and important the deity in the eyes of its followers. This being the case, one can understand

---

[14] An interesting text that sheds light on this matter is found in 1 Thessalonians where Paul writes: "For we never used either words of flattery, as you know, or a cloak for greed, as God is witness; nor did we seek glory (*doxan*) from men, whether from you or from others, though we might have *made demands* (*en barei einai*; been with weight; exercised heaviness [weightiness]) as apostles of Christ. But we were gentle (*nēpioi*; childlike and thus acting as your "juniors") among you, like a nurse taking care of her children." (2:5-7) Notice how "glory" (*doxan*) and "being with weight" (*en barei einai*) function as the two sides of the same coin in this context.

how the heavy statue of a deity would be burdensome on those who had to carry it around during socio-religious processions or military campaigns since it could not move around on its own:

> Bel bows down, Nebo stoops, their idols are on beasts and cattle; these things you carry are loaded as burdens on weary beasts. They stoop, they bow down together, they cannot save the burden, but themselves go into captivity ... Those who lavish gold from the purse, and weigh out silver in the scales, hire a goldsmith, and he makes it into a God; then they fall down and worship! They lift it upon their shoulders, they carry it, they set it in its place, and it stands there; it cannot move from its place. If one cries to it, it does not answer or save him from his trouble. (Is 46:1-2, 6-7)

In contradistinction with the statues of the idols, the Ezekelian God's "heaviness" (*kabod*) is paradoxically light as a cloud and thus moves on its own without the help of anyone or anything:

> As I looked, behold, a stormy wind came out of the north, and a great cloud, with brightness round about it, and fire flashing forth continually, and in the midst of the fire, as it were gleaming bronze ... Like the appearance of the bow that is in the cloud on the day of rain, so was the appearance of the brightness round about. Such was the appearance of the likeness of the glory of the Lord. (Ezek 1:4, 28)

> Then the Spirit lifted me up, and as the glory of the Lord arose from its place, I heard behind me the sound of a great earthquake (3:12)

> Now the cherubim were standing on the south side of the house, when the man went in; and a cloud filled the inner court. And the glory of the Lord went up from the cherubim to the threshold of the house; and the house was filled with the cloud, and the court was full of the brightness of the glory of the Lord. (10:3-4)

> Now the glory of the God of Israel had gone up from the cherubim on which it rested to the threshold of the house; and he called to the man clothed in linen, who had the writing case at his side. (9:3; see also 10:18)

> And the glory of the Lord went up from the midst of the city, and stood upon the mountain which is on the east side of the city. (11:23)

As pointed out earlier, this explains the repeated phraseology of approximation when describing God and his throne, especially in the concluding verses of chapter 1:

> And above the firmament over their heads there was the *likeness* of a throne, in *appearance* like sapphire; and seated above the *likeness* of a throne was a *likeness as it were* of a human form. And upward from what had the *appearance* of his loins I saw *as it were* gleaming bronze, like the *appearance* of fire enclosed round about; and downward from what had the *appearance* of his loins I saw *as it were* the *appearance* of fire, and there was brightness round about him. Like the *appearance* of the bow that is in the cloud on the day of rain, so was the *appearance* of the brightness round about. Such was the *appearance* of the *likeness* of the glory of the Lord. And when I saw it, I fell upon my face, and I heard the voice of one speaking. (1:26-28)

These verses not only seal the detailed aural "description" of the Ezekelian God, but also introduce the message of the entire book. The use of throne, human form, and loins impresses on the hearers that there is indeed a divine "presence." The (burning) fire that was introduced in verse 4, and referred to in verse 13, reappears again in verse 27, however this time in conjunction with the (beneficent) rainbow (v.28). Given that the divine message entrusted to Ezekiel is essentially one of utter condemnation (2:10), the author intentionally chose to link the brightness connected with God to fire (v.27), which underscores the aspect of judgment inherent in fire that burns, rather than to beneficent instruction linked to the light of teaching. Listen to Isaiah:

> It shall come to pass in the latter days that the mountain of the house of the Lord shall be established as the highest of the mountains, and shall be raised above the hills; and all the nations shall flow to it, and many peoples shall come, and say: "Come, let us go up to the mountain of the Lord, to the house of the God of Jacob; that he may teach us his ways and that we may walk in his paths." For out of Zion shall go forth the law, and the word of the Lord from Jerusalem. He shall judge between the nations, and shall decide for many peoples; and they shall beat their swords into plowshares, and their spears into pruning hooks; nation shall not lift up sword against nation, neither shall they learn war any more. O house of Jacob, come, let us walk in the light of the Lord. For thou hast rejected thy people, the house of Jacob, because they are full of diviners from the east and of soothsayers like the Philistines, and they strike hands with foreigners. Their land is filled with silver and gold, and there is no end to their treasures; their land is filled with horses, and there is no end to their chariots. Their land is filled with idols; they bow down to the work of their hands, to what their own fingers have made. So man is humbled, and men are brought low—forgive them not! Enter into the rock, and hide in the dust from before the terror of the Lord, and from the glory of his majesty. (Is 2:2-10)

The light of the Lord's law, intended to "teach us his ways and that we may walk in his paths," can turn into a destructive fire of punishment should we not abide by the divine instruction:

> Why will you still be smitten, that you continue to rebel? The whole head is sick, and the whole heart faint. From the sole of the foot even to the head, there is no soundness in it, but bruises and

sores and bleeding wounds; they are not pressed out, or bound up, or softened with oil. Your country lies desolate, your cities are burned with fire; in your very presence aliens devour your land; it is desolate, as overthrown by aliens. (Is 1:5-7)

Just as earlier in Ezekiel 1:4, again we hear in 1:26-28 of a cloud in conjunction with fire and the divine brightness. The importance of that triad is betrayed in that its two occurrences bracket the chapter as an *inclusio*. However, the cloud in verse 28 is associated with "the bow ... on the day of rain." Like the fire, the bow works in two different ways, however, the sequence in each case is oppositional to the other. Fire basically lights up an area, but should one not pay attention, its effect could be calamitous. The bow is essentially an aggressive weapon and only secondarily refers to the rainbow, a sign of hope for better days. Thus, the bow picks up on the meaning of destruction associated with fire in that it recalls the siege launched by God against his city Jerusalem (4:1-3).[15] Yet, through its association with the cloud and the day of rain, it recalls the rainbow as a harbinger of God's mercy after his devastating punishment with the flood:

> And God said, "This is the sign of the covenant which I make between me and you and every living creature that is with you, for all future generations: I set my bow in the cloud, and it shall be a sign of the covenant between me and the earth. When I bring clouds over the earth and the bow is seen in the clouds, I will remember my covenant which is between me and you and every living creature of all flesh; and the waters shall never again become a flood to destroy all flesh. When the bow is in the clouds, I will look upon it and remember the everlasting covenant between God

---

[15] See, e.g., where God is depicted as a warrior with a bow: "If a man does not repent, God will whet his sword; he has bent and strung his bow" (Ps 7:12); "He [viz. the Lord] makes wars cease to the end of the earth; he breaks the bow, and shatters the spear, he burns the chariots with fire!" (Ps 46. 9)

and every living creature of all flesh that is upon the earth." (Gen 9:12-16)

Consequently, the bow, mentioned at the end of the introductory chapter that presages Ezekiel's entire message, functions as the seed of hope for better days *after and beyond* the impending divine punishment through siege and war. That hope will be realized at the time of restoration (chs. 33-40) when God will make an everlasting covenant of peace (34:25; 37:26) and will be shepherding his new people, Gentiles as well as Judahites and Ephraimites, as his own flock (Ezek 34; 37), under the aegis of this new covenant. With the entire scenario of the book having been set, Ezekiel is now ready to listen to the divine voice: "And when I saw it, I fell upon my face, and I heard the voice of one speaking." (1:28b)

2
The Commissioning of Ezekiel

The divine word is communicated to Ezekiel in conjunction with divine spirit, thus fully bestowing on Ezekiel divine authority; indeed, the word that orders the prophet to stand up from his prostration (2:1) enables him to do so by the spirit (v.2). A classic mistake in traditional Christian theology, which is rooted in misguided mysticism, is to believe that what happened to Ezekiel could happen to any of us, or that we are potentially entitled to the same experience of Ezekiel. Nothing is farther from the truth of the matter. In each of the prophetic books God has only one representative who stands alone against all others. Indeed, it is only Ezekiel who is on God's side not only against the rebellious people (2:3-8; 3:4-9), but also against the equally rebellious "elders" (9:4-6; 14:1-3; 20:1-3) and even prophets (13:1-16) and prophetesses (vv.17-23). Ezekiel alone has God's spirit:

> The word of the Lord came to me: "Son of man, prophesy against the prophets of Israel, prophesy and say to those who prophesy out of their own minds: 'Hear the word of the Lord!' Thus says the Lord God, Woe to the foolish prophets who follow their own spirit, and have seen nothing! ... They have spoken falsehood and divined a lie; they say, 'Says the Lord,' when the Lord has not sent them, and yet they expect him to fulfill their word. Have you not seen a delusive vision, and uttered a lying divination, whenever you have said, 'Says the Lord,' although I have not spoken?" (13:1-3, 6-7)

Furthermore, Ezekiel alone has the power to dispense that spirit through his word—just as God himself does—as is clearly the case in chapter 37:

> The hand of the Lord was upon me, and he brought me out by the Spirit of the Lord, and set me down in the midst of the valley; it was full of bones. And he led me round among them; and behold, there were very many upon the valley; and lo, they were very dry. And he said to me, "Son of man, can these bones live?" And I answered, "O Lord God, thou knowest." Again he said to me, "Prophesy to these bones, and say to them, O dry bones, hear the word of the Lord. Thus says the Lord God to these bones: Behold, I will cause breath to enter you, and you shall live. And I will lay sinews upon you, and will cause flesh to come upon you, and cover you with skin, and put breath in you, and you shall live; and you shall know that I am the Lord." So I prophesied as I was commanded; and as I prophesied, there was a noise, and behold, a rattling; and the bones came together, bone to its bone. And as I looked, there were sinews on them, and flesh had come upon them, and skin had covered them; but there was no breath in them. Then he said to me, "Prophesy to the breath, prophesy, son of man, and say to the breath, Thus says the Lord God: Come from the four winds, O breath, and breathe upon these slain, that they may live." So I prophesied as he commanded me, and the breath came into them, and they lived, and stood upon their feet, an exceedingly great host. (vv. 1-10)

Without the word proffered through Ezekiel's mouth the very dry bones would not have been filled with God's spirit that granted them flesh as well as breath. So, when it comes to God's intervention in his created realm, it is always his word of command that initiates the movement of the spirit, the mighty wind of 1:4, whether unto destruction (5:2; 12:14; 13:11, 13; 17:10, 21; 19:12) or unto revival as in chapter 37. This priority even applies to the relation between God and Ezekiel: the mention of the word (1:3) precedes that of the spirit (v.4), and it is when God speaks (2:1) that his spirit enters Ezekiel (v.2). Notice further the high incidence—no less than seven times—of the verbs "say" and "speak" in 2:1-4.[1] The divine plan is initiated by God's word to Ezekiel (1:3) and ends with the revival of the dry bones without making any of the raised persons new prophets *à la* Ezekiel, who remains God's sole prophet in this book. Much less do the rest of us, hearers of the text, have direct access to God's life-giving spirit except through his word handed to Ezekiel as a scroll fully written on both sides, that is to say, to which nothing could possibly be added (2:9-10). Only Ezekiel is summoned by the divine word to dispense it and, through it, dispense the divine spirit. His hearers *throughout the ages* remain mere recipients of the words unto life that would save them from the death received as punishment for not having hearkened to that same word. However, they are never granted such life, which is an act of sheer divine mercy, in order to become like Ezekiel, initiators of a new scripture. In the Book of Ezekiel it is only Ezekiel who is raised to speak the already written word (2:1-3:1). All others who receive, hearken to, and ultimately obey that word become the people of the Ezekelian God, and he their God (11:19-20). However, such turn of the heart and return to God, as betrayed by the high incidence of the phrase "my people" which has a positive connotation on God's lips, will not take place until the end of the Ezekelian story in chapters 34-39.[2] For the time being, at the outset of that same story, "the house of Israel" to whom Ezekiel is sent (3:1) is "a rebellious house" (2:5,

---

[1] The choice of seven times may actually be intended by the author since the numeral seven reflects the fullness of the divine when it comes to God's dealings with the created realm.

[2] 34:30; 36:8, 12, 28; 37:12, 13, 23, 27; 38:14, 16; 39:7.

6, 7, 8: see also v.3), "impudent and stubborn" (v.4), "of a hard forehead and of a stubborn heart" (3:7).

Why the hyperbolic metaphor of a written scroll (2:9-10) to be eaten by Ezekiel (3:1-3) rather than God putting his spoken words in his mouth, as he did with Jeremiah (Jer 1:9)?[3] Both Jeremiah and Ezekiel deal with the divine punishment of Jerusalem and its aftermath; however, Jeremiah speaks from within the still standing Jerusalem, whereas Ezekiel, already in exile, speaks to the exiles after its fall. In other words, the destruction of that city which is foretold in Jeremiah is assumed in Ezekiel. In Jeremiah, there is always hope for a positive response to the word, which is evident in the prophet's repeated call for a "return" to the Lord.[4] In Ezekiel, the fate of Jerusalem is already "sealed," just as are the divine "words of lamentation and mourning and woe" and thus of doom, in a scroll already *written* "on the front and on the back" (Ezek 2:10). Once spread before his eyes (3:1) the prophet could only read aloud God's message to the exiles concerning the already doomed Jerusalem and warn them that their fate would be similar to that of their "fathers" (2:3) if they follow the same path of "impudence and stubbornness" (v.4). As we shall see in chapters 16, 20, and 23, the experience of the "fathers" is offered to the exiles as an example *not* to be followed.

The divine decision that a written scroll be handed down to Ezekiel finds a precedent in the Book of Jeremiah itself. When one keeps in mind the canonical as well as chronological sequence of first Jeremiah then Ezekiel, one will notice that the non-exemplary behavior of the fathers is already underscored in

---

[3] Notice the intended correspondence in that the hand of God administers the message in both cases.
[4] 3:12, 14, 22; 4:1; 15:19; 18:11; 25:5.

The Commissioning of Ezekiel

Jeremiah. Furthermore, that behavior forces Jeremiah's hand to transform his words, which are the words God himself put into his prophet's mouth (Jer 1:9), into a written scroll for the following generations:

> In the fourth year of Jehoiakim the son of Josiah, king of Judah, this word came to Jeremiah from the Lord: "Take a scroll and write on it all the words that I have spoken to you against Israel and Judah and all the nations, from the day I spoke to you, from the days of Josiah until today. It may be that the house of Judah will hear all the evil which I intend to do to them, so that every one may turn from his evil way, and that I may forgive their iniquity and their sin." Then Jeremiah called Baruch the son of Neriah, and Baruch wrote upon a scroll at the dictation of Jeremiah all the words of the Lord which he had spoken to him … Then all the princes sent Jehudi the son of Nethaniah, son of Shelemiah, son of Cushi, to say to Baruch, "Take in your hand the scroll that you read in the hearing of the people, and come." So Baruch the son of Neriah took the scroll in his hand and came to them. And they said to him, "Sit down and read it." So Baruch read it to them. When they heard all the words, they turned one to another in fear; and they said to Baruch, "We must report all these words to the king." … Then the king sent Jehudi to get the scroll, and he took it from the chamber of Elishama the secretary; and Jehudi read it to the king and all the princes who stood beside the king. It was the ninth month, and the king was sitting in the winter house and there was a fire burning in the brazier before him. As Jehudi read three or four columns, the king would cut them off with a penknife and throw them into the fire in the brazier, until the entire scroll was consumed in the fire that was in the brazier. Yet neither the king, nor any of his servants who heard all these words, was afraid, nor did they rend their garments … Now, after the king had burned the scroll with the words which Baruch wrote at Jeremiah's dictation, the word of the Lord came to Jeremiah: "Take another scroll and write on it all the

former words that were in the first scroll, which Jehoiakim the king of Judah has burned. And concerning Jehoiakim king of Judah you shall say, 'Thus says the Lord, You have burned this scroll, saying, "Why have you written in it that the king of Babylon will certainly come and destroy this land, and will cut off from it man and beast?" Therefore thus says the Lord concerning Jehoiakim king of Judah, He shall have none to sit upon the throne of David, and his dead body shall be cast out to the heat by day and the frost by night. And I will punish him and his offspring and his servants for their iniquity; I will bring upon them, and upon the inhabitants of Jerusalem, and upon the men of Judah, all the evil that I have pronounced against them, but they would not hear.'" Then Jeremiah took another scroll and gave it to Baruch the scribe, the son of Neriah, who wrote on it at the dictation of Jeremiah all the words of the scroll which Jehoiakim king of Judah had burned in the fire; and many similar words were added to them. (Jer 36:1-4, 14-16, 21-24, 28-32)

Thus the hearer of scripture has already been prepared by Jeremiah to accept more readily and without "rebelliousness" (Ezek 2:3-8; 3:9, 26-27) the non-retractable harsh words of Ezekiel.[5]

---

[5] A detailed analysis of the original Hebrew of Ezekiel 2-3 will readily show the futility of traditional theological endeavors that deal with the "correct" understanding of the "Godhead" and expression of true faith. Such discussions originated in the early Gnostic-philosophical debates among Rabbinic as well as Christian intellectuals in Alexandria, the city of Philo and Origen. These endeavors have sapped the mental energy of the "theologians" and "believers" to our present day. Rather than edifying the hearers with the content and *message* of the biblical text, these debates endorse preconceived theological ideas and often end up promoting self-righteousness. Such is a far cry from the intention of the scriptural text that is essentially an *indictment* against its hearers with the aim that they change *their* incorrect *behavior*. The irony in this matter is that Ezekiel 2-3 foresees that the hearers will not heed this prophetic message.

The Commissioning of Ezekiel

As is clear from the overwhelming, if not outright boring,[6] repetition in chapters 2 and 3, Ezekiel's mission is to proclaim to all nations throughout the ages the reason behind the Lord's decision to destroy his city of Jerusalem and to exile its remaining inhabitants. Although the exiles are the original addressees, we are told repeatedly that they would not hearken to the message: "And whether they hear or refuse to hear (for they are a rebellious house) they will know that there has been a prophet among them" (2:5); "And you shall speak my words to them, whether they hear or refuse to hear; for they are a rebellious house" (v.7); "And he said to me, 'Son of man, go, get you to the house of Israel, and speak with my words to them. For you are not sent to a people of foreign speech and a hard language, but to the house of Israel—not to many peoples of foreign speech and a hard language, whose words you cannot understand. Surely, if I sent you to such, they would listen to you. But the house of Israel will not listen to you; for they are not willing to listen to me.'" (3:4-7a) The last passage corroborates that Ezekiel's ultimate mission is to communicate God's message not only to the exiles, but to all nations who, we are told, would be more willing to accept it.[7] The Book of Ezekiel, as we shall see, is about how God will realize his plan. Through his punishment of Jerusalem and the scattering of its survivors among the nations, God will cast his net of salvation over all those, Judahites and non-Judahites, who will prove willing to hearken to Ezekiel's message and, by so doing, will "walk in my statutes and keep my ordinances and obey them;

---

[6] I am using "boring" here in the sense of "drilling (into)." However, I opted for "boring" because the scriptural "drilling (into)" is done through repetitiveness, which is "boring" for those who are at the receiving end, as any child would vouch for.

[7] This is precisely what Paul will point out in 1 Corinthians 14 and in Romans 9-11.

and they shall be my people, and I will be their God" (Ezek 11:20).

This ultimate goal, which can be secured exclusively through obedience to the words of Ezekiel, explains why the prophetic message takes precedence over anything else, including the original addressees' refusal to abide by it: "I send you to them; and you shall say to them, 'Thus says the Lord God.' And whether they hear or refuse to hear (for they are a rebellious house) they will know that there has been a prophet among them … And you shall speak my words to them, whether they hear or refuse to hear." (2:4b-5, 7a) Indeed, the behavior of the recipients is a secondary aside compared with the duty to relay the "law and teaching of the Lord." We hear this in the *maskil* (instructional teaching) of Psalm 78. The content of this *maskil* is the scriptural story of perennial disobedience, yet the introduction, which covers over eleven percent of the entire psalm, clearly states the ultimate object of this lengthy recitation of stubbornly unrepentant behavior:

> Give ear, O my people, to my teaching; incline your ears to the words of my mouth! I will open my mouth in a parable; I will utter dark sayings from of old, things that we have heard and known, that our fathers have told us. We will not hide them from their children, but tell to the coming generation the glorious deeds of the Lord, and his might, and the wonders which he has wrought. He established a testimony in Jacob, and appointed a law in Israel, which *he commanded our fathers to teach to their children; that the next generation might know them, the children yet unborn, and arise and tell them to their children,* so that they should set their hope in God, and not forget the works of God, but keep his commandments; and *that they should not be like their fathers, a stubborn and rebellious generation,* a generation whose heart was not steadfast, whose spirit was not faithful to God. (Ps 78:1-8)

The Commissioning of Ezekiel

Compare the closeness in terminology of this psalm with that found in Ezekiel. The combination of *mašal* (parable; allegory) and *ḥidah* (riddle; dark saying) is found only in Psalm 49:4; 78:2, and Ezekiel 17:2 in the entire body of scripture; however, it is only in the last two instances that they refer to the instruction to be relayed down through the generations. The instruction revolves around the rebellious behavior of Israel against God: "I will open my mouth in a parable (*mašal*); I will utter dark sayings (*ḥidot*; plural of *ḥidah*) from of old" (Ps 78:2); "Son of man, propound a riddle (*ḥidah*), and speak an allegory (*mašal*) to the house of Israel." (Ezek 17:2).

But if Ezekiel's assumption is that the addressed children of the "rebellious fathers" are themselves charged with "rebellion," then what is the use of the already written scroll and in which sense is that scroll Israel's scripture? The solution to these two intertwined questions will help us understand Ezekiel's strange attitude toward the exiles, that is, his relentless harshness toward people who are already being punished and for what appears to be the fault of their forebears! Such an attitude sounds at best enigmatic and at worst unthinkable in our days when psychological verbiage speaks of "considerateness," "empathy," understanding," and "positive reinforcement." Our immediate reaction, as modern readers, is to ask, "How does Ezekiel expect his addressees to even hear him out, let alone listen to his bidding?" The answer to all these questions is rooted in the fact that the message is delivered as a scroll filled on both sides, that is to say, a message that is complete and, as such, cannot be altered through changes, additions, or subtractions. The reason behind such an "etching in stone" is that the main content of the message relates to an already elapsed event that *cannot* possibly be changed: the fall of Jerusalem and the exile of king and priest to Babylonia. Furthermore—and this is the essential point—not only the fall, but also its triggering cause is "sealed." That cause, according to Ezekiel, is not Babylonian military superiority, but rather the Lord's punishing *his own city* for the disobedience of its citizens, the king and the people alike, to his express will articulated in his commandments to them: "Thus says the Lord God: This is Jerusalem; I have set her in the center of the nations, with countries round about her. And she has wickedly rebelled against my ordinances more than the nations, and against my statutes more than the countries round about her, by rejecting my ordinances and not walking in my statutes." (5:5-6) Thus, what happened and what *cannot* be changed is not only the fall of Jerusalem, the Lord's city, but that it fell because of its citizens' misbehavior. Put otherwise, Jerusalem fell at its own Lord's hand after he, as judge, indicted the citizens and issued the verdict of "guilty" against them. It is precisely that *entire* story which is consigned in the divine scroll as "words of lamentation and mourning and woe" (2:10).

Such a story cannot possibly be but an instructional parabolic—or rather hyperbolic as is usually the case in scripture—rendition of the facts, and not a mere description of a city's siege and fall, since how can one possibly show, let alone "prove," that it is the Lord who punished the city and with no less than a siege that he orchestrated through his prophet's hand, which is a stand-in for his divine hand (1:3; 2:9; 3:14):

> And you, O son of man, take a brick and lay it before you, and portray upon it a city, even Jerusalem; and put siegeworks against it, and build a siege wall against it, and cast up a mound against it; set camps also against it, and plant battering rams against it round about. And take an iron plate, and place it as an iron wall between you and the city; and set your face toward it, and let it be in a state

of siege, and press the siege against it. This is a sign (*'ot*) for the house of Israel. (4:1-3)

The use of the noun "sign" to describe the divine action corroborates this understanding of the text. The Hebrew *'ot* refers to the value allocated to an event, whether that event is miraculous or not. The LXX rendering of *'ot* as *sēmeion* confirms this understanding since it is from the same root as the verb *sēmainō* (give a sign, give as sign, signify). Consequently, an *'ot* does not simply point to an event, it includes the meaning associated with that event as well, as per the originator of that *'ot*.[8] The message of an instructional story is blatantly evident[9] to the hearer and does not need to be "figured out." This is contrary to what is done in classic theological thinking whereby a theologian tries to dig out the "hidden" meaning of the text.[10] This latter approach actually contradicts the express intention of scripture, making out of it a treatise for the intellectuals rather than a simple address to the common hearers instructing them on how to behave correctly in view of God's judgment of their actions. This is stressed ad nauseam in Deuteronomy. Indeed, there is nothing to cogitate about when one is faced with "ordinances and statutes." As the adage goes, one is to "just do it!"

---

[8] Such should not come as a surprise to my readers since every language has its own repertoire of nouns of that sort. Take for instance the English "instruction" which refers to the content of the teaching or command as well as to the act of delivering it.

[9] As is clear from Ezekiel's hyperbolic statement, "For you are not sent to a people of foreign speech and a hard language, but to the house of Israel—not to many peoples of foreign speech and a hard language, whose words you cannot understand. *Surely, if I sent you to such, they would listen to you.*" (3:5-6)

[10] The Hebrew *ḥidah* translated as "riddle" or "dark saying" has nothing to do with hiddenness of meaning; rather, as I shall explain later when dealing with Ezek 17:2, the intention is to "engage" or "draw the attention of" the hearer.

The matter of "ordinances and statutes" is precisely the reason for Ezekiel's extreme harshness on those already being punished. God is planning to release the exiles in order to give them another chance to abide by his will, which their fathers did not do. This intention is at its clearest in Ezekiel 11 where the fathers' disobedience to the divine "ordinances and statutes" is brought up just before God's invitation to the exiles to abide by those same rules, with the express proviso that should they not hearken to God's bidding, they in turn would be struck down:

> You shall fall by the sword; I will judge you at the border of Israel; and you shall know that I am the Lord. This city shall not be your caldron, nor shall you be the flesh in the midst of it; I will judge you at the border of Israel; and you shall know that I am the Lord; for you have not walked in my statutes, nor executed my ordinances, but have acted according to the ordinances of the nations that are round about you. … Therefore say, "Thus says the Lord God: I will gather you from the peoples, and assemble you out of the countries where you have been scattered, and I will give you the land of Israel." And when they come there, they will remove from it all its detestable things and all its abominations. And I will give them one heart, and put a new spirit within them; I will take the stony heart out of their flesh and give them a heart of flesh, that they may walk in my statutes and keep my ordinances and obey them; and they shall be my people, and I will be their God. But as for those whose heart goes after their detestable things and their abominations, I will requite their deeds upon their own heads, says the Lord God. (11:10-12, 17-21)

Though the second chance is freely given, it is not free of the "charge" to abide by the same commandments the previous generation disobeyed. It is in this sense that the divine word is "eternal" and "unchanging," and applies to all upcoming generations, and not in the sense that it contains "the truth regarding the deity" as has become the case in classical theology. The divine word's value is "eternal," that is to say, valid for all human generations, because the deity, in fact any deity of the Ancient Near East, is essentially a judge whose word stands forever once it is uttered, and this applies even more to the God who judges everyone including all other deities as though they were mere human beings (Ps 82).

This explains why the freely granted second chance is cast in terms of the same unchanging *law* as is clear from the passage that deals with the thorny issue of the children being punished for the sins of their parents, which is a detailed expansion of Ezekiel 11:18-21:

> The word of the Lord came to me again: "What do you mean by repeating this proverb concerning the land of Israel, 'The fathers have eaten sour grapes, and the children's teeth are set on edge'? As I live, says the Lord God, this proverb shall no more be used by you in Israel. Behold, all souls are mine; the soul of the father as well as the soul of the son is mine: the soul that sins shall die. If a man is righteous and does what is lawful and right ... walks in my statutes, and is careful to observe my ordinances—he is righteous, he shall surely live, says the Lord God. If he begets a son who is a robber, a shedder of blood ... shall he then live? He shall not live ... He has done all these abominable things; he shall surely die; his blood shall be upon himself. But if this man begets a son who sees all the sins which his father has done, and fears, and does not do likewise ... observes my ordinances, and walks in my statutes; he shall not die for his father's iniquity; he shall surely live. As for his father, because he practiced extortion, robbed his brother, and did what is not good among his people, behold, he shall die for his iniquity. Yet you say, 'Why should not the son suffer for the iniquity of the father?' When the son has done what is lawful and right, and has been careful to observe all my statutes, he shall surely live. The soul that sins shall die. The son shall not suffer for

the iniquity of the father, nor the father suffer for the iniquity of the son; the righteousness of the righteous shall be upon himself, and the wickedness of the wicked shall be upon himself. But if a wicked man turns away from all his sins which he has committed and keeps all my statutes and does what is lawful and right, he shall surely live; he shall not die. None of the transgressions which he has committed shall be remembered against him; for the righteousness which he has done he shall live. Have I any pleasure in the death of the wicked, says the Lord God, and not rather that he should turn from his way and live? But when a righteous man turns away from his righteousness and commits iniquity and does the same abominable things that the wicked man does, shall he live? None of the righteous deeds which he has done shall be remembered; for the treachery of which he is guilty and the sin he has committed, he shall die. Yet you say, 'The way of the Lord is not just.' Hear now, O house of Israel: Is my way not just? Is it not your ways that are not just? When a righteous man turns away from his righteousness and commits iniquity, he shall die for it; for the iniquity which he has committed he shall die. Again, when a wicked man turns away from the wickedness he has committed and does what is lawful and right, he shall save his life. Because he considered and turned away from all the transgressions which he had committed, he shall surely live, he shall not die. Yet the house of Israel says, 'The way of the Lord is not just.' O house of Israel, are my ways not just? Is it not your ways that are not just? Therefore I will judge you, O house of Israel, every one according to his ways, says the Lord God. Repent and turn from all your transgressions, lest iniquity be your ruin. Cast away from you all the transgressions which you have committed against me, and get yourselves a new heart and a new spirit! Why will you die, O house of Israel? For I have no pleasure in the death of any one, says the Lord God; *so turn, and live.*" (18:1-5, 9-10, 13-14, 17-32)

Consequently, the matter of the "new heart and new spirit" is not magical in the sense that the new situation is a given, as is generally understood not only by those "born again" but also by other traditional Christian denominations. If that were indeed the case, then God would be robbed of his essential feature, that of a judge. To the contrary, the new situation is an unwarranted as well as an unexpected chance to implement the gift of a "new heart and new spirit" by abiding by God's eternal law, which is precisely why it is an act of sheer grace(fulness) on God's part for the new generation—and everyone hearing scripture is a member of the scriptural new generation.[11] It is only when those who have been granted the second chance effectively abide by God's ordinances and statutes that they will be God's people and he their God (Ezek 11:20; 14:11).

Thus, what Ezekiel is plainly and repeatedly saying runs against the grain of classical theology that insists that the scriptural church (*ekklēsia*) is per se the "people of God" and even, as some maintain, the "heavenly city" itself. The scriptural church, as its appellation *ekklēsia* reflects, is the one "called" by the "caller" (*kalōn*) to do his bidding, and not the one who, as such, does his bidding. In other words, the church is the congregation of those who are called, in the sense of invited, and not necessarily a congregation of those who responded to the divine call.[12]

---

[11] Such was fully understood by Paul who referred to that new situation as being unconditionally bound by the "*law* of Christ" (Gal 6:2) and the "*law* of the spirit of life" (Rom 8:2). That is why, according to Paul, one is to "*walk* according to the spirit" granted by God (Gal 5:16, 25; Rom 8:4). This is an apostolic command, not solely a mere description of an attitude, which Paul would *repeat* to his hearers with the threatening warning that, if they do not do so, they might "not inherit" the promised "kingdom of God" (Gal 5:21).

[12] This is clear in the parable of the marriage feast. It starts with "The kingdom of heaven may be compared to a king who gave a marriage feast for his son, and sent his servants to call (*kalesai*) those who were invited (*keklēmenous*; called) to the marriage feast; but they would not come. Again he sent other servants, saying, 'Tell those who

The fact that the essential function and thus "reality" of a deity is its being a judge, and the resulting concern that not all those who are called will be found innocent, on the one hand, and the universality of the realm of the scriptural God (Ps 82), on the other hand, explains the special features of Ezekiel's message. Unlike the other prophets, Ezekiel's interest goes beyond Samaria and Jerusalem to include Sodom (Ezek 16:46-63). To be sure, the other prophets underscore that the realm of their God extends over the faraway superpowers (Egypt, Assyria, Babylon) as well as over the immediate neighbors (Edom, Moab, Ammon, Philistia, Damascus); Isaiah even refers to Jerusalem being like Sodom (Is 1:9-10; 23:14). However, Ezekiel alone includes Sodom, a ghost from the past, under God's net and speaks of her as the "sister" of Samaria and Jerusalem and, in fact, their "younger" sister (16:46 and 61). In so doing, he is squeezing Jerusalem between a rock and a hard place. Not only was Jerusalem supposed to have learned a lesson from the fate of her "elder" sister (vv.46, 61), Samaria (v.51), but, had she had "eyes to see and ears to hear," she would have remembered the fate of her "younger" sister who was punished by God long ago, and at a very tender age, for a much lesser misdemeanor:

> And your elder sister is Samaria, who lived with her daughters to the north of you; and your younger sister, who lived to the south of you, is Sodom with her daughters. Yet you were not content to walk in their ways, or do according to their abominations; within a very little time you were more corrupt than they in all your ways.

---

are invited (*keklēmenois*; called) ...'" (Mt 22:2-4a) but it ends with "For many are called (*klētoi*; invited), but few are chosen" (v.14). However, what is most striking in this parable is that some of those who were already "in" end up being thrown "out" (vv.12-13), thus stressing the teaching that ultimately it is "not every one who *says* to me, 'Lord, Lord,' shall enter the kingdom of heaven, but he who *does the will* of my Father who is in heaven" (7:21). This is precisely what the judgment of the new covenant over *all nations* will be about (25:31-46).

As I live, says the Lord God, *your sister Sodom and her daughters have not done as you and your daughters have done.* (vv.46-48)

The teaching is clear: Jerusalem has no valid excuse whatsoever, and her exiled children had better heed Ezekiel's warning since it is definitely an unexpected chance given them after God's full verdict of "three strikes" against the three "sisters." This will become clear in chapter 20 where the "liberating" exodus—both the initial one and the upcoming one—is described in terms of judgment rather than salvation (vv.32-38). It will be during that upcoming exodus that God will "liberate" his people by purging from them those who rebelled against his "ordinances and statutes." As he promised earlier, "… those whose heart goes after their detestable things and their abominations, I will requite their deeds upon their own heads, says the Lord God." (11:21)

Can one push the matter a step further and ask whether based on the past experience Ezekiel surmised that the exiles he was addressing would ultimately be disobedient to God, or that he knew they were rebellious? If the latter were the case, then the prophet's message would be both more pertinent and more forceful since he would be addressing a reality rather than a putative situation. Chapter 20, which is at the heart of the first part of the book (chapters 1-39) and thus forms its core,[13] provides the answer:

> Wherefore say to the house of Israel, Thus says the Lord God: Will you defile yourselves after the manner of your fathers and go astray after their detestable things? When you offer your gifts and sacrifice your sons by fire, you defile yourselves with all your idols to this day. And shall I be inquired of by you, O house of Israel? As I live, says the Lord God, I will not be inquired of by you.

---

[13] See *OTI*₃ 132.

> What is in your mind shall never happen—the thought, 'Let us be like the nations, like the tribes of the countries, and worship wood and stone.' (20:30-32)

The exiles—at least many of them—*were* committing the same sin as their fathers. That meant they were not taking seriously the second chance offered them simply by the fact that rather than being exterminated during the siege through famine, illness or sword, as their co-citizens had been, they had been exiled yet left alive. So Ezekiel was not only warning them, but also chastening, if not outright condemning, them. Indeed, the culprits were headed toward destruction as is evident in the following verses:

> As I live, says the Lord God, surely with a mighty hand and an outstretched arm, and with wrath poured out, I will be king over you. I will bring you out from the peoples and gather you out of the countries where you are scattered, with a mighty hand and an outstretched arm, and with wrath poured out; and I will bring you into the wilderness of the peoples, and there I will enter into judgment with you face to face. As I entered into judgment with your fathers in the wilderness of the land of Egypt, so I will enter into judgment with you, says the Lord God. I will make you pass under the rod, and I will let you go in by number. I will purge out the rebels from among you, and those who transgress against me; I will bring them out of the land where they sojourn, but they shall not enter the land of Israel. Then you will know that I am the Lord. (20:33-38)

By the same token, Ezekiel is leaving the same message for all upcoming generations who might consider missing the second chance.

Still, Ezekiel goes one unexpected step further. He posits that, while the "fathers" *were still in Egypt*, they were guilty then and there of the same idolatry as that perpetrated by his contemporaries whether in Jerusalem or in Babylonia:

> ... thus says the Lord God: On the day when I chose Israel, I swore to the seed of the house of Jacob, making myself known to them in the land of Egypt, I swore to them, saying, I am the Lord your God. On that day I swore to them that I would bring them out of the land of Egypt into a land that I had searched out for them, a land flowing with milk and honey, the most glorious of all lands. And I said to them, Cast away the detestable things your eyes feast on, every one of you, and do not defile yourselves with the idols of Egypt; I am the Lord your God. But they rebelled against me and would not listen to me; they did not every man cast away the detestable things their eyes feasted on, nor did they forsake the idols of Egypt. (20:5-8, see also Hos 11:1-2)

In so doing, Ezekiel was pushing the situation of "second chance" as far back as the "election" of Israel at the exodus (Ezek 20:5; see also Hos 11:1). In other words, the election itself was already the "second chance," thus putting the recipients of the prophetic message of any generation in the vulnerable position of facing God's condemnation should they not heed that message.

In Ezekiel 16, where the three "sisters" are accused of idolatry, we hear the following: "Thus says the Lord God to Jerusalem: Your origin and your birth are of the land of the Canaanites; your father was an Amorite, and your mother a Hittite ... Behold, every one who uses proverbs will use this proverb about you, 'Like mother, like daughter.' You are the daughter of your mother, who loathed her husband and her children; and you are the sister of your sisters, who loathed their husbands and their children. Your mother was a Hittite and your father an Amorite." (vv.3, 44-45) According to Deuteronomy 7:1-4; 20:16-18 and Judges 3:4-7, the Canaanites, the Amorites, and the Hittites are precisely peoples whose deities the Israelites were strictly forbidden to follow since doing so would mean blatant idolatry, and yet, according to Ezekiel, Jerusalem was their "progeny." However, and more importantly, the Israelites' "father" *in Canaan* is none other than Abraham and their "mother" none other than Sarah. That would mean that idolatry was a trait that went back to Abraham himself! Consequently, the "second chance" situation is pushed farther back in time to the "origin" and "utter beginning." Given the seriousness of the matter, one might ask if this view is supported elsewhere in scripture, and indeed it is, in Joshua 24:

> Then Joshua gathered all the tribes of Israel to Shechem, and summoned the elders, the heads, the judges, and the officers of Israel; and they presented themselves before God. And Joshua said to all the people, "Thus says the Lord, the God of Israel, 'Your fathers lived of old beyond the Euphrates, Terah, the father of Abraham and of Nahor; and they served other gods ... Now therefore fear the Lord, and serve him in sincerity and in faithfulness; put away the gods which your fathers served beyond the River, and in Egypt, and serve the Lord. And if you be unwilling to serve the Lord, choose this day whom you will serve, whether the gods your fathers served in the region beyond the River, or the gods of the Amorites in whose land you dwell; but as for me and my house, we will serve the Lord...' But Joshua said to the people, "You cannot serve the Lord; for he is a holy God; he is a jealous God; he will not forgive your transgressions or your sins. If you forsake the Lord and serve foreign Gods, then he will turn and do you harm, and consume you, after having done you good." And the people said to Joshua, "Nay; but we will serve the Lord." Then Joshua said to the people, "You are witnesses against yourselves that you have chosen the Lord, to serve him." And they said, "We are witnesses." He said, "Then put away the foreign gods which are among you, and incline your heart to the Lord, the

God of Israel." And the people said to Joshua, "The Lord our God we will serve, and his voice we will obey." So Joshua made a covenant with the people that day, and made statutes and ordinances for them at Shechem. And Joshua wrote these words in the book of the law of God; and he took a great stone, and set it up there under the oak in the sanctuary of the Lord. And Joshua said to all the people, "Behold, this stone shall be a witness against us; for it has heard all the words of the Lord which he spoke to us; therefore it shall be a witness against you, lest you deal falsely with your God." (vv.1-2, 14-15, 19-27)

From this passage it is evident that (1) the "gods" Abraham served beyond the Euphrates were honored by his "children" while in Egypt (compare with Ezek 20:7); (2) those "gods" have been lingering all along among the "children" since Joshua is asking that they be removed in Canaan; and (3) functionally, these same "gods" are equivalent with those of the Amorites.[14]

Thus scripture is not descriptive but rather it is prescriptive. It is a hyperbolic story conceived in such a way that not only posits its contemporary addressees in a "second chance" situation, but it also *does not allow* any excuse whatsoever for their impudence in refusing the message even though they stand in a long "genealogy" of people "of a hard forehead and of a stubborn heart" (Ezek 3:7). The intention is to always put any and every later hearer of the same scroll in the position of being offered a "second chance." Therefore, when the text is read aloud in any congregation, the idea of a first chance is a figment of the hearers' imagination since, *in the scriptural story*, it has already been given and is thus *behind* them. This feature is so pervasive in scripture that it becomes a crimson thread that goes back

---

[14] The closeness between Joshua 24 and Ezekiel is betrayed through the mention of "elders" at the head of the list of addressees (Josh 24:1; see also 23:2), when "the elders" are the prophet's primary concern as we shall see later.

beyond Abraham to the pre-election period that deals with the "nations" in general (Gen 1:1-10:26). Since Noah and his wife, his three sons and their wives, were the only human beings who bridged the flood period in their lifetime, no other hearer of the scriptural story, who by definition is post-diluvial, could say that either the divine punishment or the cause thereof spoken of in Genesis 6 applies to him. The result is that any *hearer* and thus addressee of the parabolic story is faced with the post-diluvial "second chance" which is linked to a covenant (Gen 6:18; 9:9-17). It is the sins of the pre-diluvial "fathers" that put every hearer in the predicament of the "second chance."

The same situation pertains to the story of the beginnings. All humans addressed by the biblical story, beginning with Cain (4:1), Abel (v.2), and Seth (v.25), are by definition *already* "at the east of the garden of Eden" where the Lord God "placed the cherubim, and a flaming sword which turned every way, to guard the way to the tree of life" (3:24). They are *outside* Eden because of Adam's disobedience *in* that garden just as the exiles are in Babylon because of their fathers' stubbornness in Jerusalem.[15] Still—actually because of that—we have no excuse according to Ezekiel's God who said to the exiles:

> What do you mean by repeating this proverb concerning the land of Israel, 'The fathers have eaten sour grapes, and the children's teeth are set on edge'? As I live, says the Lord God, this proverb shall no more be used by you in Israel. Behold, all souls are mine; the soul of the father as well as the soul of the son is mine: the soul that sins shall die. (Ezek 18:2-4)

---

[15] As Paul will eventually succinctly and aptly put it, "one man's trespass led to condemnation for all men" (Rom 5:18a).

3
God's Glory is Independent of the Temple

The original vocabulary of chapters 2 and 3, which comprise Ezekiel's commissioning, is replete with interconnected wordplay used to establish in the minds of hearers the full identity between the person of the prophet and his message. In other words, the Book of Ezekiel *is* Ezekiel to the extent that there is no other Ezekiel "out there." Both his name and his commissioning embrace his entire being *as prophet* and this is all there is to him. Ezekiel exists only as the prophet whose person and mission lie within the confines of the scroll of Ezekiel and nowhere else. In other words, Ezekiel has neither father nor mother; he was "conceived" by the scripture writers. As discussed in chapter one, even Ezekiel's father was "conceived" as an "element" of the Ezekelian story. The case of Ezekiel is similar to that of Moses: Moses *is* the five books of the Law.[1]

It is only by listening to the scriptural text *in the original Hebrew* that one will readily be "hit" by its simple and straightforward content that is meant to lead to repentance unto salvation through divine mercy. Any other approach to scripture will distort its original meaning and purpose. There is neither a

---

[1] The same applies to the phrase "The Prophets" which is a reference to the Prophetic Books. This reality is also reflected in two New Testament passages: "As it is written *in Isaiah the prophet*, Behold, I send my messenger before thy face, who shall prepare thy way; the voice of one crying in the wilderness: Prepare the way of the Lord, make his paths straight— "(Mk 1:2-3); "As indeed he [God] says *in Hosea*, Those who were not my people I will call 'my people,' and her who was not beloved I will call 'my beloved.' And in the very place where it was said to them, 'You are not my people,' they will be called 'sons of the living God.'" (Rom 9:25-26)

mental "God," let alone a mental "word" (Hebrew *dabar*; Greek *logos* or *rhēma*); there are only the scriptural words (Hebrew *debarim*; Greek *logoi* or *rhēmata*) as they are written (Hebrew *ketubim*; Greek *grammata*). Hence "Blessed is the man ... whose delight is in the law of the Lord, and on his law he meditates[2] day and night." (Ps 1:1, 2)

The staple of the book, which appears at the outset of Ezekiel's commissioning (2:1) and pervades the entire book ad nauseam (93 times in 48 chapters), is the prophet's appellation as "son of man." Only he is addressed in this manner. Considering that in the entire scripture, both Old and New Testaments, it occurs only once more as an address in Daniel 8:17, it is hard to imagine that this phrase is not at the core of Ezekiel's message. Indeed, immediately after a lengthy chapter where God is introduced as the only universal deity residing above the firmament, the prophet is addressed by that same God with the belittling "son of man" to indicate that he is simply a human being, which befits his lowly attitude of full prostration (1:28). This is in contradistinction to his former status as priest and thus one of God's "holy ones" serving around the king whose designation is "son of God." It is in this capacity of utter unworthiness that Ezekiel is called to stand up on his feet in order to address with full divine authority all other "sons of man" in the nations as well as in Israel. This divine repeated appellation used throughout the book is intended to be a constant reminder to the prophet that he would never cease to be a mere "son of man." He will never go back to his original status even in the new temple (40-48). He will not be allowed to rise

---

[2] Actually "meditates" is misleading since it reflects a personal input on the part of the reciter. The Hebrew *hagah* means "spell, enunciate" and thus connotes a repetition of the exact *written* words by heart, from memory.

God's Glory is Independent of the Temple

above his brethren; in fact, he will be forced to realize that he is no better than his fellow exiles since he will be made by God to be the "prototype" exile (12:3-7). On the other hand, the utter demeaning of God's sole plenipotentiary emissary fits another premise of the book, namely, that all "pride" shall be brought to naught: God needs to keep Ezekiel "under his thumb" at least until the message is delivered in its entirety. At the end of the message God will allow only the waters that will flow out of his new temple to "rise high" (47:5), the reason being that they will feed the trees whose leaves will be meant for healing (v.12). The land that is fed by those waters will be an open pasture with no "raised" buildings made by the hands of "sons of man." The sheer presence of God, as shepherd in the midst of his sheep (ch.34), will function as the sole city—the "high-rise"—in that land (48:35).

Ezekiel is sent to the house of Israel because they are "nations[3] of rebels (*goyim hammoredim*), who have rebelled (*maredu*) against me; they and their fathers have transgressed (*paše'u*) against me to this very (*'eṣem*; bone) day. The sons also are impudent (*qeše panim*; hard of face) and stubborn (*ḥizqe leb*; with a rigid heart)." This statement is squeezed between the repeated phrase "I am sending (*šoleaḥ*) you to…" and ending with "and you shall say to them, 'Thus says the Lord God.'" (2:3-4). The original Hebrew of these two verses is much more compelling than the translations. A detailed study of the original will readily show that they introduce the entire book.

---

[3] RSV has "a nation." However, the Hebrew has the plural *goyim*, not the singular *goy*.

As in most of the prophets,[4] Israel's sin is essentially that of *peša'*, which is the rebellion of children against the authority of the father, an action that disturbs the order and the "peace" (*šalom*) necessary for the maintenance of life. This explains why the destruction of the wicked children[5] is necessary for the final divine restoration of peace. Yet, here in Ezekiel, this basic transgression is specifically presented as one of *marad* (standing up against), which corresponds to pride and arrogance. Still, what is stunning is that the "children of Israel" are indicted as "rebellious nations (*goyim*)" or "nations of rebels" in the plural rather in the singular *goy* (nation) which, technically, would have been more appropriate.[6] This choice is clearly deliberate since in the rest of the book the very frequent occurrence of *goyim* refers exclusively to the other nations. The unmistakable intention here is to equate the value of Israel with that of the other nations who do not know God's will inscribed in the Law. This is similar to what Jeremiah writes: "Behold, the days are coming, says the Lord, when I will punish all those who are circumcised but yet uncircumcised—Egypt, Judah, Edom, the sons of Ammon, Moab, and all who dwell in the desert that cut the corners of their hair; for all these nations are uncircumcised, and all the house of Israel is uncircumcised in heart." (9:25-26) In Ezekiel 2:2, Israel is accused of behaving like the nations described in Psalm 2:1: "Why do the nations (*goyim*) conspire, and the peoples (*'ummim*) plot in vain?" It is only when whoever among the members of "the nations" of Israel will welcome the second chance of doing God's bidding that they will become his "people" (11:20; 14:11).

---

[4] See, e.g., Is 1:2, 28; Jer 2:8, 29; Ezek 2:3; Hos 7:13; 8:1; Am 1:3, 6, 9, 11, 13; Mic 1:5 [twice], 13; Zeph 3:11.
[5] The definition of wicked (*reša'im*) is "traitors," as I explain further below.
[6] See, e.g., Is 2:4; 10:6; 58:2; 65:1; Jer 5:9, 29; 7:28; 9:9.

God's Glory is Independent of the Temple

The prophets did teach that the same God could become the fiercest enemy of those who are "his," that is, those who were entrusted with his "words"[7] through Moses. As we hear in Amos and Isaiah:

> Thus says the Lord: "For three transgressions of Israel, and for four, I will not revoke the punishment ... Behold, I will press you down in your place, as a cart full of sheaves presses down. Flight shall perish from the swift, and the strong shall not retain his strength, nor shall the mighty save his life; he who handles the bow shall not stand, and he who is swift of foot shall not save himself, nor shall he who rides the horse save his life; and he who is stout of heart among the mighty shall flee away naked in that day," says the Lord. (Am 2:6a, 13-16)

> For he said, Surely they are my people, sons who will not deal falsely; and he became their Savior. In all their affliction he was afflicted, and the angel of his presence saved them; in his love and in his pity he redeemed them; he lifted them up and carried them all the days of old. But they rebelled and grieved his holy Spirit; therefore he turned to be their enemy, and himself fought against them. (Is 63:8-10)

The entities "Israel" and "nations" are exclusively scriptural, that is to say, textual and literary realities and not tangible historical ones. It is the scriptural text that posits who, when, how, and on which conditions God's people are or, more precisely, become indeed his. For the scriptural God is the universal God of all peoples and could openly say to the same "children of Israel" addressed by Ezekiel (2:3): "'Are you not like the Ethiopians to me, O children of Israel?' says the Lord. 'Did I not bring up Israel from the land of Egypt, and the Philistines from Caphtor and the Syrians from Kir?'" (Amos 9:7) Ezekiel

---

[7] See Rom 3:2.

goes to the extreme to make this point by completely omitting Babylon from the list of nations that fall under divine retribution (chs. 25-32). In fact, the king of Babylon is depicted as God's "friendly client" who does God's bidding in the chastisement of Jerusalem, just as Cyrus will be when he restores that same city (Is 44:28-45:1)! It is as though Babylon did nothing wrong in bringing to naught the Lord's city and in fact acted out of obedience to him (Ezek 17). Thus her behavior is a far cry from that of the obstinately recalcitrant Jerusalem.

Ezekiel's extreme stand surpasses even the teaching in Jonah. Jonah is summoned to offer Nineveh, Assyria's capital who destroyed Samaria, a call to repent from her evil deeds,[8] albeit not those against Samaria. Nineveh is not presented as having done anything wrong in destroying Samaria, still Nineveh is asked to repent of her "other" evil deeds. In Ezekiel, Babylon appears as totally blameless! Since Ezekiel cannot conceivably be accused of having a soft heart—"Behold, I have made your face hard against their faces, and your forehead hard against their foreheads. Like adamant harder than flint have I made your forehead" (3:8-9a)—his rationale must lie elsewhere. He is sent to the children of Israel in order to unveil their "wickedness," since only they, technically speaking, can be wicked (*reša'im*; plural of *raša'*), whereas the nations are usually evil (*ra'im*; plural of *ra'*).

Scripturally, an evil one is an overarching description of anyone who does something "bad, evil" which is the opposite of the "good" (*ṭob*), as in the general terminology of "(the) good and (the) evil" (Gen 2:9, 17; 3:5, 22; 50:20; 2 Sam 14:17; 1 Kg 3:9). The evil one is *obviously* recognizable in the same way as a

---

[8] Not "wickedness" as in RSV.

declared enemy would be. The wicked one, however, is a friend, an insider, who turns against his colleague, and thus is a "traitor." From the scriptural perspective an Israelite or a Judahite is either *yašar* (straight, upright, straightforward, forthcoming; truthful) or conversely *raša'* (deceitful; devious; wicked; treacherous; unfaithful). Ezekiel's mission is to show the "children of Israel" that by rebelling against God's authority (Ezek 2:2) they are wicked and not truthful toward their Lord. Such becomes clear when one investigates the references to "wickedness" in the Book of Ezekiel.

Except for four times (13:22; 21:25, 29; 31:11), all other 30 instances of the root *raša'* (wicked, wickedness) are found in chapters 3 (7 times), 5 (once), 7 (twice), 18 (6 times), 33 (14 times).[9] By far the highest incidence (27 times in chapters 3, 18, and 33) occurs in conjunction with Ezekiel's mission as a "watchman" (3:17; 33:2, 6, 7) who is to warn the wicked that they have a chance to repent. If he is remiss in forewarning them, he will have to answer to God; the reason being "Have I any pleasure in the death of the wicked, says the Lord God, and not rather that he should turn from his way and live?" (18:23); "For I have no pleasure in the death of any one, says the Lord God; so turn, and live" (v.32); "Say to them, As I live, says the Lord God, I have no pleasure in the death of the wicked, but that the wicked turn from his way and live; turn back, turn back from your evil ways; for why will you die, O house of Israel?" (33:11)

The instances of "wicked" in 5:6 and 7:11 fit the scenario of watchman since the former is addressed to the "wicked rebels" of Jerusalem and the latter to the land of Israel (7:2). The end punishment in 7:21 is described in the most belittling way

---

[9] I am following the count in the original Hebrew.

possible in that the idols erected by the wicked of the land will be handed over for profanation not simply to the foreigners, but more specifically to the wicked among these: "And I will give it into the hands of foreigners for a prey, and to the wicked of the earth for a spoil; and they shall profane it."

The remaining four occurrences of "wicked" confirm our findings: 13:22 is a criticism against the false prophets who are not doing what they are supposed to do: "Because you have disheartened the righteous falsely, although I have not disheartened him, and you have encouraged the wicked, that he should not turn from his wicked way to save his life"; 21:25 is an indictment of the wicked prince of Israel, while verse 29 contains a similar accusation against the wicked Ammonites who are punished by the same "sword" that the Babylonians will use to destroy Jerusalem (ch.21); and 31:11 speaks of the same fate that befalls Egypt for its wickedness at the hand of the same Babylonians, thus underscoring that even the mighty and seemingly impregnable Egypt will succumb to God's verdict "because it towered high and set its top among the clouds, and its heart was proud of its height" (v.10). The message to the children of Israel is clear: the one universal God whose throne is above the firmament will wield the same sword of justice, with which he hit Jerusalem and Judah, against all other nations, be they as little as Ammon or as powerful as Egypt. All rebellious wicked will undergo the same fate at the hand of Babylonians who alone bowed down submissively to the will of God and was not punished. The hearers can "pout" all they want, if they so choose, as Jonah did (4:9); the Lord will dismissively thrust aside their complaint as he did with Jonah (vv.10-11).

Indeed, the negative attitude of the hearers is blatantly dismissed as immaterial for God's cause. He already knows that

God's Glory is Independent of the Temple 75

the addressees are intent on not receiving the message. God is not sending Ezekiel for their sake, but rather for all upcoming generations who would know that a prophet has spoken (Ezek 2:5). The phrasing of this is blatantly demeaning to the children of Israel: Ezekiel will be remembered as having spoken not "to them" (*lahem*) but "among them" (*betokam*; in the midst of them). Put otherwise, by preempting their negative response as irrelevant, God is dismissing them even as recipients. Hence, unlike Jeremiah 36 where the scroll is produced toward the end of the prophet's mission because his message was repeatedly refused, in Ezekiel the already written scroll is the triggering factor of the prophet's mission. The "omega" in Jeremiah becomes the "alpha" in Ezekiel. The difference in perspective is reflected in the two narratives; whereas Jeremiah goes through so many emotional and personal experiences, Ezekiel never flinches in his resolve since his commission was phrased in unwavering terms:

> And you, son of man, be not afraid of them, nor be afraid of their words, though briers and thorns are with you and you sit upon scorpions; be not afraid of their words, nor be dismayed at their looks, for they are a rebellious house. (Ezek 2:6)

> Behold, I have made your face hard (*ḥazaqim*; plural of *ḥazaq*[10]) against their faces, and your forehead (*meṣaḥ*) hard (*ḥazaq*) against their foreheads. Like adamant harder (*ḥazaq*) than flint have I made your forehead; fear them not, nor be dismayed at their looks, for they are a rebellious house. (3:8-9)

The adjective *ḥazaq* is from the same root as the verb *ḥazaq*, which is a part of the prophet's name *yeḥezqe'l*. The reason behind this divine decision to be harsh is precisely because of the

---

[10] The reason is that "face" in Hebrew is a noun in the plural form, *panim*.

attitude ascribed to them: "The people (*habbanim*; the children) also are impudent (*qeše panim*; tough, difficult of face) and stubborn (*ḥizqe leb*; hard of heart)" (2:4a); "But the house of Israel will not listen to you; for they are not willing to listen to me; because all the house of Israel are of a hard forehead (*ḥizqe meṣaḥ*) and of a stubborn heart (*qeše leb*)." (3:7) Put in plain terms, if the children of Israel want to play tough, God will show them, through the medium of Ezekiel, what real toughness is all about.

When one considers that "face" and "forehead" are the two sides of the same literary coin, one realizes that it is "heart" that Ezekiel wanted to bring to the fore, especially that it occurs with both adjectives *ḥizqe* and *qeše* which are used to describe Israel's disobedience. It is the "wanton (*zoneh*; harloting) heart" of the exiles that God himself will break (6:9) because its "hardness" exceeded every measure so that it became "of stone." God does this in order to put in its stead a heart of "flesh" as a heart ought to be (11:19) when he will gather and assemble those same exiles (v.17). That this is indeed God's plan in Ezekiel is evident in the fact that between the mention of "heart" in 2:4[11] and 3:7 on the one hand, and its occurrence no less than three times in 11:19, that noun is found only in 6:9. The close interconnection between 6:9 and 11:19 is corroborated in the similar phraseology referring to the idols as "abominations":

> Yet I will leave some of you alive. When you have among the nations some who escape the sword, and when you are scattered through the countries, then those of you who escape will remember me among the nations where they are carried captive,

---

[11] Where RSV has "The people also are impudent and stubborn" (2:4a) the original Hebrew reads "The children are hard of face and stubborn of *heart*."

when I have broken their wanton heart which has departed from me, and blinded their eyes which turn wantonly after their idols; and they will be loathsome in their own sight for the evils which they have committed, for all their abominations. (6:8-9)

Therefore say, "Thus says the Lord God: I will gather you from the peoples, and assemble you out of the countries where you have been scattered, and I will give you the land of Israel." And when they come there, they will remove from it all its detestable things and all its abominations. And I will give them one heart, and put a new spirit within them; I will take the stony heart out of their flesh and give them a heart of flesh, that they may walk in my statutes and keep my ordinances and obey them; and they shall be my people, and I will be their God. But as for those whose heart goes after their detestable things and their abominations, I will requite their deeds upon their own heads, says the Lord God. (11:17-21)

God's harshness against the children of Israel does not spare Ezekiel. While God punishes only the others, he summons his prophet in no uncertain terms not to be recalcitrant (2:8a). However, the obedience required of him is not on the level of action since he will be the prototype of all exiles. Rather his obedience concerns the commission assigned to him, namely, that of conveying the message even though it will not be hearkened to (v.8b). In other words, he is not allowed to use the hard heartedness of the exiles as an excuse to say, "What for, then?" His mission is not a call to action but to speech. Among all prophets, his particular commissioning is rendered in the most extreme of hyperboles: he is to *eat* the scroll containing the divine words so that, every time he opens his mouth—and he has to open it by God's command—he would be merely regurgitating those words (3:1). It is as though God is commanding him just to open his mouth in order for his mission to be accomplished! And what excuse could he have had when the scroll was "in my mouth as sweet as honey" (3:3b). Disregarding how it felt in his stomach (v.3a)—and, according to his later colleague, it was bitter (Rev 10:9-10)—it would be sweet in the mouth. The moral of the divine message is clear: "Ezekiel, make sure to keep those words in your mouth as often as you can; they are meant to be uttered for the others to hear; they are not meant for your own delight. You are my mouthpiece, my (voice's) alter ego (3:7a) for the children of Israel and for all subsequent hearers."

One should also notice that the command "eat" is issued no less than four times (2:8; 3:1 [twice], 3), the final time with the addition "and fill your stomach." The hearer cannot miss that the intention of the last comment is to underscore that the words of God, whatever their content, are Ezekiel's sole food, literally his "bread of life," which makes the matter more extreme than in the case in Moses: "And he humbled you and let you hunger and fed you with manna, which you did not know, nor did your fathers know; that he might make you know that man does not live by bread alone, but that man lives by everything that proceeds out of the mouth of the Lord." (Deut 8:3) What one hears in Ezekiel is closer to what one finds in another prophetic book, where the words of the Lord are a matter of actual physical life and death:

> Behold, the days are coming, says the Lord God, when I will send a famine on the land; not a famine of bread, nor a thirst for water, but of hearing the words of the Lord. They shall wander from sea to sea, and from north to east; they shall run to and fro, to seek the word of the Lord, but they shall not find it. In that day the fair virgins and the young men shall faint for thirst. (Amos 8:11-13)

God's Glory is Independent of the Temple 79

On the other hand, those same words, whatever their content, are "sweet" to the palate and here Ezekiel is echoed by the Psalmist: "the ordinances of the Lord are true, and righteous altogether. More to be desired are they then gold, even much fine gold; sweeter also than honey and drippings of the honeycomb" (Ps 19:9b-10); "How sweet are thy words to my taste, sweeter than honey to my mouth!" (119:103). Thus Ezekiel is reminded that he is to live by those words while enjoying their sweetness. The utterances of God carry their own reward and, if so, then Ezekiel is to endorse them fully and without any complaint: "Moreover he said to me, 'Son of man, all my words that I shall speak to you receive in your heart, and hear with your ears.'" (Ezek 3:10) It is with such unwavering attitude that he is to "go, get you to the exiles, to your people, and say to them, 'Thus says the Lord God'; whether they hear or refuse to hear" (v.11).

It is interesting to note that in a divine address to Ezekiel the phrase "your people" occurs seven times in the book (3:11; 13:17; 33:2, 12, 17, 30; 37:18), the first six of which are within a divine indictment against the people. The last occurrence of "your people" (37:18) is in conjunction with the divine restoration of the dry bones into "the whole house of Israel" (37:11) whom God refers to twice as "my people" (vv.12, 13). So we have an odyssey that starts with divine punishment and ends with a divinely granted new start. Keeping this in mind, one cannot help but be struck with the expression *'eṣem hayyom hazzeh* in 2:3 that is translated "this very day" although its literal rendering would be "the bone of this day."[12] What makes its use important is that, outside the Pentateuch and Joshua, it is encountered only in Ezekiel in the Old Testament. Thus, it is

---

[12] "Bone" would stand for "core," "center," "body" and thus "full reality."

special to him in the Prophets and, consequently, it must be functional in his story line. A closer look at its three occurrences[13] and their positions will readily show that it is indeed so. The first one in 2:3 is *'ad 'eṣem hayyom hazzeh* (until this very day; to this very day) whereas the following ones are *be'eṣem hayyom hazzeh* (on that very day; that very day) with a specific reference to a dated day:

> In the ninth year, in the tenth month, on the tenth day of the month, the word of the Lord came to me: "Son of man, write down the name of this day, this very day. The king of Babylon has laid *siege to Jerusalem* this very day." (24:1-2)

> In the twenty-fifth year of our exile, at the beginning of the year, on the tenth day of the month, in the fourteenth year *after the city was conquered*, on that very day, the hand of the Lord was upon me, and brought me in the visions of God into the land of Israel, and set me down upon a very high mountain, on which was a structure like a city opposite me. (40:1-2)

So in the story "this very day" goes through a three-step cadence. It is because "they [the children of Israel] and their fathers have transgressed against me to this very day" that the Lord decides on two specific days, one to destroy his unfaithful city and the land around it, and the other to start erecting upon a very high mountain his own city, "the Lord is there," set in the center of pasture land where the people lie in God's peace (47:13-48:29)[14], a city not made by the hand of man (48:30-35). The oneness of the story can be seen in that (1) the two days of divine intervention mention the destruction of Jerusalem and (2)

---

[13] I am omitting the fourth (24:4a) which is just a reference to "the name of that very day" and is immediately followed in the same verse (4b) with "(on) that very day."

[14] Chapters 40-48 form a unit that begins with the mention of the divine city in 40:2 and ends with a reference to same in 48:35, which is also the end of the book.

the story line is bracketed between "and the hand of the Lord was upon him there" (1:3) and "the hand of the Lord was upon me" (40:1) which account for the first and the last of the seven occurrences of the phrase "the hand of the Lord being upon Ezekiel," the others being at 3:14, 22; 8:1; 33:22; 37:1. Of further note is that the first "day" of divine intervention introduced with "bone" (24:2) is followed with an intensive reference to broken "bones" (vv.4, 5 [twice], 10). The same is repeated in conjunction with the second "day" of divine intervention introduced with "bone" (40:1) since the new people who will populate the land in chapter 48 are none other than "all the house of Israel" that is made out the dry "bones" which are referred to no less than eight times in chapter 37 (vv.1, 3, 4 [twice], 5, 7, 11 [twice]).

Ezekiel uses the term "bone" to express the idea of "this very day" in order to pique the curiosity of his hearers, which will not be sated until they are faced with the wake-up call of seeing their own "bones" scattered (6:5). This calamity, in turn, will prove to be just a foretaste of chapter 24 when, after a long silence of 18 chapters regarding this matter[15] and thus a misleading respite, they will be suddenly and literally bombarded with four references to their broken "bones" on "the very day" God will execute his judgment against his city. They will be left crushed and hopeless for another 13 chapters, and then they will be stunned to hear that their very dry bones are being "reassembled" and "covered" with an array of sinews, flesh, and skin, and made alive by the "spirit" that will be breathed upon them through the prophet's mouth (37:8-10). Still, 6:5 has another function, that of securing the bridge also between chapters 37 and 40. Indeed, the passing reference to "bones" in 6:5 appears within an

---

[15] Between 6:5 and 24:4 there is no reference to "bones."

indictment of the (many) "mountains of Israel" (vv.1 and 2), whereas the vision of hope concerning the new city of God takes place "on a (one) very high mountain" (40:2).

A study of the content and vocabulary of the rest of chapter 3 will further confirm that the first three chapters "look ahead" and function as an introduction to the entire story line of the book and, in a sense, encapsulate and control it as well. In this sense the original verse 3:12 is the most pregnant in meaning.[16] Its literal rendering would be: "Then the Spirit (*ruaḥ*; wind) lifted me up, and I heard behind me the sound (*qol*; voice) of a great earthquake (*ra'aš*):[17] the glory of the Lord is more blessed than its place (*maqom*)."[18] The *ruaḥ*, which controlled chapter 1 and raised Ezekiel on his feet in 2:2 in order that he be commissioned, intervenes to carry him away on the chariot (3:13) that is steered by the *ruaḥ* (1:20). The interconnection between 2:2 and 3:12 is corroborated in that it is the same *qol* (voice in 1:28 and sound in 3:12) that is behind both events. As was the case with "bone," the noun *ra'aš* also spans the entire Ezekelian story. Besides 3:12-13 it is found twice more in 12:18 and 37:7, and it is the *ra'aš* that controls the outcome of both events depicted in the story. Ezekiel, and through him the inhabitants of the doomed Jerusalem with its land, will feel the quake's devastating effect:

---

[16] I refer to the original because virtually all translations misrepresent, if not outright massacre, this verse. I do not intend to burden my readers with discussing and refuting those translations.

[17] I used the colon since the following statement is the content of what the sound or voice was saying.

[18] The Hebrew comparative is missed given that it is rendered through the plain adjectival form followed by the preposition *min* (from). This explains why, e.g., the LXX has "blessed is the glory of the Lord from its place," meaning probably "when it moves from its place," which would in turn explain why RSV supplied the verb "arose" (as the glory of the Lord *arose* from its place).

Moreover the word of the Lord came to me: "Son of man, eat your bread with quaking (*ra'aš*), and drink water with trembling and with fearfulness; and say of the people of the land, Thus says the Lord God concerning the inhabitants of Jerusalem in the land of Israel: They shall eat their bread with fearfulness, and drink water in dismay, because their land will be stripped of all it contains, on account of the violence of all those who dwell in it. And the inhabited cities shall be laid waste, and the land shall become a desolation; and you shall know that I am the Lord." (12:17-20)

However, the following and final *ra'aš* will have a beneficent effect and, no less, in conjunction with *qol*, *ruaḥ*, and "bones":

Thus says the Lord God to these bones: "Behold, I will cause breath (*ruaḥ*) to enter you, and you shall live. And I will lay sinews upon you, and will cause flesh to come upon you, and cover you with skin, and put breath (*ruaḥ*) in you, and you shall live; and you shall know that I am the Lord." So I prophesied as I was commanded; and as I prophesied, there was a noise (*qol*), and behold, a rattling (*ra'aš*); and the bones came together, bone to its bone. And as I looked, there were sinews on them, and flesh had come upon them, and skin had covered them; but there was no breath (*ruaḥ*) in them. Then he said to me, "Prophesy to the breath (*ruaḥ*), prophesy, son of man, and say to the breath (*ruaḥ*), Thus says the Lord God: Come from the four winds (*ruḥot*, plural of *ruaḥ*), O breath (*ruaḥ*), and breathe upon these slain, that they may live." So I prophesied as he commanded me, and the breath (*ruaḥ*) came into them, and they lived, and stood upon their feet, an exceedingly great host. (37:5-10)

Finally, in its turn, *maqom* brackets the entire story. Since the Lord's glory resides "above the firmament" on a throne that is in a "cloud" (1:25-28), it is not bound to the earthly "place" but descends as a "cloud":

> Then the priests brought the ark of the covenant of the Lord to its place (*maqom*), in the inner sanctuary of the house, in the most holy place, underneath the wings of the cherubim. For the cherubim spread out their wings over the place (*maqom*) of the ark, so that the cherubim made a covering above the ark and its poles ... And when the priests came out of the holy place, a cloud filled the house of the Lord, so that the priests could not stand to minister because of the cloud; for the glory of the Lord filled the house of the Lord. (1 Kings 8:6-7, 10-11)

God is about to show this to the children of Israel who thought he was bound to the temple:

> Do not trust in these deceptive words: "This is the temple of the Lord, the temple of the Lord, the temple of the Lord." For if you truly amend your ways and your doings, if you truly execute justice one with another, if you do not oppress the alien, the fatherless or the widow, or shed innocent blood in this place (*maqom*), and if you do not go after other Gods to your own hurt, then I will let you dwell in this place (*maqom*), in the land that I gave of old to your fathers for ever. (Jer 7:4-7)

At the end of the Ezekelian story God will establish his "place" in conjunction with the terminology of glory and spirit and with a reminder of the destruction of the city pursuant to the prophetic vision at Chebar:

> Afterward he brought me to the gate, the gate facing east. And behold, the glory of the God of Israel came from the east; and the sound of his coming was like the sound of many waters; and the earth shone with his glory. And the vision I saw was like the vision which I had seen when he came to destroy the city, and like the vision which I had seen by the river Chebar; and I fell upon my

face. As the glory of the Lord entered the temple by the gate facing east, the Spirit lifted me up, and brought me into the inner court; and behold, the glory of the Lord filled the temple. While the man was standing beside me, I heard one speaking to me out of the temple; and he said to me, "Son of man, this is the place of my throne and the place of the soles of my feet, where I will dwell in the midst of the people of Israel for ever. And the house of Israel shall no more defile my holy name, neither they, nor their kings, by their harlotry, and by the dead bodies of their kings, by setting their threshold by my threshold and their doorposts beside my doorposts, with only a wall between me and them. They have defiled my holy name by their abominations which they have committed, so I have consumed them in my anger." (43:1-8)

Thus, the glory of the Lord is more blessed than its or his abode.[19] The centrality of this statement is that it imposes lengthy patience on its hearers to understand its meaning. The "blessing" disappears after 3:12 until it is heard again in chapter 34—and twice in a row so that it will not be passed over—in conjunction with the land of peace, where it is clear, just as it was in Genesis 1, that the blessing lies in the fruits of the earth bestowed on the humans and animals that enable them to live:

> I will make with them a covenant of peace and banish wild beasts from the land, so that they may dwell securely in the wilderness and sleep in the woods. And I will make them and the places round about my hill a blessing; and I will send down the showers in their season; they shall be showers of blessing. And the trees of the field shall yield their fruit, and the earth shall yield its increase, and they shall be secure in their land; and they shall know that I am the Lord, when I break the bars of their yoke, and deliver them from the hand of those who enslaved them. (Ezek 34:25-27)

---

[19] In the Hebrew original *mekomo* (his/its place) the suffix *o* can refer to either *yahweh* or *kabod* that are both in the masculine grammatical gender; Hebrew has only two genders, the masculine and the feminine.

The test for the people as to whether they are acknowledging in thanksgiving the divine gift of blessing is for them to share it with "the Levitical priests, the sons of Zadok" who are in charge of God's sanctuary (44:15), yet who have no inheritance:

> They shall have no inheritance; I am their inheritance: and you shall give them no possession in Israel; I am their possession. They shall eat the cereal offering, the sin offering, and the guilt offering; and every devoted thing in Israel shall be theirs. And the first of all the first fruits of all kinds, and every offering of all kinds from all your offerings, shall belong to the priests; you shall also give to the priests the first of your coarse meal, that a blessing may rest on your house. (44:28-30)

Since the glory of the Lord is more blessed and thus greater that the temple itself, the odyssey of Ezekiel starts in Chebar, where God's chariot is first spotted by the prophet, and not in Jerusalem, which is already in the past tense since the mission is to the exiles (3:15), the living remnant of that city. Ezekiel's mission is not an easy one; that is why he embarks on it not so wholeheartedly: "I went in bitterness in the heat of my spirit." (3:14b) It is as though his "spirit" was recalcitrant against the "spirit" of the Lord. That is why we are told again and in no uncertain terms that the Lord's hand prevailed on him. The wordplay in the original is powerful: "... the hand of the Lord being strong (*ḥazaqah*; hard, harsh, overpowering, holding tight) upon me." (v.14c) Thus God has the upper hand! In any case, the prophet is fated by his assigned name. Even if the outcome is that he would remain seven full days "overwhelmed" (*mašmim*; stupefied, devastated) among the exiles (v.15b), not being able to open his mouth, God will be sure to give him a nudge at the end of that period: "And at the end of seven days, the word of the Lord came to me." (v.16)

Ezekiel is sent to the exiles who are said to be residing at *tel-'abib* (v.15a). This name is unique in scripture and thus is evidently functional in Ezekiel. It is made out of the two nouns, *tel* meaning a mound of ruins[20] and *'abib* referring to the ripe ears of grain (Ex 9:31; Lev 2:14) and thus to the March/April period of the grain harvest. One can surmise that the immediate reason for Ezekiel's feeling of overwhelming stupefaction and devastation has to do with the noun *tel*; he felt that his mission was futile since his addressees were living in a place of ruin and would never get out of it given that they were bound to refuse his message. This surmise becomes virtually an assured fact when one remembers Jeremiah's oracle against Rabbah of the Ammonites where the Lord says "it shall become a *desolate mound* (*tel šemamah*; a mound of desolation), and its villages shall be burned with fire" (Jer 49:2); the noun *šemamah* is from the same root as the adjectival participle *mašmim* that described Ezekiel's status (Ezek 3:14): seeing the devastation, he felt devastated. Still, the month of *'abib* is the month of the exodus out of Egypt (Ex 13:4; 23:15; 34:18; Deut 16:1), and thus its mention opens a door in the mind of the hearers for eventual salvation. One can see how this wordplay rejoins that of "bone": out of a heap (*tel*) of bones God, in his own time, will bring about a new people (Ezek 37:1-14). However, for the time being, the exiles are in the *tel* where the sins of their fathers (*'abot*) brought them; the pun is unmistakable since the first syllable in both nouns, *'ab,* means "father."

The phrase "the end of seven days" betrays the allotted time after which God decides to have Ezekiel start his mission.

---

[20] See Deut 13:16 (You shall gather all its spoil into the midst of its open square, and burn the city and all its spoil with fire, as a whole burnt offering to the Lord your God; it shall be a heap (*tel*) for ever, it shall not be built again); Josh 8:28 (So Joshua burned Ai, and made it for ever a heap (*tel*) of ruins, as it is to this day).

"Seven" is the expression of divine fullness. Indeed the beginning of the actual mission is evident in the use of the first in a lengthy series of "the word of the Lord came *to me*" (3:16). Its earlier use was merely the statement of the narrator: "the word of the Lord came *to Ezekiel the priest*, the son of Buzi" (1:3). Ezekiel is assigned to be the "watchman" for the house of Israel (3:17). The uniqueness of this mission is obvious in that, among all the prophets, he alone is given this title by God himself. All instances of watchman occur in two texts that are parallel, if not analogous, in content, one at the beginning (3:17), and the other at the end (33:2, 6, 7) of the story of punishment and restoration. The close connection between the two passages is underscored by the same verbatim divine address, "son of man, I have made you a watchman for the house of Israel," which is found in its first and last instances (3:17a; 33:7a).[21] What is impressive is that, in both cases, the assignment of the watchman is to "speak" rather than "act," which corroborates our findings earlier regarding 3:1-9. Ezekiel's mission as watchman is not to watch the actions of the house of Israel, but rather to watch his words to them: "whenever you hear a word from my mouth, you shall give them warning from me." (3:17b and 33:7b) He is not accountable for their actions, but for whether or not he would have told them what God is asking him to:

> If I say to the wicked, "You shall surely die," and you give him no warning, nor speak to warn the wicked from his wicked way, in order to save his life, that wicked man shall die in his iniquity; but *his blood I will require at your hand*. But if you warn the wicked, and he does not turn from his wickedness, or from his wicked way, he shall die in his iniquity; but *you will have saved your life*. Again, if a righteous man turns from his righteousness and

---

[21] "you" is omitted after "I have made" by RSV in 33:7, but it appears in the Hebrew in both cases.

commits iniquity, and I lay a stumbling block before him, he shall die; because you have not warned him, he shall die for his sin, and his righteous deeds which he has done shall not be remembered; but *his blood I will require at your hand*. Nevertheless if you warn the righteous man not to sin, and he does not sin, he shall surely live, because he took warning; and *you will have saved your life*. (3:18-21)

If I say to the wicked, O wicked man, you shall surely die, and you do not speak to warn the wicked to turn from his way, that wicked man shall die in his iniquity, but *his blood I will require at your hand*. But if you warn the wicked to turn from his way, and he does not turn from his way; he shall die in his iniquity, but *you will have saved your life*. (33:8-9)

Should Ezekiel abide by his assignment, he will be relieved of all accountability since the responsibility will then lie with the wicked. This is clear from the term '*awon* used to refer to his "iniquity" (3:18, 19; 33:8, 9). The Hebrew '*awon* has the same connotation as the English "guilt," and is often translated as such, which reflects both the sinful action and the responsibility therefor and thus the punishment it entails;[22] hence the expressions "to bear (carry) one's guilt"—corresponding to the Hebrew *naśa' 'awon* that is often found in scripture—and "to be guilty of something one did."

The last verses of chapter 3 (vv.22-27) set the stage for the entire book. First, given Ezekiel's difficult mission, we hear again that the Lord's hand is upon him (v.22a), which is an expression of God's power; the initiative is never left to the prophet. This time we learn that Ezekiel is sent specifically to the *biq'ah* (plain) whose mention is repeated (vv.22b and 23), which reflects its

---

[22] That '*awon* has both these connotations, is borne out by the fact that in 4:4-6 it is translated all five times as "punishment."

importance for the author. Indeed, as with many of the previous terms, the noun *biq'ah* brackets the Ezekelian story: after its passing occurrence in 8:4, where reference is specifically made to 3:22-23, it appears twice again in chapter 37 (vv.1 and 2; translated as "valley" in RSV)[23] to indicate the locale of the dry bones and their raising. The Hebrew *biq'ah* means "spot" and thus refers to a small area that can be spotted at a distance due to its interest for the beholder in spite of its insignificance. It is much less impressive than an oasis where a water pond is evident. The *biq'ah* is a small area that can minimally sustain life due to the little water that runs through it. The famous large plain between the Lebanon and Anti-Lebanon mountain chains is known as the Beqaa (or Bekaa) Valley and, in the original Arabic, *wady 'al-biqa'*, *biqa'* being the plural of *biq'at*, which corresponds to the Hebrew *biq'ah*. An aerial view or a view from the high chain of Lebanese mountains will show intermittent green "spots" of agriculture amid either mountainous or arid spans of land. Whereas an oasis, though a far cry from a city, still blossoms with life, a *biq'ah* is more a "promise" of life. Hence the choice is clearly intentional: there will be life *if* and *when* God wills it! The hearers of Ezekiel cannot possibly miss the point since they already heard in scripture's first book that the exact same *biq'ah* (plain; Gen 11:2)[24] was arrogantly used by humankind "to build ourselves a city, and a tower with its top in the heavens and ... make a name for ourselves" (v.4). Further, that same location was the land of Nimrod, "the first on earth to be a mighty man" (10:8). In Hebrew *nimrod* means "we (shall)

---

[23] It is worth noting once more the predicament of translations which very often cover up intentional essential interconnections in the original.

[24] In Gen 10:9 we hear that Babel (Babylon) was "in the land of Shinar" where the *biq'ah* lay (11:2). A further reason for the unmistakable connection is that this is the only instance of *biq'ah* in the Pentateuch until Deut 8:7.

God's Glory is Independent of the Temple 91

rebel," and a derivative of that same verb (*marad*) is used twice in Ezekiel 2:3 to describe the attitude of the children of Israel. The Lord, however, did not shy from bringing to naught humankind's schemes (Gen 11:5-9), so let the exiled addressees and any hearers of Ezekiel beware!

In order to underscore that we are still at the outset of Ezekiel's mission, the hearers are faced again with the same basic features that marked the introductory chapter 1: "So I arose and went forth into the plain; and, lo, the glory of the Lord stood there, like the glory which I had seen by the river Chebar; and I fell on my face. But the Spirit entered into me, and set me upon my feet; and he spoke with me and said to me." (Ezek 3:23-24) However, this time, the prophet is asked to keep quiet *until* he is prompted by the Lord to speak, another stratagem to make the hearers fully realize that Ezekiel is under God's full control, unlike "the foolish prophets who follow their own spirit" and say "thus says the Lord" when he has not spoken (13:3, 7b). Although having eaten the scroll, Ezekiel is still not lord over it. The scroll contains God's words and God alone decides when they are to be dispensed. The purpose of Ezekiel's silence is to allow the exiles to continue doing what they are doing and not allow them to cover up their rebelliousness. Thus whenever God would chastise, he would be "justified in his sentence and blameless in his judgment" (Ps 51:4b):

> And you, O son of man, behold, cords will be placed upon you, and you shall be bound with them, so that you cannot go out among the people; and I will make your tongue cleave to the roof of your mouth, so that you shall be dumb and unable to reprove them; for they are a rebellious house. But when I speak with you, I will open your mouth, and you shall say to them, 'Thus says the Lord God'; he that will hear, let him hear; and he that will refuse

to hear, let him refuse; for they are a rebellious house. (Ezek 3:25-27)

This approach rejoins that in Isaiah 6:

> And he said, "Go, and say to this people: 'Hear and hear, but do not understand; see and see, but do not perceive.' Make the heart of this people fat, and their ears heavy, and shut their eyes; lest they see with their eyes, and hear with their ears, and understand with their hearts, and turn and be healed." Then I said, "How long, O Lord?" And he said: "Until cities lie waste without inhabitant, and houses without men, and the land is utterly desolate, and the Lord removes men far away, and the forsaken places are many in the midst of the land. And though a tenth remain in it, it will be burned again, like a terebinth or an oak, whose stump remains standing when it is felled." (vv.9-13)

Ezekiel will function as a watchman when his mouth will be opened (Ezek 3:27a); then the hearers will freely choose their own way (v.27b); the prophet will not be accountable for their actions as per God's word in vv.17-21. With this matter cleared, Ezekiel's mission of dispensing the divine "words of lamentation and mourning and woe" (2:10) is on its way.

Part II

The Ezekelian Story

4
The Ezekelian Story

As is the case in Jeremiah, and more so in Ezekiel where Babylon plays the role of God's obedient servant,[1] it is imperative first and foremost to drill into the hearers' conscience that the fall of the two sisters, Samaria (the capital of the Kingdom [house] of Israel) and Jerusalem (the capital of the Kingdom [house] of Judah), was of their own doing, or rather the doing of their own deity, the judge of all.[2] By reminding the exiles of the one behind the destruction of their city and, by the same token, the author of their scattering, the tone is set: in the future they are to deal with him and him alone, as he holds their fate in his "hand." But why would the author include the long forgotten older sister Samaria that fell to the Assyrians? Once again the answer lies in realizing that he is looking ahead to the end of the story, as is systematically the case with all major terminology in the text. As we shall see in detail in chapters 16 and 23, the children of the younger sister will not be allowed to gloat: the sin of their "mother" is greater than that of their "aunt." The ultimate intent is to prepare them for the final message of salvation: they shall be restored together as one family of "brethren." Indeed, immediately after the passage of the dry bones and their raising (37:1-14) we hear:

> The word of the Lord came to me: "Son of man, take a stick and write on it, 'For Judah, and the children of Israel associated with him'; then take another stick and write upon it, 'For Joseph (the stick of Ephraim) and all the house of Israel associated with him';

---

[1] See my earlier comments on this matter in chapter 3.
[2] See excursus below concerning the two Kingdoms of Israel and Judah.

and join them together into one stick, that they may become one in your hand. And when your people say to you, Will you not show us what you mean by these? say to them, Thus says the Lord God: Behold, I am about to take the stick of Joseph (which is in the hand of Ephraim) and the tribes of Israel associated with him; and I will join with it the stick of Judah, and make them one stick, that they may be one in my hand. When the sticks on which you write are in your hand before their eyes, then say to them, Thus says the Lord God: Behold, I will take the people of Israel from the nations among which they have gone, and will gather them from all sides, and bring them to their own land; and I will make them one nation in the land, upon the mountains of Israel; and one king shall be king over them all; and they shall be no longer two nations, and no longer divided into two kingdoms." (37:15-22)

Since God's will is already inscribed in the eternal scroll,[3] the Lord's medium is none other than Ezekiel in whose stomach lies that scroll. It is he, the prophet, who will enact the siege of Jerusalem that brought about its end (4:1-3). Furthermore, this will be a "sign" for the house of Israel (v.3b). Not only is this siege willed by God, but so are its meaning and lesson. The lesson intended is that the iniquity of both cities, cast as *'awon* (4:4-6; translated as punishment), as well as the iniquity of the exiles themselves (3:18, 19) brought all this about.

Samaria and Jerusalem, as two independent entities, are addressed separately by Ezekiel (4:4-7). What is definitely impressive is that the same Ezekiel is presented as being behind the fall of Samaria. This is a unique feature in prophetic literature; namely, that the same prophet is the messenger behind the destruction of two cities that were sacked over one hundred

---

[3] I am here plagiarizing Rev 14:6 that speaks of an "eternal gospel."

The Ezekelian Story

twenty years apart, according to the extra-scriptural as well as scriptural records! The explanation for this is linked to the fact that the message in Ezekiel is a written scroll conceived by the one seated upon the throne above the firmament, and thus it is valid for all ages and generations. In order to impress this reality upon the hearers, its effect is shown to be stretching as far back as possible, a stratagem that will culminate in chapter 16 where even the long extinct Sodom is included under its verdict. The result is that the hearers are to concede that God's indictment has always been true and, more importantly, his chastisement has consistently taken its course without faltering. Thus, for them, there is no way out.

To make his point even more pertinent, the author renders Samaria's fate in more detail (4:9-15) than that of Jerusalem (vv.16-17). However, there is no room for gloating, as will be made clear in chapters 16 and 23, wherein Jerusalem's punishment will outdo that of Samaria. For the time being, the hearers who have perceptive ears to hear (3:27) will be aware that the 390 days of Samaria's siege represent a shorter period than the 40 days of Jerusalem's siege. In scriptural metaphoric language, it is the basic numbers that have values; using their multiples is a way of stressing the point. Thus ten indicates a fullness of time, as do its multiples 100, 1000 or a myriad (10,000). The numeral four reflects totality as in the four directions of the globe (east, west, north, and south) or the four walls of a building; accordingly, forty would be an all-encompassing reality in totality and fullness.[4] Consequently, the

---

[4] Forty is used in the metaphor to describe Israel's years of wandering in the Sinai wilderness (Ex 16:35; Num 32:13; Deut 29:5; Josh 5:6), Jesus' forty days in the Judean wilderness (Mt 4:2; Mk 1:13; Lk 4:2), and his forty days of instruction to his disciples (Acts 1:3). Forty is also used in conjunction with the full adult age of an

40 days of Jerusalem's siege represent full and total divine punishment, and the 390 days of Samaria's siege indicate a lesser punishment: almost as much, but still not equal to that of Jerusalem.

In any event, Samaria will fade in the background and Jerusalem will take center stage starting with chapter 5. It is clear that Judah's fate is Ezekiel's prime concern; he is a Jerusalemite exile and, as such, his fate is intertwined with that of Judah. This is corroborated in the terminology of "stupefaction" used to describe the predicaments of their situation of "uncleanness" and "defilement" in a foreign land, which is not used in regard to the house of Israel:

> "... and I came to the exiles at Tel-abib, who dwelt by the river Chebar. And I sat there overwhelmed (*mašmim*; stupefied, horrified) among them seven days." (3:15)

> Moreover he said to me, "Son of man, behold, I will break the staff of bread in Jerusalem; they shall eat bread by weight and with fearfulness; and they shall drink water by measure and in dismay (*šimmamon*; horror, stupefaction). I will do this that they may lack bread and water, and look at one another in dismay (*našammu*; be horrified, desolate), and waste away under their punishment."[5] (4:16-17)

> And the Lord said, "Thus shall the people of Israel eat their bread unclean (*ṭame'*; defiled, impure), among the nations whither I will drive them." Then I said, "Ah Lord God! behold, I have never defiled (*meṭumma'ah*) myself; from my youth up till now I have

---

individual and thus a given generation, after which there is the return to the beginning of a new individual or a new generation.

[5] All three Hebrew terms are from the same root *šmm*.

never eaten what died of itself or was torn by beasts, nor has foul flesh come into my mouth."[6] (4:13-14)

In all cases, though, the punishment inflicted by God is famine for "bread," which occurs no less than six times in nine verses (vv.9, 13, 15, 16 [twice], 17). The intention is to bombard the hearers with the lack of this basic staple of life in order to make them realize that it is only abiding by the divine statutes and ordinances that will grant them life on any portion of earth where they might be and will protect them when God righteously judges them (5:6-8).

Excursus

The reference to two "houses," of Israel and Judah, in Ezekiel 4:4-6[7] is due to the fact that there were two separate kingdoms as is evident from the story of David's reign in 2 Samuel:

> Then all the tribes of Israel came to David at Hebron, and said, "Behold, we are your bone and flesh. In times past, when Saul was king over us, it was you that led out and brought in Israel; and the Lord said to you, 'You shall be shepherd of my people Israel, and you shall be prince over Israel.'" So all the elders of Israel came to the king at Hebron; and King David made a covenant with them at Hebron before the Lord, and they anointed David king over Israel. David was thirty years old when he began to reign, and he reigned forty years. At Hebron he reigned over Judah seven years and six months; and at Jerusalem he reigned over all Israel and Judah thirty-three years. (5:1-5)

---

[6] Both Hebrew terms are two verbal forms of the same verb *tame'*.

[7] See also Zech 10:6 (I will strengthen the house of Judah, and I will save the house of Joseph. I will bring them back because I have compassion on them, and they shall be as though I had not rejected them; for I am the Lord their God and I will answer them).

The Kingdom of Israel gelled around the two more prominent tribes of Ephraim and Manasseh, the sons of Joseph. That is why, in the prophetic books, that kingdom is also referred to as "Joseph" (Am 5:6, 15; 6:6; Ob 18) and "Ephraim" (Is 7:2-9; Jer 7:15; Hos; Zech 9:10, 13). On the other hand, due to that prominence of the tribes of Joseph among the descendants of Jacob, the Kingdom of Israel is also addressed as "Jacob" (Am 3:13-14; 6-14-7:5; Ob 17-18; Mic 5:7-8) and, by the same token, "Israel" (Mic 1:5; 2:12; 3:1, 8-9; Nah 2:2) since the latter is Jacob's other name (Gen 32:28). In turn, out of deference to the forefather Jacob the one combined "house" of Judah and Joseph is the "house of Israel" as is clear form Ezekiel 37:

> The word of the Lord came to me: "Son of man, take a stick and write on it, 'For Judah, and *the children of Israel associated with him*'; then take another stick and write upon it, 'For Joseph (the stick of Ephraim) and *all the house of Israel associated with him*'; and join them together into one stick, that they may become one in your hand. And when your people say to you, 'Will you not show us what you mean by these?' say to them, Thus says the Lord God: Behold, I am about to take the stick of Joseph (which is in the hand of Ephraim) and *the tribes of Israel associated with him*; and I will join with it the stick of Judah, and make them one stick, that they may be one in my hand. When the sticks on which you write are in your hand before their eyes, then say to them, Thus says the Lord God: Behold, I will take *the people*[8] *of Israel* from the nations among which they have gone, and will gather them from all sides, and bring them to their own land; and I will make them one nation in the land, upon *the mountains of Israel*; and one king shall be king over them all; and they shall be no longer two nations, and no longer divided into two kingdoms." (vv.15-22)

---

[8] The original Hebrew has "children."

The Divine Indictment

After having singled out famine in chapter 4 for his obvious purpose, in chapter 5 Ezekiel completes the picture by appealing to fire, sword, and exile (v.2). The Ancient Near East was filled with "city-states." A city and the few "villages" surrounding it accounted for virtually the entire population of a given area. A picture frequently encountered in scripture is the city, in effect, taking on the role of a "mother" and its citizens becoming her "children." Mother and children are the two sides of the same coin as we shall see in chapters 16 and 23. The siege is the classic scriptural metaphor for divine total punishment against a city. Since the numeral four represents totality, the calamity of a siege is usually expressed in four afflictions, the favorite cluster being famine, fire, sword, and exile. The enemy could maintain a long siege during which the beleaguered citizenry fell to famine, illness (pestilence), or death by fire or by the sword. The lucky among them were taken as prisoners into exile. However, Ezekiel prefaces all of this with a reference to shame, an element that will prove to be central in his teaching, that is, instruction through shaming. This is immediately introduced in 5:1 where Ezekiel is ordered to cut his hair and beard. It was demeaning to have one's hair and especially one's beard shaven (2 Sam 10:4-5; Ezra 9:2-3; Is 15:2-3; 50:6; Jer 48:36-37), the beard being the symbol of an elder.

The most extreme expression of shame, however, is punishment by one's own deity, that is, one's parent and protector, in front of outsiders, especially in front of one's enemies. This is precisely what God will do to Jerusalem and her children (Ezek 5:5-8), a lesson they could, or at least should, never forget. Indeed, the uniqueness of God's action is underscored in no uncertain terms: "And because of all your abominations I will do with you what I have never yet done, and the like of which I will never do again." (v.9) The famine will be so extreme that "fathers shall eat their sons in the midst of you, and sons shall eat their fathers" (v.10a). Yet, what they did in Jerusalem, that is, not having "walked in my statutes or kept my ordinances, but have acted according to the ordinances of the nations that are round about you" (v.7b), they will continue to do in the land of their punishment (20:32). But this will not matter since it was taken into consideration when God summoned Ezekiel to spell out the content of the scroll "whether they hear or refuse to hear" (2:5, 7; 3:11). Actually, according to 1 Samuel 8, God already had a full taste of this recurring attitude on the part of the children of Israel when their forefathers did the same thing as Ezekiel's contemporaries are doing:

> Then all the elders of Israel gathered together and came to Samuel at Ramah, and said to him, "Behold, you are old and your sons do not walk in your ways; now appoint for us a king to govern us like all the nations." (1 Sam 8:4-5)

God's answer to Samuel was the prototype of what he would eventually say to Ezekiel:

> And the Lord said to Samuel, "Hearken to the voice of the people in all that they say to you; for they have not rejected you, but they have rejected me from being king over them." (1 Sam 8:7)

> And he said to me ... "But the house of Israel will not listen to you; for they are not willing to listen to me." (Ezek 3:4a, 7)

The wordplay in the original, unrecognizable in RSV, reflects that the divine judgments in 5:8, 10, and 15 are in direct relation to, and thus an indictment for, the broken ordinances (vv.6 and 7). Whereas in vv.10 and 15 "judgments" is a rendering of *šephaṭim* (plural of *šepheṭ* meaning the act of judgment), in v.8 it is the Hebrew *mišphaṭim* (plural of *mišphaṭ* meaning the emitted, proclaimed judgment) that is used in the original. This same *mišphaṭim* is used four times in vv.6 and 7, and in all cases RSV translates it as "ordinances." Since *šephaṭim* in vv.10 and 15 and *mišphaṭim* in v.8 occur as complement nouns of the same verb *'aśah* (do, make, execute), their intended purpose is to stress God's intervention as judge. Consequently, the express use of *mišphaṭim* in v.8 is to underscore the justice of God since his judgment is done according to his ordinances *as laws* and thus is just to the extent that it is legal. Put otherwise, the condemned will receive only their *just* punishment. Later we shall hear another version: "I will judge you according to your ways ... I will punish you for your ways ... I will judge you according to your ways ... I will punish you according to your ways." (7:3, 4, 8, 9) The same thought is also found in 24:14b (according to your ways and your doings I will judge you) whose link to chapter 5 is evident through the use of the same verb *ḥus*: "I will execute judgments on you ... I will cut you down; my eye *will not spare* (*lo' taḥos*), and I will have no pity" (5:10-11); "I will not go back, I *will not spare* (*lo' 'aḥus*), I will not repent." (24:14a)

Chapter 5 uses the same device that we have encountered several times before, namely, the stratagem of bracketing the story. In 5:11 we find the first of seven instances of the verb *ḥamal* whose meaning is "carry the burden of something (instead of someone else, for someone else's sake)" and thus "have mercy, pity": "Wherefore, as I live, says the Lord God, surely, because you have defiled my sanctuary with all your detestable things and with all your abominations, therefore I will cut you down; my eye will not spare, and I will have no pity (*'eḥmol*)." It occurs five more times in 7:4, 9; 8:18; 9:5, 10 with exactly the same connotation as is evident in that "having no pity" is systematically paired with "the eye not sparing."[9] It then disappears until 36:21 where it is used in a positive connotation: "But I had concern (*'eḥmol*) for my holy name, which the house of Israel caused to be profaned among the nations to which they came. Therefore say to the house of Israel, Thus says the Lord God: It is not for your sake, O house of Israel, that I am about to act, but for the sake of my holy name, which you have profaned among the nations to which you came." (vv.21-22) So, ultimately, the Lord's intervention that redresses the situation is rooted in a "change of heart" on his part without being prodded by something the exiles will have done; indeed, how could "very dry bones" do anything? He will suddenly decide to bear with them and carry their burden out of sheer beneficence.

The Height of Arrogance

Chapter 6 is specifically addressed to the mountains of Israel, particularly their multiplicity. The importance given them is noticeable at the outset; not only is their mention repeated (vv.2 and 3), but the reference to them is further detailed in that they are included with "the hills, the ravines and the valleys" (v.3). The intention of this inclusion is multifaceted. First, it presents the mountains as an all-encompassing reference to the entire land as is evident in the parallel text where the cities are part of the picture: "therefore, O mountains of Israel, hear the word of

---

[9] As in the case of Ezekiel, God works through his emissaries who do exactly his bidding as alter egos would: "Then he cried in my ears with a loud voice, saying, 'Draw near, you executioners of the city, each with his destroying weapon in his hand' ... And to the others he said in my hearing, 'Pass through the city after him, and smite; your eye shall not spare, and you shall show no pity' ... 'As for me, my eye will not spare, nor will I have pity, but I will requite their deeds upon their heads.'" (Ezek 9:1, 5, 10)

The Ezekelian Story

the Lord God: Thus says the Lord God to the mountains and the hills, the ravines and the valleys, the desolate wastes and the deserted cities, which have become a prey and derision to the rest of the nations round about." (36:4) Secondly, the choice of mountains as representative of the totality has to do with their height, and thus they symbolize the arrogance of the people residing in the land. Thirdly, though the mention of "ravines (*'aphiqim*) and valleys (*ge'ayot*)" seems out of order, they reflect depth rather than elevation and thus humility rather than pride and haughtiness. Their unexpected inclusion serves to enhance the elevation of the mountains and the hills, hence their addition is functional. This is corroborated by the following factors:

1. In Ezekiel one finds by far the highest incidence of *'aphiqim* in the Prophets, seven compared to once in Isaiah and twice in Joel. Only in Ezekiel does *'aphiqim* occur in conjunction with mountains, whereas in Isaiah (8:7) and Joel (1:20; 3:18) the term refers to streams or waterbeds.

2. All instances of *ge'ayot* in Ezekiel are found together with mountains.

3. In Ezekiel 31:2-12 where both terms are used together in parallel with mountains, the immediate context clearly refers to height and haughtiness:

> "Son of man, say to Pharaoh king of Egypt and to his multitude: 'Whom are you like in your greatness? Behold, I will liken you to a cedar in Lebanon, with fair branches and forest shade, and of great height, its top

among the clouds. The waters nourished it, the deep made it grow tall, making its rivers flow round the place of its planting, sending forth its streams to all the trees of the forest. So it towered high above all the trees of the forest; its boughs grew large and its branches long, from abundant water in its shoots. All the birds of the air made their nests in its boughs; under its branches all the beasts of the field brought forth their young; and under its shadow dwelt all great nations. It was beautiful in its greatness, in the length of its branches; for its roots went down to abundant waters. The cedars in the garden of God could not rival it, nor the fir trees equal its boughs; the plane trees were as nothing compared with its branches; no tree in the garden of God was like it in beauty. I made it beautiful in the mass of its branches, and all the trees of Eden envied it, that were in the garden of God. Therefore thus says the Lord God: Because it towered high and set its top among the clouds, and its heart was proud of its height, I will give it into the hand of a mighty one of the nations; he shall surely deal with it as its wickedness deserves. I have cast it out. Foreigners, the most terrible of the nations, will cut it down and leave it. On the mountains and in all the valleys (*ge'ayot*) its branches will fall, and its boughs will lie broken in all the watercourses (*'aphiqim*) of the land; and all the peoples of the earth will go from its shadow and leave it.'"

4. Lastly, those knowledgeable in Hebrew will notice that chapter 7 proceeds on the same line of invective. Where *ge'ayot* occurs in conjunction with "mountains" (v. 16), the same indictment of haughtiness is leveled against the children of Israel in these terms: "Their beautiful ornament they used for vainglory (*ga'on*), and they made their abominable images and their detestable things of it; therefore I will make it an unclean thing to them … I will bring the worst of the nations to take possession of their houses; I will put an end to their proud (*ga'on*) might, and their holy places shall be profaned." (7:20, 24) The Hebrew root *g'(y)*— has the connotation of "haughtiness," majesty," "exaltation," "pride," "arrogance' and occurs in many forms. On the other hand, *ge'ayot* is the plural of the noun *gay'* whose root is *gy'*. The only time in scripture where *ge'ayot* (consonantal *g'yot*) is written as *ge'ayt* (consonantal *g'yt*), which links it to the root *gy'*, is in Ezekiel 6:3. The consonantal *g'yt* is very close to *g'ut* which is one of the nouns from the root *g'(y)*— connoting "haughtiness." Since this is its first occurrence in the book of Ezekiel, it is not beyond acceptable reason to assume that its consonantal writing was deliberately used to draw attention to the mountains' height and thus haughtiness, which will be brought out in chapter 7 where *ge'ayot* occurs with "mountains" (v.16) and *'aphiqim* is not included.

The mountains are linked to the "high places" (*bamot*, plural of *bamah*; 6:3, 6), "altars" (*mizbahot*, plural of *mizbeah*; vv.4, 5, 6, 13) and "idols" (*gillulim*, plural of *gillul*; vv.4, 6, 9, 13). In turn, these four elements, which appear for the first time in Ezekiel 6, are clearly connected to "abominations" (*to'abot*; plural of *to'ebah*; vv. 9, 11) that we encountered twice in vv.9 and 11 of the previous chapter. This being the case, then chapter 6 functions as an explanation of "abominations," namely, going after other deities rather than the Lord who appeared to Ezekiel without linkage to any high place or altar. Another term for such behavior is harlotry as is evident from v.9: "Yet I will leave some of you alive. When you have among the nations some who escape the sword, and when you are scattered through the countries, then those of you who escape will remember me among the nations where they are carried captive, when I have broken their wanton (*zoneh*; committing harlotry) heart[10] which has departed from me, and blinded their eyes which turn wantonly (*zonot*; commit harlotry) after their idols; and they will be loathsome in their own sight for the evils which they have committed, for all their *abominations*." (vv.8-9) Harlotry will be the express theme of the repeated parabolic story of Jerusalem in chapters 16 and 23.

It is worth noting that it is precisely the "abominations" that explain the "dismay" felt by the children of Israel (4:16, 17) and the prophet himself (3:15). The root *šmm* encountered in *mašmim* (overwhelmed; stupefied, horrified; 3:15), *šimmamon* (dismay; horror, stupefaction; 4:16), and *našammu* (be horrified, desolate, dismayed; v.17) is found thrice in chapter 6, once at the beginning (v.4) and twice in a row in the concluding verse. In all

---

[10] The same heart that earlier was said to be "hardened" (*hizqe leb*; 2:4) and "stubborn" (*qeše leb*; 3:7).

cases it refers to God's inflicting the dismay as punishment against the cause of the people's and the prophet's dismay. Their altars will be put to shame as will the land with its mountains, the high places, where the idols are situated:

> Thus says the Lord God to the mountains and the hills, to the ravines and the valleys: Behold, I, even I, will bring a sword upon you, and I will destroy your high places. Your altars shall become desolate (*našammu*), and your incense altars shall be broken; and I will cast down your slain before your idols. (vv.3b-4)

> And I will stretch out my hand against them, and make the land desolate (*šemamah*) and waste (*mešammah*), throughout all their habitations, from the wilderness to Riblah. Then they will know that I am the Lord. (v.14)

Still, chapter 6 holds two more important features. The first corroborates what we found in chapters 2 and 3: Ezekiel's message is that God himself is punishing the children of Israel for their abominations and, more importantly, through the punished Israel this message is addressed beyond Israel to all nations. Behind his breaking the incense altars (6:4) and the idols (v.6), God's real intention is to break the people's heart (v.9). He does that through the siege of their city: "by sword, by famine, and by pestilence" (vv.11-12). However, it is the fourth curse of the siege, the scattering of the survivors into exile (v.8), which will prove to be the medium for spreading God's message among the nations. Those survivors, when asked about the reason behind their exile, will have to acknowledge openly what happened, and then not only the nations, but also and primarily they themselves "shall know that I am the Lord; I have not said in vain that I would do this evil to them" (v.10). The importance of this thought is reflected in its repetition a few verses later and as the concluding statement: "And I will stretch out my hand against them, and make the land desolate and waste, throughout all their habitations, from the wilderness to Riblah. Then they will know that I am the Lord." (v.14)

The second feature, a corollary of the first, is the priority of God's words over the event. This confirms that what takes place *in scripture* does so at the direct and express dictate of God. Consequently, the priority is not the event but God's promise which precedes the event, regardless of whether what is promised is calamitous or beneficent. This feature is so predominant in Ezekiel that it recurs as a refrain in the book. Furthermore, the most frequent "they shall know that I am the Lord" is a shortened formula for "you shall know that I, the Lord, have spoken, and I have done it, says the Lord" (37:14), as is evident from the following previous instances:

> … and they shall know that I, the Lord, have spoken in my jealousy, when I spend my fury upon them. (5:13b)

> And they shall know that I am the Lord; I have not said in vain that I would do this evil to them. (6:10)

> Now I will soon pour out my wrath upon you, and spend my anger against you, and judge you according to your ways; and I will punish you for all your abominations. And my eye will not spare, nor will I have pity; I will punish you according to your ways, while your abominations are in your midst. Then you will know that I am the Lord, who smite. (7:8-9)

> This city shall not be your caldron, nor shall you be the flesh in the midst of it; I will judge you at the border of Israel; and you shall know that I am the Lord; for you have not walked in my statutes, nor executed my ordinances, but have acted according to the ordinances of the nations that are round about you. (11:11-12)

The Ezekelian Story

... and you shall know that I, the Lord, have spoken. (17:21)

Then the nations that are left round about you shall know that I, the Lord, have rebuilt the ruined places, and replanted that which was desolate; I, the Lord, have spoken, and I will do it. (36:36)

5

Abominations Bring an End to Jerusalem

From the repeated occurrence of "abominations" (*to'abot*; vv.3, 4, 8, 9, 20[1]) and the double instance of "my eye will not spare you, nor will I have pity" (vv.4 and 9), chapter 7 is unmistakably the continuation of the divine indictment that began with chapter 5. There we first heard "Wherefore, as I live, says the Lord God, surely, because you have defiled my sanctuary with all your detestable things and with all your abominations, therefore I will cut you down; my eye will not spare, and I will have no pity" (v.11). Chapter 7 functions as the finale of the trial since it is introduced as the "end" (*qeṣ*), the term that functions as the subject of the chapter (7:2 [twice], 3, 6 [twice]). The Semitic root *qṣ(ṣ)* has the meaning of cutting off and thus cutting short or putting an end to. As such, it fits the metaphor of harvest that is frequently used in scripture. At harvest time, one either cuts off, plucks, the ripe fruits or cuts down a tree that has proven fruitless. Put otherwise, at harvest the "end" can be either beneficent or menacing or, more precisely, an end that is expectedly positive can surprisingly turn sour, which is confirmed in what we hear in vv.6-7:

> An end has come, the end has come; it has awakened against you. Behold, it comes. Your doom has come to you, O inhabitant of the land; the time has come, the day is near, *a day of tumult, and not of joyful shouting* upon the mountains.

---

[1] In this verse RSV's "their abominable images" is the rendering of *ṣalme to'abotam*, literally "statues of their abominations."

The classic passage of such a state of affairs is found in Amos where we find a similar reference to both "the day of the Lord" and the "end." Moreover, in the case of "end" we have wordplay on the consonantal root *qṣ* connoting that end's direct connection with harvest:

> Woe to you who desire the day of the Lord! Why would you have the day of the Lord? It is darkness, and not light; as if a man fled from a lion, and a bear met him; or went into the house and leaned with his hand against the wall, and a serpent bit him. Is not the day of the Lord darkness, and not light, and gloom with no brightness in it? (5:18-20)

> Thus the Lord God showed me: behold, a basket of summer fruit (*qayṣ*). And he said, "Amos, what do you see?" And I said, "A basket of summer fruit (*qayṣ*)." Then the Lord said to me, "The end (*qeṣ*) has come upon my people Israel; I will never again pass by them." (8:1-2)

Since Ezekiel 7 is the last chapter that constitutes the introductory section of the first part of the book, one would expect to find another word or phrase that will have a hold on the Ezekelian story, as we have seen in the previous chapters, and indeed there is. At the outset of chapter 7 we find one of the central phrases of Ezekiel *'admat yisra'el* (v.2), which is unfortunately and misleadingly rendered as "the land of Israel" in RSV.[2] RSV does not differentiate between *'ereṣ yisra'el* (the earth of Israel) and *'admat yisra'el* (the ground of Israel), translating both of them as "the land of Israel." However, in the original Hebrew, the following is evident;

---

[2] The English "the land of" connotes piece of real estate with specific borders.

1. *'admat* is a Hebrew form, meaning "the ground of," from the original *'adamah* (earthly ground; dry ground as opposed to sea) that is the feminine of *'adam* (human being).

2. The first occurrence of *'admat yisra'el* in the book is directly linked to *ben 'adam* (son of man): "The word of the Lord came to me: 'And you, *ben 'adam*, thus says the Lord God to *'admat yisra'el.*'" (7:1-2a)

3. *'ereṣ yisra'el* is found only three times (27:17; 40:2; 47:18) compared to the twenty instances of *'admat yisra'el* spread throughout the first part of the book, chapters 1-39 (chs.7, 11, 12, 13, 18, 20, 21, 25, 33, 36, 37, 38).

4. Not only is *'admat yisra'el* a staple of Ezekiel, but it is only encountered in Ezekiel in the entire Old Testament which makes its use explicitly intentional.

The intimate relationship between *'adamah* and *'adam* is at its clearest in the story of the origin of man. The Hebrew *'adam* (man) is formed (as a potter forms a vessel from clay) out of the *'adamah* (ground). The priority of the "ground" of the earth is further underscored in that man is formed "of dust from the ground" (Gen 2:7), and he will return to dust upon his demise: "In the sweat of your face you shall eat bread till you return to the ground, for out of it you were taken; you are dust, and to dust you shall return." (3:19) The clarification that man is formed not directly out of the ground, but out of its dust, goes hand in hand with the pottery metaphor whereby a broken or unused pot may end up pulverized and not look like a vessel anymore. This fits perfectly with the belittling intention behind the epithet "son of man" in Ezekiel. As in the case of other words and phrases in Ezekiel, *'admat yisra'el* looks ahead toward its final occurrences in chapters 37 and 38. At the restoration, the dry bones will be raised and covered with sinew, flesh, and skin (37:8) and through the divine breathing (v.9) will be made into human beings (*'adam*), as in Genesis 2:7,[3] and as such will be brought into the *'admat yisra'el* (v.12).[4] This corresponds to the phraseology of the preceding chapter:

> For I will take you from the nations, and gather you from all the countries (*'araṣot*; plural of *'ereṣ* [earth]), and bring you into your own[5] land (*'admatekem*). I will sprinkle clean water upon you, and you shall be clean from all your uncleannesses, and from all your idols I will cleanse you. A new heart I will give you, and a new spirit I will put within you; and I will take out of your flesh the heart of stone and give you a heart of flesh. And I will put my spirit within you, and cause you to walk in my statutes and be careful to observe my ordinances. (36:24-27)

As is usual in Ezekiel, this statement harks back to a similar one at the beginning of the book:

> Therefore say, "Thus says the Lord God: I will gather you from the peoples, and assemble you out of the countries (*'araṣot*; plural of *'ereṣ* [earth]) where you have been scattered, and I will give you

---

[3] The correspondence is evident in the use of the same verb *naphaḥ* (breathe) in both instances.

[4] Here RSV betrays its understanding of "the land of Israel" as a deeded piece of real estate in that it adds the unwarranted "home" after the verb "bring": "Behold, I will open your graves, and raise you from your graves, O my people; and I will bring you *home* into the land of Israel."

[5] Again RSV, by adding the unwarranted "own," betrays its bias in viewing the *'admat yisra'el* as a deeded property.

the land of Israel (*'admat yisra'el*)." And when they come there, they will remove from it all its detestable things and all its abominations. And I will give them one heart, and put a new spirit within them; I will take the stony heart out of their flesh and give them a heart of flesh, that they may walk in my statutes and keep my ordinances and obey them; and they shall be my people, and I will be their God. (11:17-20)

What is striking here is that the renewed "heart of flesh" takes the place of the "heart of stone" in the *flesh* of the people, that is to say, in the people as flesh, just as *'adam* was made, which is precisely the point underscored in chapter 37. Consequently, *'admat yisra'el* is a phrase purposely coined by the author of Ezekiel to fit the message of the book and does not refer to a given piece of land, let alone country. This is corroborated in that this phrase appears for the last time, and repeated twice, in the context of the metaphoric showdown on *'admat yisra'el* between God, on the one hand, and Gog and the *'ereṣ* (earth) of Magog (38:2), where God will control the outcome through the same *ra'aš* with which he both punished Israel (12:18) and restored it (37:7):

> But on that day, when Gog shall come against the land of Israel (*'admat yisra'el*), says the Lord God, my wrath will be roused. For in my jealousy and in my blazing wrath I declare, On that day there shall be a great shaking (*ra'aš*) in the land of Israel (*'admat yisra'el*); the fish of the sea, and the birds of the air, and the beasts of the field, and all creeping things that creep on the ground, and all the men that are upon the face of the earth, shall quake at my presence, and the mountains shall be thrown down, and the cliffs shall fall, and every wall shall tumble to the ground. I will summon every kind of terror against Gog, says the Lord God; every man's sword will be against his brother. (38:18-21)

The *ra'aš* that is the product of the divine *ruaḥ* (wind; 3:12-13) is under God's control as is the *ruaḥ*. At God's will, each can have a benevolent or a destructive effect.

The content of chapter 7 corroborates that the arrogance of both the people and the "mountains" of Israel are the reason behind God's decision, and shaming them is the medium of his punishment:

> They gird themselves with sackcloth, and horror covers them; shame is upon all faces, and baldness on all their heads. (v.18)

> I will bring the worst of the nations to take possession of their houses; I will put an end to their proud might (*ge'on 'azzim*; the pride [arrogance] of the mighty ones), and their holy places shall be profaned. (v.24)

The ultimate aim of the attackers, beyond the siege and its corollaries—sword, pestilence, famine, and scattering of the survivors (vv.14-15)—is the decapitation of the city through the disempowerment of its leaders:

> Disaster comes upon disaster, rumor follows rumor; they seek a vision from the prophet, but the law perishes from the priest, and counsel from the elders. The king mourns, the prince is wrapped in despair, and the hands of the people of the land are palsied by terror. (vv.26-27a; see also the classic passage in 2 Kg 24:10-15)

6
Reprise of the Ezekelian Story

Chapters 1 through 7 culminate with the proclamation of the "end" of Jerusalem (7:1-14) as punishment for its sins of idolatry (vv.15-27). The same message is taken up in more detail in chapters 8 to 24. This is a classic device consistent in scripture whereby the second time around the same point is underscored so that there would be no misunderstanding on the hearers' part, and ultimately so that they would have no excuse nor be surprised when God's promised wrath is unleashed. Chapter 8 reprises what was started in chapter 1 by beginning with a precise dating formula and using similar phraseology to describe the divine apparition:

> In the thirtieth year, in the fourth month, on the fifth day of the month ... the word of the Lord came to Ezekiel the priest, the son of Buzi, in the land of the Chaldeans by the river Chebar; and the hand of the Lord was upon him there ... And above the firmament over their heads there was the likeness of a throne, in appearance like sapphire; and seated above the likeness of a throne was a likeness as it were of a human form. And upward from what had the appearance of his loins I saw as it were gleaming bronze, like the appearance of fire enclosed round about; and downward from what had the appearance of his loins I saw as it were the appearance of fire, and there was brightness round about him. (1:1, 3, 26-27)

> In the sixth year, in the sixth month, on the fifth day of the month, as I sat in my house, with the elders of Judah sitting before me, the hand of the Lord God fell there upon me. Then I beheld, and, lo, a form that had the appearance of a man; below what

appeared to be his loins it was fire, and above his loins it was like the appearance of brightness, like gleaming bronze. He put forth the form of a hand... (8:1-3)

Since dating was a priestly function, it is intended here also as irony: instead of portending temple service, it is auguring the demise of the temple together with all its services. In other words, it is Ezekiel "the prophet," and not Ezekiel "the priest," that is speaking here on God's behalf. In exile, it is only the prophetic voice, among the different strata of leadership, which is still functional. The phraseology of the last two verses of chapter 7 prepared for this situation:

> Disaster comes upon disaster, rumor follows rumor; they seek a vision from the prophet, but the law perishes from the priest, and counsel from the elders. The king mourns, the prince is wrapped in despair, and the hands of the people of the land are palsied by terror. (7:26-27a)

With the destruction of the city and its temple complex, the socio-religious leaders, the prophet, priest, and elders, as well as the political leaders, the king and prince, are no longer functional and are summarily dismissed. The presentation of priest and elders is outright negative, however that of the prophet is mysteriously left "hanging" in the sense that the prophet is still sought out, albeit vainly, as is clear from the context (7:26). A few verses later, the "mystery" is unveiled: Ezekiel "the priest" is nowhere to be found; his position is taken over by Ezekiel "the prophet" who is about to put to shame "the elders of the house of Israel" (8:11-12). So the prophetic voice will remain alive even in exile. As we shall see in chapter 12, Ezekiel will be the prototype of all exiles, giving them hope in that, *as a prophet*, he was exiled by God ahead of them and will ultimately sustain them after his harsh indictment of them.

In his translation to Jerusalem we are specifically told that Ezekiel sat in his house, with *the elders of Judah* sitting before him (8:1). This is a unique instance in the book; indeed, in vv.11 and 12 they are referred to as "the elders of the house of Israel" (8:11, 12), and later these same elders are dubbed "the elders of Israel" (14:1; 20:1, 3). The intention is to put pressure on the elders *in exile* by reminding them that they are the progeny of the Jerusalemite leaders who are being ruthlessly prosecuted in chapter 8. The threatening tone of the entire situation is further reflected in both the introduction of and the activity subscribed to the divine hand. It is the only instance in the book where the hand is said to be that "of the Lord God" (8:1) instead of simply "of the Lord" (1:3; 3:14, 22; 33:22; 37:1; 40:1). Also, it is the only time when the divine hand "fell" upon Ezekiel (8:1). Moreover, in God's hand lies his power expressed through the *ruaḥ* (mighty wind): "He put forth the form of a hand, and took me by a lock of my head; and the Spirit (*ruaḥ*) lifted me up between earth and heaven, and brought me in visions of God to Jerusalem."[1] (v.3) Finally, "[he] took me by a lock of my head" (v.3), an action done by God's hand, is a reminder of the prophet's name, "God holds tightly, grasps firmly."

Still, the real expression of the divine threat lies in that Judah's idolatrous behavior is arousing the jealousy of Israel's God who had warned that he was a "jealous" (*qanna'* or *qanno'*) deity. That we are dealing here with idolatry is evident in the phraseology:

> ... the Spirit lifted me up between earth and heaven, and brought me in visions of God to Jerusalem, to the entrance of the gateway

---

[1] This in turn explains the frequent Pauline parallelism between "spirit" and "power."

of the inner court that faces north, where was the seat of the image (*semel*) of jealousy, which provokes to jealousy ... Then he said to me, "Son of man, lift up your eyes now in the direction of the north." So I lifted up my eyes toward the north, and behold, north of the altar gate, in the entrance, was this image (*semel*) of jealousy. And he said to me, "Son of man, do you see what they are doing, the great *abominations* that the house of Israel are committing here, to drive me far from my sanctuary? But you will see still greater *abominations*." (vv. 3, 5-6)

Not only is there a double reference to abominations, but there is also a repeated instance of the rarely used noun *semel*, which is found three more times, in Deuteronomy 4:16 and 2 Chronicles 33:7, 15, where it denotes a graven image, an idol:

> Therefore take good heed to yourselves. Since you saw no form on the day that the Lord spoke to you at Horeb out of the midst of the fire, beware lest you act corruptly by making a graven image for yourselves, in the form of any figure (*semel*), the likeness of male or female, the likeness of any beast that is on the earth, the likeness of any winged bird that flies in the air, the likeness of anything that creeps on the ground, the likeness of any fish that is in the water under the earth. (Deut.4:15-18)

> And the image of the idol (*semel*) which he [Manasseh] had made he set in the house of God, of which God said to David and to Solomon his son, "In this house, and in Jerusalem, which I have chosen out of all the tribes of Israel, I will put my name for ever ... Then Manasseh knew that the Lord was God ... And he took away the foreign gods and the idol (*semel*) from the house of the Lord, and all the altars that he had built on the mountain of the house of the Lord and in Jerusalem, and he threw them outside of the city. (2 Chr 33:7, 12b, 15)

Why would Ezekiel accentuate the aspect of jealousy by twice referencing the *semel* as "the image (*semel*) of jealousy

Reprise of the Ezekelian Story

(*haqqin'ah*)" (Ezek 8:3, 5) and the first time with the additional emphasis "which provokes to jealousy (*hammaqneh*)" (8:3)? The explanation lies in several passages in the Law where the adjective "jealous" (*qanna'* or *qanno'*) is used to describe a feature of the scriptural God in conjunction with the worship of idols or other deities:

> You shall have no other gods before me. You shall not make for yourself a graven image, or any likeness of anything that is in heaven above, or that is in the earth beneath, or that is in the water under the earth; you shall not bow down to them or serve them; for I the Lord your God am a jealous (*qanna'*) God, visiting the iniquity of the fathers upon the children to the third and the fourth generation of those who hate me, but showing steadfast love to thousands of those who love me and keep my commandments. (Ex 20:3-6//Deut 5:8-10)

> ... for you shall worship no other god, for the Lord, *whose name is Jealous* (*qanna'*), is a jealous (*qanna'*) God. (Ex 34:14)

> For the Lord your God is a devouring fire, a jealous (*qanna'*) God. (Deut 4:24)

> You shall not go after other gods, of the gods of the peoples who are round about you; for the Lord your God in the midst of you is a jealous (*qanna'*) God; lest the anger of the Lord your God be kindled against you, and he destroy you from off the face of the earth. (Deut 6:14-15)

This teaching of the Law reverberates in both the Prior and Latter Prophets:

> But Joshua said to the people, "You cannot serve the Lord; for he is a holy God; he is a jealous (*qanno'*) God; he will not forgive your transgressions or your sins. If you forsake the Lord and serve

foreign gods, then he will turn and do you harm, and consume you, after having done you good." (Josh 24:19-20)

The Lord is a jealous (*qanno'*) God and avenging, the Lord is avenging and wrathful; the Lord takes vengeance on his adversaries and keeps wrath for his enemies. The Lord is slow to anger and of great might, and the Lord will by no means clear the guilty. His way is in whirlwind and storm (*śe'arah*)², and the clouds are the dust of his feet. (Nah 1:2-3)

Two points stand out. First, God's jealousy functions primarily against those who were made aware that he is their sole deity. Their only way to secure his love rather than his ire is to "keep his commandments" which, in turn, is their only means of loving him. Secondly, God's jealousy expresses itself in the divine punishment of a consuming fire, as occurs in a siege, and through destructive stormy wind. Both these facets are paramount in Ezekiel and explain why divine jealousy is at the outset of the prophet's communication to the exiled elders.

God's jealousy (*qin'ah*; Ezek 8:3, 5) is a central component of the Ezekelian story, and its occurrences follow the same pattern as that of other major constituents. After having stated that God would exercise his anger and fury according to his word spoken in jealousy (5:13), Ezekiel explains the reason for this jealousy (8:3, 5). In the classic parables of harlotry in chapters 16 and 23, we hear in detail that God's punishment of Jerusalem for dallying with foreign deities is due to his jealousy (16:38, 42; 23:25). However, given the strict monotheism of the scriptural God, that is to say, that he is the sole God not only of Israel, but

---

² Akin in sound and meaning to *se'arah* of Ezek 1:4: "As I looked, behold, a stormy (*se'arah*) wind came out of the north..." Sometimes the two Hebrew letters ס (*samekh*, transliterated as *s*) and שׂ (*sin*, transliterated as *ś*) are interchangeable, as in our case here.

also of the nations (Am 1-2; Jon; Ps 82), we will hear of his jealous wrath being exacted against Edom (35:11; 36:5-6), the land of Jacob's brother Esau, and even against the universal armies of Gog of Magog (38:19)—which rejoins in content Nahum's oracle against Nineveh (1:1-3). What is remarkable in the case of Gog of Magog is that we hear of the divine jealousy in conjunction with the last instance of *ra'aš* in Ezekiel:

> Thus says the Lord God: Are you he of whom I spoke in former days by my servants the prophets of Israel, who in those days prophesied for years that I would bring you against them? But on that day, when Gog shall come against the land of Israel, says the Lord God, my wrath will be roused. For in my jealousy (*qin'ah*) and in my blazing wrath I declare, On that day there shall be a great shaking (*ra'aš*) in the land of Israel; the fish of the sea, and the birds of the air, and the beasts of the field, and all creeping things that creep on the ground, and all the men that are upon the face of the earth, shall quake (*ra'ašu*) at my presence, and the mountains shall be thrown down, and the cliffs shall fall, and every wall shall tumble to the ground. (38:17-20)

Thus, on the one hand, the divine jealousy is behind the *ra'aš* associated with the divine chariot's relinquishing the temple and triggering the scattering of the people. Yet, on the other hand and at God's behest, the same *ra'aš* will bring together the scattered bones (37:7) in order to stage a manifestation of his power that even the mightiest could not withstand (38:14-20). Put otherwise, whatever the scriptural God does and whenever he acts, he does so, as Ezekiel puts it, "for the sake of my name, that it should not be profaned in the sight of the nations" (20:9, 14, 22).

Another essential and striking feature of Ezekiel is that the primary reference for "the God of Israel" is not the temple at

Jerusalem, as would have been expected in the case of city deities; rather the plain (*biq'ah*; 8:4) is the locale of his original epiphany. In other words, for Ezekiel, it is not the deity of the Jerusalem *lofty mountain* temple that appeared to him at Chebar; rather it is the God who appeared to him at Chebar *in the lowly plain* who is about to bring down the lofty temple and thus show himself as the deity of that temple in spite of all indications to the contrary. Indeed, the house of Israel tried "to drive me far from my sanctuary" by replacing God with the statue of another deity (v.6). However, such an action proved to be the demise of both that statue and Israel itself because it provoked the jealousy of God: "Then he said to me, 'Son of man, lift up your eyes now in the direction of the north.' So I lifted up my eyes toward the north, and behold, north of the altar gate, in the entrance, was this image of jealousy." (v.5; see also v.3) As we heard in 4:1-3, Ezekiel is the medium of God's intervention. Given that the slightest vacillation on Ezekiel's part is inadmissible (2:6, 8; 3:8-9), God makes sure that his prophet is fully convinced through an eye witness experience; he is indeed commanded by God to dig (*ḥatar*) a hole in the city wall (8:8) in order to go in and witness the Jerusalemites' abominations (8:7-10). Still, this text looks ahead to chapter 12 where he will be summoned by the same God to dig (*ḥatar*) another hole to go out as an exile (12:5, 7) ahead of the prince of the city who will follow (v.12).[3]

---

[3] The link between the two passages is evident in that these occurrences account for all instances of the verb *ḥatar* in Ezekiel. What makes the case even more compelling is that *ḥatar* is found only three more times in the entire Old Testament (Am 9:2; Jon 1:13; Job 24:16). In Jonah, we hear of the men "digging (plowing)" (*wayyaḥteru* from the root *ḥatar*) through the waters by rowing hard.

The handling of the prophetic vision of Jerusalem in chapter 8 is purposely cast retrospectively from the viewpoint of the exile, and thus functions as primer for the following chapters that speak of how the exile came about. Such can be already detected in the reference to Ezekiel's addressees at Chebar as being "the elders of Judah" (v.1). Other textual features corroborate this. The first is the four step introduction of Ezekiel to the abominations wrought in Jerusalem, which are divided by the triple occurrence of "you will see still greater abominations" (vv.6, 13, 15). The numeral four is reflective of universality and thus presages the scattering of the Judahites to the four corners of the earth, one for each level of abomination. Another feature are the two cardinal directions: north (vv.3, 5, 14; 9:3) and east (8:16). Both point toward Babylon that lay in the east. The invaders from the east usually attacked from the north (23:24; 26:7; see also Jer 1:13-15); the reason for this is that between the Euphrates and the land of Canaan lay the Syrian desert that was difficult for a large army to cross. So the route from Assyria and Babylon would be first north and then south toward the Mediterranean littoral and the major cities of Syria and the Lebanon and anti-Lebanon mountains. By the same token, the route of exile would be first north and then south down the Euphrates. A third feature is the mention of Tammuz (Ezek 8:14), which is unique in scripture. Tammuz was essentially a Sumerian and Babylonian deity, not part of the eastern Mediterranean plateau pantheon. His mention is clearly underscored through the definite article before his name *hattammuz*, which corresponds to *ha'elohim (the God, that is, the absolute deity)* as compared to *'elohim* (God). It is as though Ezekiel was made to witness that Tammuz literally and totally took the place of the Lord in the minds of "the house of Judah" (v.17). Indeed, this fits well with the Lord's statements that can be paraphrased: "The people are looking to the north and the east (vv.14, 16) trying to drive me far from my sanctuary (v.6); well, not only shall I make *them* go that route (11:9) but actually I shall personally lead them that way (vv.23-24)."

The last and most interesting feature is the seventy "elders of Israel" (8:11). Traditionally the numeral seventy is linked to the nations, according to Genesis 10, and as such is reflective of the scriptural God's universality.[4] The first time in scripture that we encounter the numeral seventy is in reference to the number of persons connected to Jacob and his children in Egypt, that is, away from the land of Judah and Israel and thus among the "nations": "All the persons belonging to Jacob who came into Egypt, who were his own offspring, not including Jacob's sons' wives, were sixty-six persons in all; and the sons of Joseph, who were born to him in Egypt, were two; all the persons of the house of Jacob, that came into Egypt, were seventy." (Gen 46:26-27) The intentionality of this number is borne out in its repetition at the beginning of the story of the exodus from Egypt and as an unexpected appendix to the names of Jacob's twelve children:

> These are the names of the sons of Israel who came to Egypt with Jacob, each with his household: Reuben, Simeon, Levi, and Judah, Issachar, Zebulun, and Benjamin, Dan and Naphtali, Gad and Asher. All the offspring of Jacob were seventy persons; Joseph was already in Egypt. (Ex 1:1-5)

The following time this numeral appears *before and until Ezekiel*—and again twice in a row betraying intentionality—is to

---

[4] Seventy is the multiple of seven and ten. Seven is the divine number, expressive of the fullness of divinity, while ten and multiples of ten—hundreds, thousands, etc., are generally used in reference to numbers of people and suggest a large number that represents totality.

introduce "seventy of the elders of Israel" (Ex 24:1, 9) while the Israelites were still roaming, that is, scattered outside Judah and Israel, in "the wilderness of the land of Egypt." This parallels "the wilderness of the peoples" in Ezekiel (20:35-36). The universality of the number seventy impacted the legend concerning the Septuagint (from the Latin *septuaginta* meaning seventy), a translation of the Hebrew Old Testament into Greek, produced in Alexandria[5] by seventy Jewish scholars for the Jews living outside Palestine among the Greco-Roman Gentiles.[6]

Pointing out Jaazaniah the son of Shaphan among the elders (8:11) is deliberate since both names are symbolic. Shaphan is the name of King Josiah's secretary whom the king sent with a mission to Hilkiah the high priest, which unleashed events that ended up with the discovery of the Book of the Law (2 Kg 22:3-10). His mention brackets the story from his being sent out (v.3) to his reading of the book before the king (v.10). A more expanded version of this story is found in 1 Chronicles 34:8-19. His importance is further underscored in that, after the sack of Jerusalem (2 Kg 25:8-21), it is his grandson Gedaliah whom

---

[5] In the Preface to Ecclesiaticus (Wisdom of Sirach) we hear of Egypt being the center of such translation activity: "You are urged therefore to read with good will and attention, and to be indulgent in cases where, despite our diligent labor in translating, we may seem to have rendered some phrases imperfectly. For what was originally expressed in Hebrew does not have exactly the same sense when translated into another language. Not only this work, but even the law itself, the prophecies, and the rest of the books differ not a little as originally expressed. When I came to Egypt in the thirty-eighth year of the reign of Euergetes and stayed for some time, I found opportunity for no little instruction. It seemed highly necessary that I should myself devote some pains and labor to the translation of the following book, using in that period of time great watchfulness and skill in order to complete and publish the book for those living abroad who wished to gain learning, being prepared in character to live according to the law."

[6] Luke will carry on this tradition in his take on Jesus' sending out his messengers to proclaim the gospel teaching: first we have the sending of the twelve (9:1-6) followed by another seventy (10:1-12, 17-10).

Nebuchadnezzar, king of Babylon, appoints as governor over the remnant of Judah (v.22). So Ezekiel's reference to Shaphan, who otherwise is not mentioned outside 2 Kings, Jeremiah, and 2 Chronicles, is to link him with the reason behind the fall of Jerusalem, namely, with disobedience to God's commandments. Indeed, how could the king and the people have been obedient to the ordinances inscribed in "the book of the law" (2 Kg 22:8, 11; 2 Chr 34:14, 15) when they were unaware of its existence? This "book of the law," on the other hand, is none other than Deuteronomy, as is clear from the following repeated instances found only in it:

> If you are not careful to do all the words of this law which are written in this book, that you may fear this glorious and awful name, the Lord your God ... Every sickness also, and every affliction which is not recorded in the book of this law, the Lord will bring upon you, until you are destroyed. (Deut 28:58, 61)

> The Lord would not pardon him, but rather the anger of the Lord and his jealousy would smoke against that man, and the curses written in this book would settle upon him, and the Lord would blot out his name from under heaven. And the Lord would single him out from all the tribes of Israel for calamity, in accordance with all the curses of the covenant written in this book of the law ... therefore the anger of the Lord was kindled against this land, bringing upon it all the curses written in this book (Deut 29:20-21, 27)

> ... if you obey the voice of the Lord your God, to keep his commandments and his statutes which are written in this book of the law, if you turn to the Lord your God with all your heart and with all your soul. (Deut 30:10)

> When Moses had finished writing the words of this law in a book, to the very end ... Take this book of the law, and put it by the

side of the ark of the covenant of the Lord your God, that it may be there for a witness against you. (Deut 31:24, 26)

Since the content of Deuteronomy is most fiercely anti-idolatry, it stands to reason that in the context of his sharp criticism against idolatry (Ezek 8), Ezekiel opted to refer to Shaphan by name, especially that as the king's secretary, he was supposed to be aware of all the writings of the palace-temple complex.

Another interesting aspect of Shaphan is its meaning in Hebrew, which makes it fit perfectly within the story of the discovery of the book of the law. In scripture *šaphan* occurs only four times (Lev 11:5; Deut 14:7; Ps 104:18; Prov 30:26) and refers to the rock badger: "The high mountains are for the wild goats; the rocks are a refuge for the badgers (*šephanim*)" (Ps 104:18); "the badgers (*šephanim*) are a people not mighty, yet they make their homes in the rocks." (Prov 30:26) So Shaphan, the rock badger, was able to find the book of the law among the stones of the temple building while it was being renovated:

> In the eighteenth year of King Josiah, the king sent Shaphan the son of Azaliah, son of Meshullam, the secretary, to the house of the Lord, saying, "Go up to Hilkiah the high priest, that he may reckon the amount of the money which has been brought into the house of the Lord, which the keepers of the threshold have collected from the people; and let it be given into the hand of the workmen who have the oversight of the house of the Lord; and let them give it to the workmen who are at the house of the Lord, repairing the house, that is, to the carpenters, and to the builders, and to the masons, as well as for buying timber and quarried stone to repair the house." (2 Kings 22:3-6)

However, the irony is that, in finding that book, he unleashed the curses of God inscribed therein and precipitated the undoing of that same temple he was trying to repair. The fact that the

Jerusalem leaders were not aware of the Book of the Law is a clear indication that they had never followed its injunctions. This is evident in the way with which the biblical author makes that point:

> And the king commanded all the people, "Keep the passover to the Lord your God, as it is written in this book of the covenant." For no such passover had been kept since the days of the judges who judged Israel, or during all the days of the kings of Israel or of the kings of Judah; but in the eighteenth year of King Josiah this passover was kept to the Lord in Jerusalem. (23:21-23)

In Ezekiel, it is the un-lawful behavior of the elders, including Shaphan's son, that prompted God to unleash his jealousy.

By adding the name *ya'azanyahu* (Jaazaniah), which means, "the Lord lends his ear," Ezekiel was pushing the irony to its extreme. Although the elders are excusing their appeal to other deities by saying "the Lord does not see us, the Lord has forsaken the land," the same Lord is in fact listening carefully to what they are saying and to the prayers they are addressing to those idols. And although he is hearing them, he is *not* about to lend his ear to their pleas when he will release his wrath against them: "Therefore I will deal in wrath; my eye will not spare, nor will I have pity; and though they cry in my ears (*'oznay*, from the same root *'zn* as the name *ya'azanyahu*) with a loud voice, I will not hear them." (Ezek 8:18).

Finally, the action of the elders toward the idols is described in the following way: "And before them [all the idols of the house of Israel] stood seventy men of the elders of the house of Israel, with Jaazaniah the son of Shaphan standing among them. Each had his censer in his hand, and the smoke of the cloud of incense went up." (8:11) This last phrase, "the smoke of the cloud of incense," is cumbersome, to say the least. The closest other instances are either "the cloud of the incense" (Lev 16:13) or "the smoke of the incense" (Rev 8:4) and both specifically refer to a "censer" (Lev 16:12; Rev 8:3), as Ezekiel does. In either case, the choice of words is dictated by the context. One would expect smoke with incense, and this is precisely what the Revelation passage is all about: there is no reference to either glory or cloud in the immediacy.[7] In Leviticus, on the other hand, "cloud" was intentionally chosen over "smoke" to underscore the connection with divine presence: "and the Lord said to Moses, 'Tell Aaron your brother not to come at all times into the holy place within the veil, before the mercy seat which is upon the ark, lest he die; for I will appear in the cloud upon the mercy seat ... and [Aaron shall] put the incense on the fire before the Lord, that the cloud of the incense may cover the mercy seat which is upon the testimony, lest he die.'" (16:2, 13) These are the only two instances of "cloud" in Leviticus while "glory" in this book is found only in 9:6 and 23. Since the context in Ezekiel is similar to that in Revelation, one would have expected "the smoke of the incense." Consequently, the expanded "the smoke of the cloud of incense" was formulated to underscore "cloud" and, by the same token, the level of abomination on the part of the elders. Indeed, in the larger context of chapters 8-11 that form a unit describing God's glory leaving the Jerusalem temple (8:4; 9:3; 10:4, 18, 19; 11:22, 23) because of the abominations, "cloud" is unequivocally presented as the expression of the divine glory: "Now the cherubim were standing on the south side of the house, when the man went in; and a cloud filled the inner court. And the glory of the Lord went up from the cherubim to the threshold of the house; and the house was filled with the cloud,

---

[7] The closest instances of glory are in 7:12 and 11:13, and the closest mentions of cloud are in 1:7 and 10:1.

and the court was full of the brightness of the glory of the Lord." (10:3-4) The foolish elders really thought that they could exchange God's "cloud" with that of the vanishing smoke produced by their censers!

7
God's Glory Abandons the Jerusalem Temple

Chapters 9 and 10 describe the actual chastisement of Jerusalem, culminating with God's glory leaving the temple. This mission is carried out symbolically by seven men because seven is the divine numeral. Thus, those men function in these chapters the way Ezekiel did in chapters 4-5: they are God's extended hand doing his work for him. Beside their number, this is confirmed in that their leader is said to be "a man clothed in linen (*baddim*, plural of *bad*), with a writing case at his side" (vv.2, 3). Since *bad* is specifically a priestly garment fabric (Lev 6:10; 16:4, 23, 32; 1 Sam 22:18)[1] it ensues that the "man clothed in linen" is performing a priestly function. The only two passages where *bad* occurs in conjunction with a function to be performed are found in Leviticus 6 and 16:

> The Lord said to Moses, "Command Aaron and his sons, saying, This is the law of the burnt offering (*'olah*; holocaust). The burnt offering shall be on the hearth upon the altar all night until the morning, and the fire of the altar shall be kept burning on it. And the priest shall put on his linen (*bad*) garment, and put his linen (*bad*) breeches upon his body, and he shall take up the ashes to which the fire has consumed the burnt offering on the altar, and

---

[1] In 1 Sam 2:18 "Samuel was ministering before the Lord, a boy girded with a linen ephod" in view of his destiny to take over the place of Eli the priest (3:1-4:1). Similarly, David is said to have worn a linen ephod while he was performing the function of high priest, as any king was (2 Sam 6:14//1 Chr 15:27). In both cases, the author's intention is evident in the mention of "a linen ephod," ephod being specifically a priestly garb (Ex 28:4; Lev 8:6-7; 1 Sam 2:28; 14:3; 23:6-9).

put them beside the altar. Then he shall put off his garments, and put on other garments, and carry forth the ashes outside the camp to a clean place. The fire on the altar shall be kept burning on it, it shall not go out; the priest shall burn wood on it every morning, and he shall lay the burnt offering in order upon it, and shall burn on it the fat of the peace offerings. Fire shall be kept burning upon the altar continually; it shall not go out." (Lev 6:8-13)

... and the Lord said to Moses, "Tell Aaron your brother not to come at all times into the holy place within the veil, before the mercy seat which is upon the ark, lest he die; for I will appear in the cloud upon the mercy seat. But thus shall Aaron come into the holy place: with a young bull for a sin offering and a ram for a burnt offering (*'olah*; holocaust). He shall put on the holy linen (*bad*) coat, and shall have the linen (*bad*) breeches on his body, be girded with the linen (*bad*) girdle, and wear the linen (*bad*) turban; these are the holy garments. He shall bathe his body in water, and then put them on. And he shall take from the congregation of the people of Israel two male goats for a sin offering, and one ram for a burnt offering. And Aaron shall offer the bull as a sin offering for himself, and shall make atonement for himself and for his house." (Lev 16:2-6)

In both cases the duty to be performed is the burnt offering, a sacrifice in which the oblation is totally consumed by fire with nothing remaining for either the offering person or the priest (Lev 1); moreover, the holocaust is done in conjunction with the most holy Day of Atonement when expiation is done for *all* the sins of *everyone*. Thus in Ezekiel 9-10, God is performing "without pity" (8:18; 9:5, 10) a burnt offering of the people. This is confirmed by the mention of the consuming fire that proceeds from the divine chariot itself (10:2, 6-7; see also 8:2).

What does the "mark" in 9:4 and 6 refer to and what is its function? In the original the noun translated as mark is *taw*, the last letter of the Hebrew alphabet which in the ancient script looked like an X. It would be used to make a "sign" on an item in order to point it out.[2] This is how the Septuagint understood it since it translates the *taw* into *sēmeion* (sign); the later Latin Vulgate, a Christian product, renders it as *tau*, the Latin transliteration of the Hebrew *taw*. The only other instance of *taw* is found in Job where it clearly refers to a sign in the sense of signature: "Oh, that I had one to hear me!—Here is my signature (*tawi*; my *taw*)! let the Almighty answer me!—Oh, that I had the indictment written by my adversary!" (31:35) The Jerusalem Bible that translates *taw* in Ezekiel into *croix* (cross) renders Job's *tawi* as *mon dernier mot* (my last word), which fits the context since the entire chapter contains Job's apologetic discourse that conclude with "The words of Job are ended" (v.40b). Still, given that the use of the Hebrew alphabetic letter *taw* as noun is so rare and its instance in Job is justifiable, why did Ezekiel opt for *taw* over the more usual *'ot* (sign), as the Septuagint understood it? Just as in the case of Job, Ezekiel had a specific motive.

In Ezekiel, *taw* refers to God's "signature" as his "last word" concerning the behavior of the Judahites. It is as though God went through all possible scenarios of disobedient idolatry on the part of the people—represented by the letters of the alphabet up to *taw*—and he is abhorred (*nit'ab*; passive verbal form *niph'al* from the root *t'b*) at their abhorrence-provoking abominations

---

[2] I shall not indulge here in refuting the later fantasies concerning its being a prefiguration of the New Testament cross. Should one follow that path of reading back into an older text, then one would have a license to read at will into the Old Testament almost anything one wishes or, at least, make a case for it.

(*to'abot*: plural of *to'ebah* from the root *t'b*).³ On the other hand, since *taw* is the first letter in *to'abot*, it also may have been meant as a reminder of the reason behind the need for the "mark," that is, to protect from the impending disaster "the men who sigh and groan over all the abominations" that are committed in Jerusalem (Ezek 9:4). Then the question that remains is, "A reminder to whom?" Since all the others were about to be destroyed, the obvious answer is "to those who have been marked" and, beyond them, to the eventual hearers of the story. Still, why would those who are marked for salvation need any reminder unless the threat against them is always looming on the horizon? Indeed, two chapters later we hear of "the (obviously remaining) inhabitants of Jerusalem":

> And the word of the Lord came to me: "Son of man, your brethren, even your brethren, your fellow exiles, the whole house of Israel, all of them, are those of whom the inhabitants of Jerusalem have said, 'They have gone far from the Lord; to us this land is given for a possession.' Therefore say, 'Thus says the Lord God: Though I removed them far off among the nations, and though I scattered them among the countries, yet I have been a sanctuary to them for a while in the countries where they have gone.' Therefore say, 'Thus says the Lord God: I will gather you from the peoples, and assemble you out of the countries where you have been scattered, and I will give you the land of Israel.' *And when they come there, they will remove from it all its detestable things and all its abominations.* And I will give them one heart, and put a new spirit within them; I will take the stony heart out of their flesh and give them a heart of flesh, *that they may walk in my statutes and keep my ordinances and obey them*; and they shall be my people, and I will be their God. *But as for those whose heart goes*

---

³ Formally *to'ebah* is actually the feminine participle singular of the active verbal form *qal* whose passive verbal form is the *niph'al*. Thus, *to'ebah* means an abhorrence-provoking action.

after their detestable things and their abominations, I will requite their deeds upon their own heads, says the Lord God." (11:14-21)

Thus the *taw* is to *remain* a permanent reminder not to fall prey to the *to'abot*, but to stay obedient to God's statutes and ordinances. Even those who are marked are not exempt from the value or meaning of that mark!

The God of Ezekiel is the Sole Deity

The function of chapter 10 is to ascertain once more and in a very elaborate manner that the God who appeared to Ezekiel at Chebar is the primary reference as to what the deity of the Jerusalem temple is all about. Put otherwise, the Lord whose habitation is primarily the temple of Jerusalem did not end in exile, dragged there by the deity and the king of Babylon. Rather the God who appeared from above the firmament to Ezekiel in chapter 1, and is the sole deity of all nations, is abandoning the temporary building erected against his will (2 Sam 7; Is 66:1-2a) and into which he conceded to abide (2 Sam 6:1-19). He is in no need of the prayers and sacrifices offered there (Is 1:11-15; 66:3). The extensive repetition of the details in Ezekiel 10 that have been mentioned in chapter 1 seems unnecessary at face value, yet when one remembers 1 Samuel 8 where the people requested that they be "like all the nations" (v.5), one realizes that such repetition is necessary due to the extreme recalcitrance of the hearers. In Ezekiel's mind, the deity that appears at Chebar takes priority over the one that resides in Jerusalem:

> Then the glory of the Lord went forth from the threshold of the house, and stood over the cherubim. And the cherubim lifted up their wings and mounted up from the earth in my sight as they went forth, with the wheels beside them; and they stood at the door of the east gate of the house of the Lord; and the glory of the

God of Israel was over them. *These were the living creatures that I saw underneath the God of Israel by the river Chebar; and I knew that they were cherubim.* (10:18-20)

The importance, if not centrality, of this Ezekelian teaching will be delivered no less than three times (chs.16, 20, 23) in an overbearingly detailed and repetitive way so that even a hearer who plugs his ears cannot possibly miss it. Moreover, it is precisely this view that will infuse the classic scriptural story that God as *yahweh* (the Lord) first appeared and revealed his will expressed in ordinances in the wilderness: "And God said to Moses, 'I am the Lord (*yahweh*). I appeared to Abraham, to Isaac, and to Jacob, as God Almighty, but by my name the Lord (*yahweh*) I did not make myself known to them.'" (Ex 6:2-3) It is this appearance of his that controls both the past of the people in Egypt and their future in Canaan. This point is stressed in that all the men of war who were brought out of Egypt did not enter Canaan:

> So Joshua made flint knives, and circumcised the people of Israel at Gibeath-haaraloth. And this is the reason why Joshua circumcised them: all the males of the people who came out of Egypt, all the men of war, had died on the way in the wilderness after they had come out of Egypt. Though all the people who came out had been circumcised, yet all the people that were born on the way in the wilderness after they had come out of Egypt had not been circumcised. For the people of Israel walked forty years in the wilderness, till all the nation, the men of war that came forth out of Egypt, perished, because they did not hearken to the voice of the Lord; to them the Lord swore that he would not let them see the land which the Lord had sworn to their fathers to give us, a land flowing with milk and honey. So it was their children, whom he raised up in their stead, that Joshua circumcised; for they were uncircumcised, because they had not been circumcised on the way. (Josh 5:3-7; see also Deut 2:14-18).

Additionally, this passage corroborates the understanding of the function of the "mark" on the forehead in chapter 9.

8
Witnessing the Abominations in Jerusalem

The beginning of chapter 11 (vv.1-13) is a reprise of chapters 8 and 9. However, whereas in chapter 8 God's *ruaḥ* carries Ezekiel in order to eye-witness both the abominations committed in Jerusalem and the divine judgment through the seven emissaries, here God implements the verdict through Ezekiel himself, as was the case in chapters 4 and 5. This literary device is used to impress upon the hearers that Ezekiel had no choice but to comply with his mission, as was repeatedly stressed in chapters 2 and 3. Specifically, the prophet had no choice because he witnessed the abominations with his own eyes, so even if the thought crossed his mind to intercede, as Jeremiah tried to do and was shut out by God himself (Jer 7:16-18), it is literally out of the question here. This explains why Ezekiel implements his mission unwaveringly, his face hard against their faces and his forehead hard against their foreheads, and without being dismayed at their looks (3:8-9). For him, the case is closed.

The same twenty-five men of 8:16 are revisited, and we are told that among them were "Jaazaniah the son of Azzur, and Pelatiah the son of Benaiah, princes of the people" (11:1). As in the case of Jaazaniah the son of Shaphan in 8:11, all the names used here are metaphoric and thus functional within the context. This time around Jaazaniah[1] is the son of Azzur (*'azzur*); the

---

[1] In 11:1 we have *ya'azanyah* instead of *ya'azanhayu* in 8:11. The former is simply a shortened form of the latter, which explains why RSV translates both into Jaazaniah in both cases.

Hebrew *'azzur* is from the root *'azar* (to help) and recalls, sound wise, the passive participle *'azur* meaning "the one who is helped." The combination of the two names connotes someone in need of the help of the Lord who hearkens to his prayer; the first person that comes to mind is the king: "Give the king thy justice, O God, and thy righteousness to the royal son! May he judge thy people with righteousness, and thy poor with justice!" (Ps 72:1-2) This is confirmed by the second pair of names. Both *pelaṭyahu* (Pelatiah) and *benayahu* (Benaiah) are connected to a building: *pelaṭyahu* is from the verb *palaṭ* (to level, to flatten) and means "the Lord levels" and *benayahu* is from the verb *banah* (to build) and means "the Lord builds." It is as though the Lord is leveling the uneven ground in order to build upon it. This again brings to mind the building of the temple which is a kingly duty; however, such an endeavor cannot be done without the Lord's specific help: "Unless the Lord builds the house, those who build it labor in vain." (Ps 127:1)[2] Nevertheless, instead of at least one of them being "king," we hear that Jaazaniah and Pelatiah were "princes" of the people. Is there a reason behind this?

Ezekiel's extreme abhorrence of anything that is even potentially arrogant—cities, temples, mountains, heights—obviously includes the person of the king as "son of god." The scriptural prophets and scripture in general are notoriously anti-kingly. Any monarch was prone to assume that he was as divine as his deity and to forget that he was simply a *locum tenens* bound to die and leave the throne to another "son of god." However, Ezekiel stands unique in the way he deals with kingship: he simply ignores it; it is as though it is not worth

---

[2] It is interesting to note that both psalms—and only they in the Psalter—are ascribed to Solomon, the prototype king as he is presented in 1 Kg 3-10.

mentioning. Such is belittling at its utmost! A quick survey of the book will corroborate this state of affairs.

Throughout Ezekiel the noun "king" is used profusely to refer to the monarchs of other nations: Babylon (17:12, 16: 19:9; 21:19, 21; 24:2; 26:7; 29:18, 19: 30:10, 24, 25; 32:11), Tyre (28:12), Egypt (29:2, 3; 30:21, 22, 24, 25; 31:2; 32:2),[3] Edom (32:29), the earth in general (27:33; 28:17), the coastlands (27:35), many peoples (32:10). Of note are the many references to the king of Babylon, who functions as the obedient servant of the Lord. In comparison, the king of Judah is mentioned a few times and always in demeaning situations (1:2; 7:27; 17:12,[4] 16). In fact Ezekiel prefers to refer to the Judean leader as *śar* (chief; leader; prince; 11:1; 22:27) and more often as *naśi'* (prince; chief; 12:10, 12; 19:1; 21:12, 25; 22:6, 25,[5] 27). To be sure, the leaders of other nations are also referred to as "princes,"[6] especially in the case of the mighty leader Gog of Magog (38:2, 3; 39:1) and his supporters (39:18). What is striking though is the lack of instances where a Judahite leader is referred to as king in a positive connotation. It is as though Ezekiel, in an oblique way, is conveying the message that, in Judah, the Lord God is exclusively the King. This is fully transparent in the following statement:

> Wherefore say to the house of Israel, Thus says the Lord God: Will you defile yourselves after the manner of your fathers and go astray after their detestable things? When you offer your gifts and sacrifice your sons by fire, you defile yourselves with all your idols to this day. And shall I be inquired of by you, O house of Israel?

---

[3] In 29:14-15 there is a reference to Egypt as kingdom.
[4] In v.14 we hear of the kingdom of Judah being humbled.
[5] The Hebrew has instead "the conspiracy of her prophets" here.
[6] Ezek 26:16; 27:21; 28:2; 30:13; 32:29, 30.

As I live, says the Lord God, I will not be inquired of by you. What is in your mind shall never happen—the thought, "Let us be like the nations, like the tribes of the countries, and worship wood and stone." As I live, says the Lord God, surely with a mighty hand and an outstretched arm, and with wrath poured out, I will be king (*'emlok*; I will rule as a king would) over you. I will bring you out from the peoples and gather you out of the countries where you are scattered, with a mighty hand and an outstretched arm, and with wrath poured out; and I will bring you into the wilderness of the peoples, and there I will enter into judgment with you face to face. As I entered into judgment with your fathers in the wilderness of the land of Egypt, so I will enter into judgment with you, says the Lord God. (20:30-36)

In the age of restoration, God will take over total control. God turns the tables against the "shepherds" of Israel by dismissing them from their positions of leadership and takes their place as the sole shepherd: "I myself will be the shepherd of my sheep." (34:15a) Being the deity, he will obviously implement his rule through an earthly representative who necessarily will likewise be a shepherd, just as the monarch is king after the manner of his deity: "And I will set up over them one shepherd, my servant David, and he shall feed them: he shall feed them and be their shepherd." (v.23) However—and this is what is stunning—although the Lord will be God of his people, his representative will be a prince, and not the expected king, which again expresses Ezekiel's abhorrence of that noun: "And I, the Lord, will be their God, and my servant David shall be prince (*naśi*) among them; I, the Lord, have spoken." (v.24) When this statement is iterated at the end of chapter 37 it is phrased thusly: "My servant David shall be king (*melek*) over them; and they shall all have one shepherd ... and David my servant shall be their prince (*naśi*) for ever." (vv.24a, 25b) It is the last part of a statement that carries the weight, especially since it reflects a lesser title. Ezekiel did not say, "David will be prince, nay even a king"; rather he began with king and then reverted to prince which was earlier introduced in chapter 34. Since the hearers already know that David will be prince, why did Ezekiel throw in "king" only to end up with the expected prince? He did so in view of chapters 38-39. In spite of all appearances to the contrary, the mighty prince, Gog of Magog (38:2, 3; 39:1), is not so impressive when compared to the shepherd God who raises the dry bones. Put otherwise, the humble shepherd David is the real king as is his shepherd God! The superiority of "prince" over "king" in the new Israel is sealed in the final chapters 40-48 where the new king-like figure is the "prince," and that he is mentioned as such no less than seventeen times,[7] while reference to kings is made in the most negative way possible; even their dead bodies are unwelcome in the new Jerusalem:

> While the man was standing beside me, I heard one speaking to me out of the temple; and he said to me, "Son of man, this is the place of my throne and the place of the soles of my feet, where I will dwell in the midst of the people (children) of Israel for ever. And the house of Israel shall no more defile my holy name, neither they, nor their kings, by their harlotry, and by the dead bodies of their kings, by setting their threshold by my threshold and their doorposts beside my doorposts, with only a wall between me and them. They have defiled my holy name by their abominations which they have committed, so I have consumed them in my anger. Now let them put away their idolatry and the dead bodies of their kings far from me, and I will dwell in their midst for ever." (43:6-9)

---

[7] 44:3; 45:7, 8, 9, 16, 17, 22; 46:2, 4, 8, 10, 12, 16, 17, 18; 48:21, 22.

The statement in 11:3 in both its parts, "The time is not near to build houses" and "this city is the caldron, and we are the flesh," has always been a *crux interpretum*, a difficult puzzle for interpreters. Many solutions are advanced but none is satisfactory. The reason for this is the chronic lack of consideration on the part of exegetes toward the personal names within the story. When one considers that the name Pelatiah, son of Benaiah, relates to building then one can follow the story line. The prince Pelatiah is expressly punished with death at the end of the passage (v.13). The prince, a stand-in for the king, and his entourage are misleading the people (v.2) by presenting themselves as the victims of the siege (v.3) and thus not being able to build (a pun on Pelatiah, son of Benaiah) houses *beqarob*. The Hebrew *beqarob* means either "any time soon" ("the time is not near" in RSV) or "in the midst (of the city)." Either way, the effect is the same: "we, the leaders, will not be able to carry on our life." However, God calls their bluff and cunning: it is they, the overseers of the temple service, who are bringing the calamity on the city through their idolatrous behavior. The inhabitants of the city are the real victims: "You have multiplied your slain in this city, and have filled its streets with the slain. Therefore thus says the Lord God: Your slain whom you have laid in the midst of it, they are the flesh, and this city is the caldron." (vv.6-7a) It is the common people who will be left in the dilapidated city, without buildings to house them. As for the leaders, some of them will survive in exile (2 Kg 24:14-16: Ezek 17:12), and in honor nonetheless (2 Kg 25:27-30), and even one of them will end up on the throne (24:17; Ezek 17:13). The divine punishment of 11:7b-11 is intended to void the leaders' statement of verse 3. They will neither remain in the city nor reach the exile destination but will be felled "at the border of Israel," which is mentioned twice for underscoring:

... but you shall be brought forth out of the midst of it. You have feared the sword; and I will bring the sword upon you, says the Lord God. And I will bring you forth out of the midst of it, and give you into the hands of foreigners, and execute judgments upon you. You shall fall by the sword; I will judge you at the border of Israel; and you shall know that I am the Lord. This city shall not be your caldron, nor shall you be the flesh in the midst of it; I will judge you at the border of Israel. (vv.7b-11)

Verse 13a confirms that it is specifically Pelatiah the son of Benaiah who dies, the prince whose name is directly related to the statement of verse 3a concerning building. The divine punishment is aimed at countering the princely bluff. Ezekiel fully got the message of the punishment's finality and is literally taken aback. His reaction is the typical gesture of one facing the weighty presence (*kabod*) of God: "Then I fell down upon my face, and cried with a loud voice, and said, 'Ah Lord God! wilt thou make *a full end* of the remnant of Israel?'" (v.13b)

However, as is usual in scripture, self-righteousness prevails. The spared people assumed that God's gift to them is their own property or personal possession, thus they did not perceive the reason for the divine punishment: "Son of man, your brethren, even your brethren, your fellow exiles, the whole house of Israel, all of them, are those of whom the inhabitants of Jerusalem have said, 'They have gone far from the Lord; to us this land (*'ereṣ*; earth) is given for an inheritance (*moraŝah*; patrimony).[8]'" (v.15) Whereas possession reflects personal ownership of a property, an inheritance or a patrimony means that the piece of land is a family estate bequeathed by the father to whomever he *chooses*, yet it remains a *family* estate. Those who live on it do not own it; they just enjoy it. The sin of the inhabitants of Jerusalem lies in

---

[8] RSV's translation of *moraŝah* into "possession" is misleading, to say the least.

their assumption that the exiles are forever gone and, consequently, those who remain there are the sole "owners" of the land of Judah. "Not so," says God who is alive and well[9] and makes it clear that the decision of inheritance is his to make at all times. His scattering part of the inhabitants of Jerusalem and Judah is just a stage in a grandiose plan that encompasses not only all of Judah (vv.16-21), but also both the forgotten Ephraim (the kingdom of Israel; 37:15-28) and the rest of the nations as Isaiah openly teaches (42:6-7; 49:6; 66:12-20). This divine plan is evident in the way the Lord God corrects the Jerusalemites' thinking that the exiles "have gone far (*raḥaqu*; *qal* form of the verb *raḥaq*) from the Lord" (Ezek 11:15). In actuality it was the Lord God who "removed them far off (*hirḥaqtim*; *hiph'il* form of the same verb) among the nations" (v.16a). However, at the same time, he has been a protective "sanctuary (*miqdaš*) to them" (v.16b). The second stage of God's plan is to gather those whom he has exiled in order to grant them as a gift "the land (*'adamah*; ground) of Israel" (v.17).[10] Still, this gift is not unconditional as is usually assumed. To the contrary, first those who are gathered will have to "remove from it all its detestable things and all its abominations" (v.18) in order for God to be able to implement the last stage of his plan: "I will give them one heart, and put a new spirit within them; I will take the stony heart out of their flesh and give them a heart of flesh." (v.19) But even that divine action has a purpose, which is apparent from the use of the strong Hebrew conjunction *lema'an* (in order that; so that) introducing the concluding

---

[9] In Ezekiel we find 16 instances of "as I live" (*ḥay-'ani*; living I am) on God's lips compared to only 11 in the rest of the Old Testament.

[10] As I mentioned earlier, by translating both *'ereṣ* and *'adamah* into "land" RSV not only blurs the intended nuance but misleads the hearers into endorsing blatant political Zionism.

clause. The aim is "that they may walk in my statutes and keep my ordinances and obey them" (20a) and only if that condition is met "they shall be my people, and I will be their God" (v.20b). The proof that the gift is not unconditional is corroborated in the last part of the statement containing the divine plan, namely, a judgment that will punish those who would not abide by God's statutes and ordinances: "But as for those whose heart goes after their detestable things and their abominations, I will requite their deeds upon their own heads, says the Lord God." (v.21) In turn, this elucidates that "the whole house of Israel, all of them" (v.15) is not inclusive; rather it is all-encompassing of those who will have passed the test of judgment, as will become evident in a later passage that uses a similar terminology:

> I will bring you out from the peoples and gather you out of the countries (*'araṣot*; earths) where you are scattered, with a mighty hand and an outstretched arm, and with wrath poured out; and I will bring you into the wilderness of the peoples, and there I will enter into judgment with you face to face. As I entered into judgment with your fathers in the wilderness of the land of Egypt, so I will enter into judgment with you, says the Lord God. I will make you pass under the rod, and I will let you go in by number. *I will purge out the rebels from among you, and those who transgress against me*; I will bring them out of the land (*'ereṣ*; earth) where they sojourn, *but they shall not enter the land* (*'adamah*) *of Israel*. Then you will know that I am the Lord. As for you, O house of Israel, thus says the Lord God: Go serve every one of you his idols, now and hereafter, if you will not listen to me; but my holy name you shall no more profane with your gifts and your idols. For on my holy mountain, the mountain height of Israel, says the Lord God, *there all the house of Israel, all of them, shall serve me in the land* (*'ereṣ*);[11] there I will accept them, and there I will require your

---

[11] The *'ereṣ* as *'adamah* (v.38).

contributions and the choicest of your gifts, with all your sacred offerings. (20:34-40)

The divine plan will unfold in the future. For the time being, Ezekiel's mission is among his fellow exiles. That is why, after having been taken by the *ruah* from Chebar to Jerusalem to eyewitness the abominations there, he is now transported back to Chebar through the medium of the same *ruah* (11:24). Once there, he is left on his own to accomplish his mission (v.25). As for "the glory of the God of Israel" that was hovering over Jerusalem all through chapters 8-11 (8:4; 9:3; 10:19), it "went up from the midst of the city, and stood upon the mountain which is on the east side of the city" (11:23) and would remain there until 43:2. Then, Ezekiel will be brought to same spot at which he was in Jerusalem (The Spirit lifted me up, and brought me to the east gate of the house of the Lord, which faces east; 11:1) and where he beheld "the glory of the God of Israel" (And the cherubim lifted up their wings and mounted up from the earth in my sight as they went forth, with the wheels beside them; and they stood at the door of the east gate of the house of the Lord; and the glory of the God of Israel was over them; 10:19) in order to witness its return into the city:

> Afterward he[12] brought me to the gate, the gate facing east. And behold, the glory of the God of Israel came from the east; and the sound of his coming was like the sound of many waters; and the earth shone with his glory. And the vision I saw was like the vision which I had seen when he came to destroy the city, and like the vision which I had seen by the river Chebar; and I fell upon my face. As the glory of the Lord entered the temple by the gate facing

---

[12] "a man, whose appearance was like bronze, with a line of flax and a measuring reed in his hand" (40:3).

east, the Spirit lifted me up, and brought me into the inner court; and behold, the glory of the Lord filled the temple. (43:1-5)

Ezekiel Leaves Jerusalem

In addressing the exiles, Ezekiel is asked to play the role of an exile in order to make his message more pertinent. The punishment is all-encompassing and the prophet himself is not exempt from it: the book's opening unequivocally states that Ezekiel "was among the exiles by the river Chebar" (1:1). In chapter 12 the hearers are asked to recall the beginning of the book—twice in a row the exiles are specifically addressed as "a rebellious house" (*bet meri*; 12:3), exactly as was the case in chapters 2 (vv.5 and 6) and 3 (vv.26 and 27). So here Ezekiel is recalling his own exile in order to remind them of theirs, with the hope this time that "*perhaps* (*'ulay*) they will understand, though they are a rebellious house" (12:3b). This is the only instance of the adverb *'ulay* in Ezekiel and its use within the context of these few opening verses implies that this time round the rebellious house had better heed the message.

Earlier, the prophet entered the city through a hole he dug in its wall, unbeknown to anyone since he was on a scouting mission (8:8). However, this time, the same action is to be carried out specifically "in their sight," an action which is underscored through its occurrence seven times in five verses (12:3 [twice], 4 [twice], 5, 6, 7). In the Hebrew original, this is even more striking: "in their sight" in Hebrew is "to their eyes." The message opens thus: "Son of man, you dwell in the midst of a rebellious house, who have *eyes to see, but see not*, who have ears to hear, but hear not; for they are a rebellious house." (vv.2-3a) The verb that is translated as "understand" in verse 3b (RSV) is "see" in Hebrew. Still, Ezekiel was to leave the city "at evening in their sight, as men do who must go into exile" (v.4b); in other words, he was not just performing a role of a fugitive going the way of exile, but he in fact was one. This is further underscored through two extra literary devices. First, he was to cover his face that he may not see[13] (anymore) the earth he was leaving behind for good and, even more, "as a sign for the house of Israel" (v.6), that is, as the prototype exile. The value of that sign will be clarified later: "Say, 'I am a sign for you: as I have done, so shall it be done to them; they shall go into exile, into captivity.'" (v.11) Secondly, although he packed his baggage during the day, he was not to leave until evening and, specifically, "in the dark" (v.7) according to God's command (v.6).

The phrase "in the dark" seems to have another purpose. The Hebrew *'alaṭah* is found only four times in scripture, once in Genesis 15:17 and thrice here in Ezekiel 12 in the prepositional form *be'alaṭah* (in the dark; vv.6, 7, 12). The repetition in vv.6 and 7 concerning Ezekiel is clearly intended to stress that factor. The description of the prophet's exile is meant as prototype of the prince's, as is obvious from the close parallelism in the terminology describing the fate of each as well as the actual textual link between their predicted fortunes:

> "You shall bring out your baggage by day in their sight, as baggage for exile; and you shall go forth yourself at evening in their sight, as men do who must go into exile. Dig through the wall in their sight, and go out through it. In their sight you shall lift the baggage upon your shoulder, and carry it out in the dark; you shall cover your face, that you may not see the land; for I have made you a sign for the house of Israel." And I did as I was commanded. I brought out my baggage by day, as baggage for exile, and in the evening I dug through the wall with my own hands; I went forth

---

[13] Notice again the literary play on "not seeing."

in the dark, carrying my outfit upon my shoulder in their sight. In the morning the word of the Lord came to me: "Son of man, has not the house of Israel, the rebellious house, said to you, 'What are you doing?' Say to them, 'Thus says the Lord God: *This oracle concerns the prince in Jerusalem and all the house of Israel who are in it.' Say, 'I am a sign for you: as I have done, so shall it be done to them; they shall go into exile, into captivity.'* And the prince who is among them shall lift his baggage upon his shoulder in the dark, and shall go forth; he shall dig through the wall and go out through it; he shall cover his face, that he may not see the land with his eyes." (12:4-12)

In other words, the phrase "in the dark" seems to be functional in the prince's case. Earlier in 8:12, we have the only other instance of "in the dark" in Ezekiel. Although the original there is *baḥošek* (in the darkness), given that the subject in 8:12 and 12:12 is Jaazaniah the son of Shaphan, one can surmise that the connection between the two instances was on the author's mind:

> And before them stood seventy men of the elders of the house of Israel, with Jaazaniah the son of Shaphan standing among them. Each had his censer in his hand, and the smoke of the cloud of incense went up. Then he said to me, "Son of man, have you seen what the elders of the house of Israel are doing in the dark (*baḥošek*), every man in his room of pictures? For they say, 'The Lord does not see us, the Lord has forsaken the land.'" (8:11-12)

> And the prince who is among them shall lift his baggage upon his shoulder in the dark (*be'alaṭah*), and shall go forth; he shall dig through the wall and go out through it; he shall cover his face, that he may not see the land with his eyes. (12:12)

Since one of the two princes of 11:1, Pelatiah the son of Benaiah, is said to have died in v.13, then the prince of 12:12 is none other than the remaining one, Jaazaniah the son of Shaphan.

Thus, having perpetrated his abominations "in the dark," he will be exiled also "in the dark."

The question that remains, however, is why the author used the rare *'alaṭah* in chapter 12 instead of the common *ḥošek*, especially since he just did so in chapter 8 to speak of the same person. The intent here is to stress the nuance that *'alaṭah* carries when compared to *ḥošek*. The latter refers to complete darkness as in opposition with light (Gen 1:4-5). The former indicates the period of sundown or nightfall as can be gathered from its use in Genesis: "When the sun had gone down and it was dark (*'alaṭah*), behold, a smoking fire pot and a flaming torch passed between these pieces." (15:17) Thus, *'alaṭah* represents the prelude to *ḥošek*, just as the announcement of total destruction precedes the actual disaster. Indeed, the way to exile is the first step toward death in that exile: "And I will spread my net over him [the prince], and he shall be taken in my snare; and I will bring him to Babylon in the land of the Chaldeans, yet he shall not see it; and he shall die there." (Ezek 12:13) In scripture *ḥošek* occurs frequently as the expression of full punishment (see, e.g., Joel 2:1-3; Zeph 1:14-17). Its only other use later in Ezekiel will confirm this connotation: "When I blot you [Pharaoh] out, I will cover the heavens, and make their stars dark; I will cover the sun with a cloud, and the moon shall not give its light. All the bright lights of heaven will I make dark over you, and put darkness (*ḥošek*) upon your land, says the Lord God." (32:7-8) Consequently, the author wanted to underline the prince's belittlement in having to escape through a hole in the wall in the dark instead of exiting officially through the city gate. This was just the tip of the iceberg; his capital punishment would be death, which rejoins the earlier prediction that the leaders would fall by the sword "at the border of Israel" (11:10-11).

However, even the demise of the prince (12:13) and his entourage (vv.14-15) will not be the last chapter in their "story." It will live on through the few whom God will have spared so that they could spread that story among the nations where they will have been dispersed (v.16). The mission of the spared will specifically be "that (*lema'an*; with the purpose of) they confess (*yesapperu*; recount openly and in detail) all their abominations among the nations where they go." This way, not only those dispersed "shall know that I am the Lord" (v.15) but also the nations themselves who had not previously known him will "know that I am the Lord" (v.16) This reading takes exception with RSV's which considers that the second "know that I am the Lord" is addressed to the few Judahites that are spared: "But I will let a few of them escape from the sword, from famine and pestilence, that they may confess all their abominations among the nations where they go, and may know that I am the Lord." (v.16) This is the accepted understanding of most translations. However, the Jerusalem Bible and also two French translations, *Traduction Oecuménique de la Bible* and *Bible en français courant*, take exception to that evaluation. The original text seems to support either possibility.

That the nations will "know that I am the Lord" is what we find unequivocally at the end of the Ezekelian story: "In the latter days I will bring you against my land, that the nations may know me, when through you, O Gog, I vindicate my holiness before their eyes" (38:16); "So I will show my greatness and my holiness and make myself known in the eyes of many nations. Then they will know that I am the Lord" (v.23); "And my holy name I will make known in the midst of my people Israel; and I will not let my holy name be profaned any more; and the nations shall know that I am the Lord, the Holy One in Israel." (39:7) Given that the study of the odyssey of central words or phrases spans or brackets the Ezekelian story, it seems possible that the author already had in mind in 12:16 that the nations would ultimately "know that I am the Lord." One can make the case that this possibility is actually a probability. Looking carefully at chapters 38-39 one discovers that they essentially give the reason behind the nations' confession that the Lord is the universal God:

> And I will set my glory among the nations; and all the nations shall see my judgment which I have executed, and my hand which I have laid on them. The house of Israel shall know that I am the Lord their God, from that day forward. And the nations shall know that the house of Israel went into captivity for their iniquity, because they dealt so treacherously with me that I hid my face from them and gave them into the hand of their adversaries, and they all fell by the sword. I dealt with them according to their uncleanness and their transgressions, and hid my face from them. (39:21-24)

The nations would know that the house of Israel was sent into captivity for their iniquity and that the Lord hid his face from them. The exiles spared would confess "all their abominations *among the nations where they go*" (12:16). This thought, which will be expanded upon in chapter 39, can also be found previous to 12:12:

> Therefore thus says the Lord God: Because you are more turbulent than the nations that are round about you, and have not walked in my statutes or kept my ordinances, but have acted according to the ordinances of the nations that are round about you; therefore thus says the Lord God: Behold, I, even I, am against you; and I will execute judgments in the midst of you *in the sight of the nations*. And because of all your abominations I will do with you what I have never yet done, and the like of which I will never do again. (5:7-9)

You shall be a reproach and a taunt, a warning and a horror, *to the nations round about you*, when I execute judgments on you in anger and fury, and with furious chastisements—I, the Lord, have spoken—(5:15)

Yet I will leave some of you alive. When you have among the nations some who escape the sword, and when you are scattered through the countries, then those of you who escape *will remember me among the nations* where they are carried captive, when I have broken their wanton heart which has departed from me, and blinded their eyes which turn wantonly after their idols; and they will be loathsome in their own sight for the evils which they have committed, for all their abominations. And they shall know that I am the Lord; I have not said in vain that I would do this evil to them. (6:8-10)

Thus, this concern of the author, along with his other major interests, is found throughout the book.

The reason for God's extreme punishment against the inhabitants of Jerusalem (12:19a) as well as against the prophet himself (v.18) is due to "the violence of all those who dwell in it [the land]" (v.19b). Violence (*ḥamas*) is precisely the reason given in the chapter regarding the "end" addressed to the "ground of Israel" (*'admat yisra'el*; 7:2) (v.11 and 23) and in the beginning of the section (chs. 8-12) that deals with the reason behind the dispersion of its inhabitants (8:17). The noun occurs once more at the end of the book, in conjunction with the princes (45:9), in order to bring back to mind the magnitude of the princes' sin that was behind the divine punishment:

Then he said to me, "Have you seen this, O son of man? Is it too slight a thing for the house of Judah to commit the abominations which they commit here, that they should fill the land with violence (*ḥamas*), and provoke me further to anger? Lo, they put the branch to their nose." (8:17)[14]

Thus says the Lord God: Enough, O princes of Israel! Put away violence (*ḥamas*) and oppression (*šod*), and execute justice and righteousness; cease your evictions of my people, says the Lord God. (45:9)

Except for its occurrence in 28:16 in an address to Tyre, the arrogant city par excellence to which the prophet dedicated seventy-six verses (26:1-28:19), *ḥamas* is confined to the five mentioned instances. The same feature of bracketing Ezekiel's message applies to it, which makes it a classic example of prime concern for the prophet. Consequently, it would behoove us to delve into its meaning.

Let us begin with a classic passage: "Proclaim to the strongholds in Assyria, and to the strongholds in the land of Egypt, and say, 'Assemble yourselves upon the mountains of Samaria, and see the great tumults within her, and the oppressions (*'ašuqim* from the root *'ašaq*) in her midst. They do not know how to do right,' says the Lord, 'those who store up violence (*ḥamas*) and robbery (*šod*) in their strongholds.'" (Am 3:9-10) A few verses later the root *'ašaq* occurs in the following context: "Hear this word, you cows of Bashan, who are in the mountain of Samaria, who oppress (*'ošeqot*) the poor, who crush the needy, who say to their husbands, 'Bring, that we may drink!'" (4:1) It is clear from these texts that *ḥamas* refers to the action of forced violence or oppression that a more powerful person inflicts on a less fortunate one. Such is corroborated in Ezekiel 45:9 where the same couple *ḥamas* and *šod* is found, with

---

[14] Jaazaniah the son of Shaphan, referred to in v.11, is later introduced, together with Pelatiah the son of Benaiah, as "princes of the people" (11:1).

their opposites being justice and righteousness that would require following the rules of equity rather than taking advantage of the weaker person. This understanding is further confirmed in 7:11 (Violence has grown up into a rod of wickedness; none of them shall remain, nor their abundance, nor their wealth; neither shall there be preeminence among them) and 28:16 (In the abundance of your trade you were filled with violence) where violence is clearly linked to richness and preeminence, that is to say, to a position allowing one to take advantage for one's own benefit at the expense of someone less privileged. Still, what makes violence tantamount to idolatrous abomination in God's eyes (8:17) is that his law is contravened by the priests, the very people whose duty is to uphold it: "Her (the earth's, *'ereṣ*, which is a feminine noun in Hebrew) priests have done violence to (*ḥamesu*; from the verb *ḥamas*) my law and have profaned my holy things." (22:26a) God's law requires that the less fortunate—alien, poor, widow, orphan—be cared for. It is no wonder then that the divine indictment is phrased in the following way by Ezekiel's contemporary:

> The word that came to Jeremiah from the Lord: "Stand in the gate of the Lord's house, and proclaim there this word, and say, Hear the word of the Lord, all you men of Judah who enter these gates to worship the Lord. Thus says the Lord of hosts, the God of Israel, Amend your ways and your doings, and I will let you dwell in this place. Do not trust in these deceptive words: 'This is the temple of the Lord, the temple of the Lord, the temple of the Lord.' For if you truly amend your ways and your doings, if you truly execute justice one with another, if you do not oppress (*ta'ašoqu*) the alien, the fatherless or the widow, or shed innocent blood in this place, and if you do not go after other gods to your own hurt, then I will let you dwell in this place, in the land that I gave of old to your fathers for ever." (Jer 7:1-7)

9
The False Prophets

The passage 12:21-28 serves as introduction to chapter 13 where the false prophets and prophetesses in Jerusalem are harshly criticized for propagating teachings not sanctioned by God. In it we hear for the first time mention of *mašal* (proverb), which is a staple of Ezekiel's teaching. Given that the Semitic *mašal* is much more versatile than its English translation "proverb," it is imperative to make a few explanatory comments concerning that word. The *mašal* encompasses the entire gamut of our English "adage," "saying," "example," "proverb," "fable," "parable," "simile," "verisimilitude," even "story," so long as the common denominator is instruction. Put more straightforwardly, a *mašal* is "instructional" material that spans the full array from a simple statement to a full-fledged story, as is evidenced in the scriptural Book of Proverbs, whose Hebrew title is *mišle šelomoh*, the *mešalim*[1] (plural of *mašal*) of Solomon. This book contains the lengthy instruction regarding the "good wife" covering 22 verses (31:10-31) as well as one verse instructional statements, and they are all *mešalim*.

Because it is essentially instructional, a corollary aspect of the *mašal* is that its value is intrinsic and does not need to be validated for or by the addressees. The hearers of a *mašal* listen to it and abide by its instruction to their own benefit, or disregard its message to their own detriment. That is why the Book of Proverbs is part of what is referred to as Wisdom Literature and, conversely, the other books of that same section of scripture

---

[1] Its construct state form is *mišle*, which is the form *mešalim* takes when followed by a noun complement.

(Job; Ecclesiastes; Wisdom of Solomon; Wisdom of Sirach) are filled with "proverbs." In other words, the *mašal*, much like a fable of Aesop or an adage, is the classic medium of wisdom, the opposite of which is folly. Folly, in turn, can be misleading when it uses the garb of wisdom, the *mašal*, to find currency. However, one cannot afford to wait and see whether a given saying will be proven correct or incorrect, since in the meantime disaster may strike. That is why a foolish saying is not to be corrected; rather it has to be silenced and replaced with a wholesome saying. This is precisely what the Lord is doing in 12:21-28 and throughout chapter 13, especially that the misleading proverb herein is challenging the teaching God entrusted to Ezekiel through the "visions" he was privy to at Chebar (1:1).

Ezekiel's non-commissioned opponents were issuing a "proverb" challenging God's decision promulgated by Ezekiel, to raze "the ground of Israel" (*'admat yisra'el*; 12:22a). The content of that misleading proverb was "The days grow long, and every vision comes to nought," meaning that the vision received by Ezekiel is false since the "end" announced in chapter 7 has not yet occurred and the days continue to roll by. So God commands Ezekiel to silence that proverb which is rooted in a "false vision or flattering divination" (12:24), and summons him to emit a counter-proverb: "The days are at hand, and the fulfillment of every vision" (v.23b). It is worth noting that the Hebrew term rendered as "the fulfillment of" is actually *debar* (the word [matter] of). This is a clear indication, as explained in the discussion of the "vision" of chapter 1, that the vision of Ezekiel was not so much a projection of his own imagining—as he claims is the case with his opponents—but it was delivered through the word of the Lord (*debar yahweh*; v.3). That such was on the author's mind is corroborated in what God says in the following verse: "But I the Lord will speak (*'adabber*) the word (*dabar*) which I will speak (*'adabber*), and it will be performed. It will no longer be delayed, but *in your days*, O rebellious house, I will speak (*'adabber*) the word (*dabar*) and perform it, says the Lord God." (12:25) What is even more impressive is that the entire divine statement to Ezekiel in vv.22-25 is introduced as "the word of the Lord" (*debar yahweh*; v.21).

Scripture is supposed to be read aloud by a reader and thus heard by others. Underscoring a point is done through repetition as we do when we communicate orally. This is precisely what we hear in vv.26-28, which are essentially a carbon copy of the previous vv.21-25. However, in view of the following chapter where the harangue is specifically against prophets (*nebi'im* from the root *nb'*) and prophetesses, the author slips in the participle *nibba'* (he prophesies; from the same root *nb'*) when speaking of Ezekiel at the end of v.27.

The divine address of chapter 13 is divided between prophets (vv.1-16) and prophetesses (vv.17-23). A different metaphor is used in each case, however they both boil down to the same effect: leading or condemning the people to disaster and death. The prophets do it through deception while the prophetesses do it by means of incantation that is not allowed in the Law. The reason behind the falseness of their prophecy lies in that they "prophesy out of their own minds (*leb*; heart)" (vv.2 and 17). The Hebrew *leb* means "core, center" and refers to the "mind" of the human beings with which they think, will, act, and feel; that is why, as we heard earlier, in order to renew the exiles, God will have to "break their heart":

> Yet I will leave some of you alive. When you have among the nations some who escape the sword, and when you are scattered through the countries, then those of you who escape will remember me among the nations where they are carried captive,

when I have broken their wanton heart which has departed from me, and blinded their eyes which turn wantonly after their idols; and they will be loathsome in their own sight for the evils which they have committed, for all their abominations. And they shall know that I am the Lord; I have not said in vain that I would do this evil to them. (6:8-10)

The source behind the erring of their heart is that these false prophets "follow (*holekim 'aḥar*; walk after) their own spirit (*ruḥam*)" (13:3). God alone is *ru'aḥ* (spirit) whereas the human being is merely *nepheš* (breath, breathing, soul).[2] "Following their own spirit" simply means "not following God's spirit." Such is corroborated in the further explication that by doing so they "have seen (*ra'u*) nothing," which is clearly contrary to Ezekiel's visions (*mar'ot*; from the same *ra'ah* root as *ra'u*) in 1:1. Put otherwise, although they assumed or rather wanted the others to believe that their visions were prompted by the divine spirit as were Ezekiel's visions, this was not the case. Any of their visions are merely "false vision or flattering divination" (12:24; see also 13:6, 23). In the case of the false prophets the irony is that their actions will not stop God's plan of destruction, but actually will play into his hand. Indeed, trying to patch up a breach in the city walls by daubing them with whitewash might fool the citizens, but it could not avert the divine "stormy wind (spirit)" (*ruaḥ se'arot*) that God is unleashing (v.13), which is the same spirit Ezekiel had witnessed in 1:4 and by whose power he was sent on his mission (2:2). The "peace" (13:10) those bogus prophets are selling to the citizens of Jerusalem is simply false peace (v.16).

---

[2] See my comments in *C-1Cor* pp.59-69.

The False Prophets

The prophetesses are using the other side of the same coin of deception—they are resorting to witchcraft. What makes their case even more alarming is that it goes against what Ezekiel, as watchman, is supposed to be doing, that is, propping up the righteous to proceed ahead and inviting the wicked to change their ways (3:16-21). The prophetesses are doing just the opposite: "... you have disheartened the righteous falsely, although I have not disheartened him, and you have encouraged the wicked, that he should not turn from his wicked way to save his life." (13:22)

10
Ezekiel's First Encounter with the Exiles

A major turning point in the book occurs in chapter 14. First we hear of the initial encounter between Ezekiel and the exiles (vv. 1-11); secondly, the prophet establishes unequivocally the personal accountability of each and every individual for the punishment one incurs. The exiles can no longer blame their exile in Babylon on the sins of their "fathers" (vv. 12-23).

As mentioned earlier in conjunction with chapter 8, by referring to both the leaders of Jerusalem and those in exile as "elders of Israel," Ezekiel was establishing the connection between their situations. Indeed, in Babylon as well as in Jerusalem it is the sin of idolatry that is pervading; notice the high incidence of "idols" and the allusion to such idolatry as "abomination," both of which were encountered earlier in reference to the sins perpetrated in Jerusalem:

> Any man of the house of Israel who takes his idols into his heart and sets the stumbling block of his iniquity before his face, and yet comes to the prophet, I the Lord will answer him myself because of the multitude of his idols, that I may lay hold of the hearts of the house of Israel, who are all estranged from me through their idols. Therefore say to the house of Israel, Thus says the Lord God: Repent and turn away from your idols; and turn away your faces from all your abominations. (14:4-6)

Furthermore, the parallelism is also and most importantly evident in that the elders of Israel in exile were "sitting" (v.1) in the presence of Ezekiel, just as were the elders of Judah (8:1). The Lord's reaction is one of extreme irritation: "should I let myself be inquired of at all by them?" (14:3b) In the parallel situation of chapter 20 where the elders also "sat before me" (v.1), we hear the more expanded version of the divine reaction: "Is it to inquire of me that you come? As I live, says the Lord God, I will not be inquired of by you. Will you judge them, son of man, will you judge them?" (vv.3b-4a) The reason for such a strong reaction is that sitting is the position a judge takes when he faces (sits before) those whom he is about to judge. So, the elders were about to emit judgment on God's representative, and if so, then on God himself, and God was not about to allow that to happen. In 20:1, we are told explicitly "certain of the elders of Israel came to inquire of the Lord, and sat before me." Unfortunately, the English "inquire of" does not render accurately the Hebrew *daraš* whose meaning is "study intensively, in detail" and thus "examine thoroughly," which is precisely what the judge does: he inquires in a pertinent manner not to learn something to his own personal benefit, but in order to make a decision concerning the person of his inquiry.[1] So, a more accurate rendition of 20:1-4 would be:

> In the seventh year, in the fifth month, on the tenth day of the month, certain of the elders of Israel came to scrutinize the Lord, and sat before me. And the word of the Lord came to me: "Son of man, speak to the elders of Israel, and say to them, Thus says the Lord God, Is it to scrutinize me that you come? As I live, says the Lord God, I will not be scrutinized by you. Will you judge them, son of man, will you judge them?"

That it is God, through his representative, whom the elders are attempting to scrutinize is corroborated three verses later: "For

---

[1] Another example would be the difference between an inquiry by a traveler intended for his own benefit and thus does not entail an assessment of the answer, on the one hand, and a policeman inquiry aimed at assessing the person whom he is questioning, on the other hand.

any one ... who comes to a prophet to inquire for himself of me, I the Lord will answer him myself." (14:7)

Immediately after the address in the plural to the elders (v.6), the text turns to the singular to speak not only of "any one" (vv.7-8) but also of "the prophet" (v.9), instead of "the prophets," as was done in the previous chapter. This is to prepare for the following passage (vv.12-23) that will stress individual responsibility. Both the threat (v.7 and v.9a) and the punishment (v.8 and 9b) are addressed to the individual person and to the individual prophet as well; moreover, the guilt of each will be his own: "And they shall bear their punishment (*'awon*; guilt, burden)—the punishment (*'awon*) of the prophet and the punishment (*'awon*) of the inquirer shall be alike." (v.10) However, there is more to this than meets the ear at first hearing. A closer look at the passage, especially in the original, will reveal a few more important features.

The general appeal cast in the plural is a command where the root *šub* occurs thrice: "Repent (*šubu*; turn around, return [assumedly, to me]) and turn away (*hašibu*; make turn [assumedly, yourselves or your faces]) from your idols; and turn away (*hašibu*; make turn) your faces from all your abominations." (v.6) The radicalism of the command stressing an unconditional and total turnabout has to do with the fact that it is addressed to each and every one of "the house of Israel," and is also required of "the strangers (*ger*)[2] that sojourn (*yagur*) in Israel" (v.7). The significance of this is that God's earth where his plan will be realized is *'admat yisra'el* (the ground of Israel), that is, his plan is inclusive of every *'adam* (human being). Indeed, "So you shall divide this land among you according to

---

[2] RSV translated the singular *ger* (stranger) into "strangers," understanding it as a generic singular.

the tribes of Israel. You shall allot it as an inheritance for yourselves and for the aliens (*gerim*) who reside (*garim*) among you and have begotten children among you. They shall be to you as native-born sons of Israel; with you they shall be allotted an inheritance among the tribes of Israel. In whatever tribe the alien (*ger*) resides (*gar*), there you shall assign him his inheritance, says the Lord God" (47:21-23). In chapter 14 we can see once more the literary device of looking ahead to the end of the story, which does not finish with the demise of Jerusalem and Judah. Repentance is only one of many steps in God's plan. The fall of Jerusalem will produce exiles who, in turn, will be threatened with punishment should they follow the way of their predecessors. Such punishment, however, will not be the end of the Ezekelian story. The besieged citizens of Jerusalem will be "a reproach and a taunt, a warning (*musar*; instruction) and a horror, to the nations round about you" (5:15). Furthermore, a disobedient exile will be "cut off from the midst of my people" and as such made into "a sign and a byword (*mešalim*; [instructional] parables)" (14:8) for future generations of "strangers" as well as Judahites.

If that is the fate of the individual exile, then the threat against Ezekiel is all the more ominous and his guilt weightier (vv.9-10). The individual exiles are many, however "the prophet" is spoken of in the singular and cannot but be Ezekiel since all the other prophets and prophetesses of Judah were already disposed of (ch.13). Ezekiel was assigned as God's sole prophet at Chebar, where he is now. That is why his "burden" (*'awon*; punishment as well as guilt) is rendered in a most extreme fashion: not only the divine hand that was earlier stretched "*to* me" (*'elay*; 2:9) will now be stretched "*against* him" (*'alaw*; 14:9b), but "if the prophet be deceived and speak a word, *I, the Lord, have deceived that prophet*" (v.9a). In other words, should Ezekiel decide to be a false prophet, God will expose him as such; his lie would be so flagrant that it could not be mistaken for the word of the Lord. Unlike the other prophets at Jerusalem, Ezekiel is under the control of God's spirit, his stomach and mouth are filled with God's words, so should Ezekiel even begin to think of faltering, God will make it so that he, God, be the originator and that, in this case, *quite literally* Ezekiel's 'awon (guilt) will be a "divine" 'awon (punishment). Ezekiel was expressly told twice not to be dismayed before the exiles (2:9; 3:6) or his fate would be similar to that of his contemporary: "But you, gird up your loins; arise, and say to them everything that I command you. Do not be dismayed by them, lest I dismay you before them." (Jer 1:17) God shall never allow his opponents to even assume that they got the best out of Ezekiel when it comes to the words that Ezekiel utters; only God, who set those words in his mouth in the first place, would be allowed to do so. God maintains such control over the prophet since his ultimate purpose is "that the house of Israel may go no more astray from me, nor defile themselves any more with all their transgressions, but that they may be my people and I may be their God, says the Lord God" (Ezek 14:11).

The second part of chapter 14 (vv.12-23) underscores God's *universal* righteousness in *all his doings*. It would be wrong to hear it as independent of the previous passage; in fact, the link between the two is safeguarded through the same avenue of punishment against any culprit: "I will stretch out my hand against him [a prophet]" (v.9) and "I will stretch out my hand against it [a land]" (v.13). Thus, just as vv.6-11 started to stress the individual accountability of each and every human being, Judahite and stranger alike, here also the universality of the divine sentence is made through the medium of three ancient non-Hebrew, non-Judahite, personalities: Noah, Daniel,[3] and Job. In the case of a siege ordained by God, they would not be able to save anyone but themselves, not even their own sons and daughters, let alone their co-citizens (vv.12-20).

The following verses 21-23 have given rise to much controversy in that they seem, at first hearing, to go against the grain of vv.12-20. These verses speak somewhat positively of the exiles who are supposed to be the tail end of the siege, as witnessed in the use of "sons and daughters" (v.22; see vv.16, 18, 20), and "a sign and a byword" for everybody else. Yet, we are told that they would be a consolation:

> For thus says the Lord God: How much more when I send upon Jerusalem my four sore acts of judgment, sword, famine, evil beasts, and pestilence, to cut off from it man and beast! Yet, if there should be left in it any survivors to lead out (*muṣa'im*; from the verb *yaṣa*) sons and daughters, when they come forth (*yoṣe'im*; from the verb *yaṣa*) to you, and you see their ways and their doings, you will be consoled (*niḥamtem*) for the evil that I have brought upon Jerusalem, for all that I have brought upon it. They will console (*niḥamu*) you, when you see their ways and their doings; and you shall know that I have not done without cause all that I have done in it, says the Lord God. (14:21-23)

How should one correctly understand these verses? As hard as it may seem to our "modern" ears, in the tradition of Ancient Near Eastern wisdom, harsh punishment carries with it a factor of consolation. Here it is reflected in the three names of Noah, Daniel, and Job. The fact that a few survivors were allowed to escape the four scourges of sword, famine, evil beasts, and pestilence is a clear "sign and parable" that God intended that a lesson be drawn from the righteous judgment he just inflicted.

---

[3] Daniel is a reference to the wise king of the Ugaritic lore, Danel.

Why? Because, as we shall hear repeatedly later, "Have I any pleasure in the death of the wicked, says the Lord God, and not rather that he should turn from his way and live?" (18:23); "For I have no pleasure in the death of any one, says the Lord God; so turn, and live" (v.32); "And you, son of man, say to the house of Israel, Thus have you said: 'Our transgressions and our sins are upon us, and we waste away because of them; how then can we live?' Say to them, As I live, says the Lord God, I have no pleasure in the death of the wicked, but that the wicked turn from his way and live; turn back, turn back from your evil ways; for why will you die, O house of Israel?" (33:10-11) Notice the thrice occurrence in the last verse of the verb *šub* (turn; turn back; return; repent) that we just encountered in 14:6, which confirms the link in thought between the two instances.

The consolation lies in that the hearers are given another chance and, more importantly, with a forewarning. The same kind of consolation is found in the classic opening of Isaiah's Book of Consolation (chs.40-66): "Comfort (*nahamu*; console), comfort (*nahamu*; console) my people, says your God. Speak *tenderly* to (*'al-leb*; to the heart of) Jerusalem, and cry to her that her warfare is ended, that her iniquity is pardoned, *that she has received from the Lord's hand double for all her sins.*" (40:1-2) Thus the punished remnant in Ezekiel will be indeed a consolation to the exiles in that they were spared by God *for the exiles' sake*. Should these not hearken to the warning, God may well "bring you out (*hoṣe'ti*; from the verb *yaṣa'*) from the peoples and gather you out of the countries where you are scattered" (20: 34), however, he will do so in order to "enter into judgment with you face to face" (v.35)! That our text here (14:21-23) has chapter 20 in mind is evident in the unexpected use of the verb *yaṣa'* twice in one verse (14:22) after the use of the verb "deliver" (*naṣal*) no less than seven times (vv.14, 16 [twice], 18 [twice], 20 [twice]). The intention is undeniable: as with the exodus from Egypt, the upcoming exodus from Babylon will be unto judgment rather than salvation (20:34-36).[4] Thus, the harshness of the lesson is for the good of the upcoming generations who must understand that their hope lies in God's justice and righteousness.[5] Ezekiel teaches repeatedly in chapter 20 that God "... *acted for the sake of my name*, that it should not be profaned in the sight of the nations among whom they dwelt." (vv.9, 14, 22)

---

[4] Paul will point out unequivocally when addressing the overconfident, yet deluded, Corinthians that what happened to others was a lesson *for his hearers' as well as his sake*: "I want you to know, brethren, that our fathers were all under the cloud, and all passed through the sea, and all were baptized into Moses in the cloud and in the sea, and all ate the same supernatural food and all drank the same supernatural drink. For they drank from the supernatural Rock which followed them, and the Rock was Christ. Nevertheless with most of them God was not pleased; for they were overthrown in the wilderness. *Now these things are warnings for us, not to desire evil as they did.* Do not be idolaters as some of them were; as it is written, 'The people sat down to eat and drink and rose up to dance.' We must not indulge in immorality as some of them did, and twenty-three thousand fell in a single day. We must not put the Lord to the test, as some of them did and were destroyed by serpents; nor grumble, as some of them did and were destroyed by the Destroyer. *Now these things happened to them as a warning, but they were written down for our instruction, upon whom the end of the ages has come.*" (1 Cor 10:1-11)

[5] Again the Apostle Paul makes this matter clear in Romans: "What if some were unfaithful? Does their faithlessness nullify the faithfulness of God? By no means! Let God be true though every man be false, as it is written, 'That thou mayest be justified in thy words, and prevail when thou art judged.' But if our wickedness serves to show the justice of God, what shall we say? That God is unjust to inflict wrath on us? (I speak in a human way.) By no means! For then how could God judge the world? ... through my falsehood God's truthfulness abounds to his glory..." (3:3-7)

11
The Parabolic Stories

The Metaphor of the Vine

Chapter 15 is an aside to the previous chapter as is evident from its conclusion: "And I will make the land (*ha'areṣ*) desolate (*šemamah*), because they have acted faithlessly (*ma'alu ma'al*), says the Lord God." (15:8) This is a compact statement of 14:13-16:

> Son of man, when a land sins against me by *acting faithlessly* (*me'al ma'al*), and I stretch out my hand against it, and break its staff of bread and send famine upon it, and cut off from it man and beast, even if these three men, Noah, Daniel, and Job, were in it, they would deliver but their own lives by their righteousness, says the Lord God. If I cause wild beasts to pass through *the land* (*ha'areṣ*), and they ravage it, and it be made *desolate* (*šemamah*), so that no man may pass through because of the beasts; even if these three men were in it, as I live, says the Lord God, they would deliver neither sons nor daughters; they alone would be delivered, but *the land* (*ha'areṣ*) would be *desolate* (*šemamah*).

This chapter 15 also functions as a hinge between the preceding and the following chapters in that it introduces the metaphor of the vine for Jerusalem and Judah. This metaphor is classic in both the Old Testament (e.g., Is 5:1-4; Jer 2:21; Ps 80:8, 14) and the New Testament (Jn 15:1-7) to speak of God's community. We shall encounter this same metaphor in chapters 17 and 19:

> Then he [a great eagle] took of the seed of the land and planted it in fertile soil; he placed it beside abundant waters. He set it like a

willow twig, and it sprouted and became a low spreading vine, and its branches turned toward him, and its roots remained where it stood. So it became a vine, and brought forth branches and put forth foliage. But there was another great eagle with great wings and much plumage; and behold, this vine bent its roots toward him, and shot forth its branches toward him that he might water it. From the bed where it was planted he transplanted it to good soil by abundant waters, that it might bring forth branches, and bear fruit, and become a noble vine. (Ezek 17:5-8)

Your mother was like a vine in a vineyard transplanted by the water, fruitful and full of branches by reason of abundant water. Its strongest stem became a ruler's scepter; it towered aloft among the thick boughs; it was seen in its height with the mass of its branches. (19:10-11)

The vine needs a lot of care before it starts producing fruit. Thus, the vine and vineyards are reflective of a long stay in a given place and, by the same token, of a lengthy time of peace and security. In the detailed description of the curses that God will inflict on those who "will not obey the voice of the Lord your God or be careful to do all his commandments and his statutes which I command you this day" (Deut 28:15), we hear the following:

Cursed shall you be in the city, and cursed shall you be in the field ... and you shall grope at noonday, as the blind grope in darkness, and you shall not prosper in your ways; and you shall be only oppressed and robbed continually, and there shall be no one to help you. You shall betroth a wife, and another man shall lie with her; you shall build a house, and you shall not dwell in it; you shall plant a vineyard, and you shall not use the fruit of it ... You shall carry much seed into the field, and shall gather little in; for the locust shall consume it. You shall plant vineyards and dress them, but you shall neither drink of the wine nor gather the grapes; for the worm shall eat them. (Deut 28:16, 29-30, 38-39)

That is why earlier the Lord specifically criticized the false prophets who were heralding "peace" when he had decided otherwise:

Because, yea, because they have misled my people, saying, 'Peace,' when there is no peace; and because, when the people build a wall, these prophets daub it with whitewash; ... The wall is no more, nor those who daubed it, the prophets of Israel who prophesied concerning Jerusalem and saw visions of peace for her, when there was no peace, says the Lord God. (Ezek 13:10, 15b-16)

Here, in chapter 15, we hear of the "vine" being set in the fire just as Jerusalem (5:2, 4) was during its siege (chs. 4-5):

Therefore thus says the Lord God: Like the wood of the vine among the trees of the forest, which I have given to the fire for fuel, so will I give up the inhabitants of Jerusalem. And I will set my face against them; though they escape from the fire, the fire shall yet consume them; and you will know that I am the Lord, when I set my face against them. (15:6-7).

The theme of the vine will be expanded upon in chapters 17 and 19.

A Story of Harlotry

A lengthy series of "parables" begins in chapter 16 and concludes in chapter 24 with the indictment of Jerusalem. The longest parabolic story of Jerusalem's abominations occurs in chapter 16. That the designation of "proverb" applies to this entire chapter is evident in the phrase "Your mother was a Hittite and your father an Amorite" that introduces the chapter: "Son of man, make known to Jerusalem her abominations, and say, Thus says the Lord God to Jerusalem: Your origin and your birth are of the land of the Canaanites; your father was an Amorite, and your mother a Hittite." (vv.2-3) The juncture at which that city's two sisters, Samaria and Sodom, are introduced as co-culprits, we hear: "Behold, every one who uses proverbs will use this proverb about you, 'Like mother, like daughter.' You are the daughter of your mother, who loathed her husband and her children; and you are the sister of your sisters, who loathed their husbands and their children. Your mother was a Hittite and your father an Amorite." (vv.44-45)

On the other hand, chapters 16-24 do not introduce a new topic, but build up on the previous section (chs. 4-14). Chapter 15 introduces the theme of the vine, which will be built upon in chapters 17 and 19. Chapter 16 expands on the theme of abominations as harlotries, which was deftly introduced early on in the previous section:

> Yet I will leave some of you alive. When you have among the nations some who escape the sword, and when you are scattered through the countries, then those of you who escape will remember me among the nations where they are carried captive, when I have broken their *wanton* (*zoneh*; playing the harlot, adulterous, fornicator) heart which has departed from me, and blinded their eyes *which turn wantonly* (*zonot*; playing the harlot) after their idols; and they will be loathsome in their own sight for the evils which they have committed, for all their abominations. And they shall know that I am the Lord; I have not said in vain that I would do this evil to them. (6:8-10)

Except for 20:30 and 43:7 and 9, the root *zanah* (commit harlotry) is found only and repeatedly in chapter 16 (12 times) and its twin chapter 23 (10 times), making it the theme of these two chapters. In turn, this fits perfectly the scriptural equivalence between apostasy, leaving the Lord for other deities, which qualified as abomination in the previous chapters, and the metaphor of the harlot or the adulterous wife (16:32; see also Ex 34:15-16; Lev 17:7; 20:5; Deut 31:16; Hos 1-2). The connection between the two is evident in the start of the indictment in chapter 16: "Son of man, make known to Jerusalem her abominations." (v.2)

Another indication that chapters 16-24 are a reprise of chapters 4-14 can be found in some interesting features of chapters 16, 20, and 23 that are three parallel renditions of the scriptural story of Israel. Why would there be three renditions of the same story within such a short interval, with two almost identical copies at either end? Although chapters 16 and 23 have overlapping content, it is only in chapter 16 that Sodom is mentioned as the youngest sister of Samaria and Jerusalem. Taking into consideration what we found earlier, namely, that Ezekiel first witnessed what was happening in Jerusalem and then he addressed the exiles, it stands to reason that chapter 16 is covering the abominations of Jerusalem before its fall. Chapter 23 is revisiting the same abominations because they are still going on among the Jerusalemite exiles and, by extension, the Samaritan exiles. This being the case, Sodom is omitted since it was destroyed and there were no survivors in exile (Jer 49:18; 50:40). While Jerusalem was still standing in Canaan among the Amorites and the Hittites (16:3, 45), she should have learned not only from the fate of Samaria, but even more so from that of Sodom. Notice that Samaria does not play a major role in chapter 16; her abominations are passed over in half a verse (v.51a), whereas those of Sodom extend over three verses (vv.48-50), and Jerusalem is explicitly said to have looked down at her (v.56). Further evidence that chapter 16 deals specifically with Jerusalem (vv.1-43) is that Samaria and Sodom are not introduced until v.45. Chapter 23, on the other hand, introduces the two sisters, Samaria and Jerusalem, as the subject matter right from the beginning (v.2). It is as though chapter 23 starts (Son of man, there were two women, the daughters of one mother; v.2) at the level of 16:44 (Behold, every one who uses proverbs will use this proverb about you, "Like mother, like daughter") and, more specifically, with an eye on their children in exile. In chapter 16 the Assyrians, who destroyed Samaria and besieged Jerusalem, do not come into the picture until v.28; whereas in chapter 23 the Assyrians are part of the picture right from the beginning (v.5), immediately after the introduction of the two sisters by name (v.4). The description of the two sisters' infatuation with the Assyrians takes over the following verses (vv.6-13).

Can one find any further indication that chapter 16 looks back to the time when the exiles' "fathers" were committing abominations in Palestine, while chapter 23 is concerned more with the Jerusalemite exiles in Babylon and the Samaritan exiles in Assyria? The phrase "your father was an Amorite, and your mother a Hittite" occurs twice in chapter 16, in v.3 to introduce Jerusalem and then in v.45 to introduce her sisters, Samaria and Sodom. Verse 3 is actually more comprehensive since it first mentions that Jerusalem's "origin and birth are of the land of the Canaanites," moving from the larger context of land to that of the family and thus encompassing all aspects of one's origin. The noun *moledot* (birth; plural of *moledet*), common in scripture, is from the root *yalad* (bear, give birth) and thus refers to either parentage (e.g., Gen 11:28; 12:1; 24:4, 7) or progeny (e.g., Gen 48:6). The following verse confirms this meaning: "And as for your birth (*moledot*), on the day you were born (*huledet* also from the root *yalad*) your navel string was not cut, nor were you washed with water to cleanse you, nor rubbed with salt, nor

The Parabolic Stories

swathed with bands." (Ezek 16:4) So the real crux in this matter is the noun *mekorot* that is translated as "origin." Although, in the entire scripture it occurs only three times, all in Ezekiel, each of those three instances is in conjunction with a different community: Jerusalem (16:3 where it is in the plural form *mekorot*), the Ammonites (21:30 where it is in the plural form *mekurot*), and Egypt (29:14 where it is in the singular form *mekurah*).[1] To say, as many interpreters do, that since *moledet* refers to the biological family *mekurah* must be connoting the geographical area of origin, is preposterous. "Origin" is nothing more than an educated guess based on the context; commentators are admittedly at a loss concerning the Hebrew root of the noun *mekorot*. Later in Ezekiel 21:30 and 29:14 we hear of "the land (*'ereṣ*) of your [their] *mekurot*" just as we do of "the land (*'ereṣ*) of your [my; our] *moledet*" (Gen 11:28; 24:7; 31:13; Ruth 2:11; Jer 22:10). Given the frequency of wordplay in scripture, and given that the word is exclusively Ezekelian, one should question whether Ezekiel used *mekurah* with intended wordplay in mind. It would behoove us to refer to three classic translations: the Greek Septuagint (LXX), the Latin Vulgate, and the English King James Version (KJV).

> ***Greek Septuagint (LXX)***: "your root (*mekorot*) and your genesis (*moledot*) [are] out of the land of Canaan" (16:3) followed by "and your genesis (*moledot*) the day you were born" (v.4); then "in your own (*mekurot*) land" (21:30); then "in the land whence they were taken (*mekurah*)" (29:14).
>
> ***Latin Vulgate***: "your root (*mekorot*) and generation (*moledot*) [are] of the Canaanite land" (16:3) followed by "and when you were born (*moledot*) on the day of your birth" (v.4); then "in the

---

[1] The vocalic *o* and *u* in Hebrew are closely related and often one reverts into the other.

land of your nativity (*mekurot*)" (21:30); then "in the land of its nativity (*mekurah*)" (29:14).

English King James: "Thy birth (*mekorot*) and thy nativity (*moledot*) is of the land of Canaan" (16:3) followed by "And as for thy nativity (*moledot*), in the day thou wast born" (v.4); then "in the land of thy nativity (*mekurot*)" (21:30); then "into the land of their habitation (*mekurah*)" (29:14).

Clearly there seems to be an overlapping of the meanings assigned to the two nouns in the Vulgate and KJV. The LXX has no overlapping, but its weakness lies in that the hearer is totally unaware that the original Hebrew uses the same noun *mekurah* in all three instances and thus misses completely the intended connection between them.

To solve the crux, it would be prudent to start our analysis by taking into consideration the entire phrase, "Your origin and your birth are of the land of the Canaanites; your father was an Amorite, and your mother a Hittite," since it has another singular feature "the land of the Canaanite."[2] Indeed, not only is this the rarer form in scripture compared to "the land of Canaan," but a few verses later the original Hebrew twice uses this latter form (16:29; 17:4).[3] How is one to take this double "oddity" back to back—*mekurah* and "the land of the Canaanite"—and find a solution that would account for both at the same time? Let us begin with the more obvious: "Canaanite" was chosen over "Canaan" in view of the immediately following "Amorite" and Hittite." Several times we encounter the

---

[2] The usual Hebrew form is in the singular *kena'ani* (Canaanite). The plural *kena'anim* (Canaanites) is encountered only thrice: Neh 9:24; Job 41:6 (translated as "merchants"); and Ob 20 (translated as "Phoenicia").

[3] RSV has instead "the trading land" (16:29) and "a land of trade" (17:4). The same kind of emendations is found in JB in both cases and in KJV in 17:4.

combination of those Gentile names after "the land of" and often in the immediate sequence Canaanite-Hittite-Amorite (Gen 15:19-21; Ex 3:8, 17; 13:5; Deut 7:1; Josh 12:8; Ezra 9:1), in addition to the many other instances where we have those names within lists of Gentile names without the specific mention of "the land of" (e.g. Ex 33:2; 34:11; Deut 20:17; Josh 3:10). So Ezekiel wanted to stress that Jerusalem and Judah were part of the amalgam of the inhabitants of Canaan, whoever they might have been ethnically. The origin of the Hittites was in Asia Minor; the Amorites were spread all over the Ancient Near East.

Such a view is intrinsic to scripture. Abraham is from the stock of Shem who is one of the three sons of Noah, who is son of Adam (Gen 5) or, in Ezekelian terminology, "son of man" (*ben 'adam*). Moreover, Abraham's *'ereṣ* (land) and *moledet* (12:1) is Haran (12:4), which is upper Mesopotamia, and, beyond that, Ur of the Chaldeans in lower Mesopotamia, which is introduced as the *'ereṣ moledet* of Haran, Abraham's brother (11:26). On the other hand, in Deuteronomy we hear that, at the offering of the first fruits of the land in Canaan, one was to pray thus: "A wandering Aramean was my father; and he went down into Egypt and sojourned there, few in number; and there he became a nation, great, mighty, and populous."(26:5). Earlier, in Genesis, Abraham sent his servant "to my country (*'ereṣ*) and to my kindred (*moledet*), and take a wife for my son Isaac" (24:4) and, in the following chapter, we are told: "and Isaac was forty years old when he took to wife Rebekah, the daughter of Bethuel the Aramean of Paddan-aram, the sister of Laban the Aramean." (25:20) All this shows that the *'ereṣ* and the *moledet* of the "father" of Samaria and Judah cover the entire area known as the Ancient Near East. Consequently, the scriptural *'ereṣ* is incorrectly translated in English as "land" that has the connotation of a piece of real estate, unless one takes it as land versus sea, in which case its meaning would be "earth," which is precisely the original understanding of *'ereṣ*, any area on earth where mammals live according to Genesis 1.

However, this same earth is introduced as *'adamah* (ground) in Genesis 1:25, just before the mention of *'adam* in vv.26 and 27, a cryptic prefiguration of what one is about to learn in 2:7, that earth as *'adamah* is the "begetter" of *'adam*: "then the Lord God formed man *(ha'adam; the man and thus any and every man)* of dust from the ground (*'adamah*), and breathed into his nostrils the breath of life; and man (*ha'adam*) became a living being." The scroll given through God's hand to Ezekiel, the "son of man" (*ben 'adam*) and thus a "mere man" (*'adam*), was about to transform *'ereṣ yisra'el* that was filled with abominations into a truly human (adamic) *'admat*[4] *yisra'el* where any and every *'adam* would live according to God's will that was expressed in another "scroll":

> The graven images of their gods you shall burn with fire; you shall not covet the silver or the gold that is on them, or take it for yourselves, lest you be ensnared by it; for it is an abomination to the Lord your God. And you shall not bring an abominable thing into your house, and become accursed like it; you shall utterly detest and abhor it; for it is an accursed thing. All the commandments which I command you this day you shall be careful to do, that you may live and multiply, and go in and possess the land which the Lord swore to give to your fathers. And you shall remember all the way which the Lord your God has led you these forty years in the wilderness, that he might humble you, testing you to know what was in your heart, whether you

---

[4] *'admat* is the form *'adamah* takes when followed by a noun complement, "Israel" in this case.

would keep his commandments, or not. And he humbled you and let you hunger and fed you with manna, which you did not know, nor did your fathers know; that he might make you know that man (*ha'adam*; *the* human being) does not live by bread alone, but that man (*ha'adam*; *the* human being) lives by everything that proceeds out of the mouth of the Lord. (Deut 7:25-8:3)

As we saw earlier, Ezekiel has been chosen to be the prototype of the *'adam* who would be humbled into doing God's bidding and, through his summons, God will break the wanton (*zoneh*; playing the harlot [with the abominations]) heart of every *'adam* into submission to him (Ezek 6:9) so that all human beings "shall know that I am the Lord" (v.10) and shall "walk in my statutes and keep my ordinances and obey them; and they shall be my people, and I will be their God" (11:20). Ezekiel's interest in all humans being brought into submission to the Lord is corroborated in the story of the tower of Babel which is an offshoot of the Ezekelian story.[5]

Where does *mekurah* fit in all this? As it stands, this word is the passive participle feminine singular of the verb *makar* meaning "sell." Accordingly, *mekurah* refers to a person or an object (of the grammatically feminine gender) that is sold and, by the same token, purchased.[6] In Hebrew, when the subject is undetermined, the grammatical masculine and feminine are equally used. The plural *mekorot/mekurot* would refer to sold items and thus purchases, and ultimately to property, and if this is the case, then one can justify the unexpected preposition *min*

---

[5] See earlier my discussion of *biq'ah* (plain, valley), pp. 89-90.
[6] This interpretation is actually betrayed in the LXX's rendering of *'ereṣ mekuratam* (the land of their *mekurah*) in Ezekiel 29:14 as "the land whence *they were taken*," thus understanding *mekurah* in the sense of "taken away, sold off."

(contracted into *me* before *'ereṣ* [the land of]), translated "of" in RSV, before "the land of the Canaanite" (*me[min] 'ereṣ hakkena'ani*). One would have expected just "the land of the Canaanite" as predicate or "in (Hebrew *be*) the land of the Canaanite." However, the preposition *min* has the connotation of "from, out of," as RSV renders it in Genesis 24:7: "The Lord, the God of heaven, who took me from my father's house and *from the land of* (*me'ereṣ*) my birth (*moladti* form *moledet*)…" Moreover, in Ezekiel 16, the preposition *min* does not fit at all after *moledot* making of the latter a secondary item; the addition of *moledot* in v.3 is only in view of the description of Jerusalem *at birth* in the following verse: "And as for your birth (*moledot*), *on the day you were born* (*huledet*, from the same root *yalad* as *moledot*) your navel string was not cut, nor were you washed with water to cleanse you, nor rubbed with salt, nor swathed with bands." (v.4) The secondary status of *moledot* is corroborated in that it occurs only here in Ezekiel and that it is in the plural form, which is unique in scripture; the obvious use of the plural *moledot* instead of the common singular *moledet* was to match the plural *mekorot*. Actually the plural *moledot* is strange considering that *moledet* is a generic singular corresponding to the equally generic singular *zera'* (sperm; progeny); one refers to the descendants as progeny, not progenies.

The only scriptural passage that fits this context is Genesis 23 where Abraham, while in "the land of Canaan" (v.2), purchases from Ephron "the Hittite" the field with the cave where he would inter his wife Sarah. Although Abraham was among Hittites who were originally from Asia Minor, he presents himself as "a stranger and a sojourner among you" (v.4). Thus, the lesson is that "the earth is the Lord's and the fullness thereof, the world and those who dwell therein" (Ps 24:1); he is, as king, the sole proprietor.[7] The corollary is that the earth as "ground" (*'adamah*) is dispensed of according to the need of the human being (*'adam*).[8] Later in Ezekiel 16, this thought is specifically reflected in the indictment of Sodom, the "sister" who early on was condemned as an exemplary warning for the other two sisters. Her "abomination" is described in the following words:

> As I live, says the Lord God, your sister Sodom and her daughters have not done as you and your daughters have done. Behold, this was the guilt of your sister Sodom: *she and her daughters had pride, surfeit of food, and prosperous ease, but did not aid the poor and needy.* They were haughty, and did abominable things before me; therefore I removed them, when I saw it. (vv. 48-50)

Such goes hand in hand with the divine indictment of Jerusalem in Jeremiah, Ezekiel's contemporary:

> Do not trust in these deceptive words: "This is the temple of the Lord, the temple of the Lord, the temple of the Lord." For if you truly amend your ways and your doings, if you truly execute justice one with another, *if you do not oppress the alien, the fatherless or the widow, or shed innocent blood in this place*, and if you do not go after other gods to your own hurt, then I will let you dwell in this place, in the land that I gave of old to your fathers for ever. (Jer 7:4-7)

In scripture, the earth on which the human being happens to reside is God's gift, and thus it is never earned, let alone one's deeded property. The children of Israel were expressly and repeatedly reminded of that *in the Law*:

---

[7] In the Semitic languages, *melek* (king) is from the root *malak* whose connotation is "possess, own, be proprietor of."
[8] I discuss this chapter in detail in my *C-Gen* where I show the wordplay that pervades the entire story.

You shall not wrong a stranger or oppress him, for you were strangers in the land of Egypt. You shall not afflict any widow or orphan. If you do afflict them, and they cry out to me, I will surely hear their cry; and my wrath will burn, and I will kill you with the sword, and your wives shall become widows and your children fatherless. (Ex 22:21-24)

You shall not oppress a stranger; you know the heart of a stranger, for you were strangers in the land of Egypt. (Ex 23:9)

And when the Lord your God brings you into the land which he swore to your fathers, to Abraham, to Isaac, and to Jacob, to give you, with great and goodly cities, which you did not build, and houses full of all good things, which you did not fill, and cisterns hewn out, which you did not hew, and vineyards and olive trees, which you did not plant, and when you eat and are full, then take heed lest you forget the Lord, who brought you out of the land of Egypt, out of the house of bondage. You shall fear the Lord your God; you shall serve him, and swear by his name. You shall not go after other gods, of the gods of the peoples who are round about you; for the Lord your God in the midst of you is a jealous God; lest the anger of the Lord your God be kindled against you, and he destroy you from off the face of the earth. (Deut 6:10-15)

You shall not pervert the justice due to the sojourner or to the fatherless, or take a widow's garment in pledge; but you shall remember that you were a slave in Egypt and the Lord your God redeemed you from there; therefore I command you to do this. When you reap your harvest in your field, and have forgotten a sheaf in the field, you shall not go back to get it; it shall be for the sojourner, the fatherless, and the widow; that the Lord your God may bless you in all the work of your hands. When you beat your olive trees, you shall not go over the boughs again; it shall be for the sojourner, the fatherless, and the widow. When you gather the grapes of your vineyard, you shall not glean it afterward; it shall be for the sojourner, the fatherless, and the widow. You shall remember that you were a slave in the land of Egypt; therefore I command you to do this. (Deut 24:17-22)

When a stranger sojourns with you in your land, you shall not do him wrong. The stranger who sojourns with you shall be to you as the native among you, and you shall love him as yourself; for you were strangers in the land of Egypt: I am the Lord your God. (Lev 19:33-34)

And when you reap the harvest of your land, you shall not reap your field to its very border, nor shall you gather the gleanings after your harvest; you shall leave them for the poor and for the stranger: I am the Lord your God. (Lev 23:22)

Genesis 23 also sheds light on why Ezekiel opts for the mother as Hittite and the father as Amorite, and not vice versa. One might have expected the opposite since the Hittites are usually mentioned before the Amorites in the list of seven nations and, as Ezekiel does in 16:3, the father is usually referred to before the mother. The reason is twofold. First of all, in the Genesis story, Sarah is buried in a Hittite field. Secondly, cities are grammatically feminine entities and thus they function as mothers of their citizens; by the same token, the three cities that are addressed would be sisters and this being the case, the proverb "like mother like daughter" (16:44) would fit better than "like father, like son." Furthermore, a city would be the wife of the monarch or the deity; that is why her sin would consist in having "loathed her husband and children (the citizens)" (v.45).

Instead of heeding the teaching of the Law—Genesis through Deuteronomy—Jerusalem is accused of having acted like the "Canaanites." In scripture, the Canaanites are notorious merchants who sell and buy for their own profit. Translations such as RSV—and also KJV and JB—often render Canaan and

Canaanite as "trader" (Is 23:8;[9] Ezek 17:4;[10] Hos 12:7;[11] Zeph 1:11;[12] Zech 14:21[13]). In that sense, Jerusalem learned that trade (*mekorot*) "from the land of Canaan" and thus became a descendant (*moledet*) of that "mother" and, along with Samaria and Sodom, became her daughter. Although it is the youngest sister Sodom and her daughters who are accused of greed and lack of generosity toward the needy (Ezek 16: 49-50), God declares to Jerusalem that "… your sister Sodom and her daughters have not done as you and your daughters have done" (v.48).

This understanding of *mekorot* in Ezekiel 16:3 is confirmed by its two other occurrences in 21:30 (*mekurot*) and in 29:14 (*mekurah*). The buying and selling in order to enhance one's possessions and thus one's power at the expense of the stranger, widow, orphan, and needy is condemned by God not only in Judah and Israel, but universally, as one learns from Amos 1-2. It is precisely this universality of God's justice that the hearers of Ezekiel will encounter soon in chapter 21. In overtaking the entire Eastern Mediterranean seaboard including Egypt, the

---

[9] "Who has purposed this against Tyre, the bestower of crowns, whose merchants were princes, whose *traders* ("Canaanites" in the original Hebrew) were the honored of the earth?" Tyre was one of the main Phoenician cities, which was known for their trading activity in the Mediterranean before the Greeks and later the Romans. It expanded its influence into Western North Africa around the famous city of Carthage that later challenged even the influence of mighty Rome.

[10] "he [a great eagle] broke off the topmost of its young twigs and carried it to *a land of trade* ("the land of Canaan" in the original Hebrew), and set it in a city of merchants."

[11] "*A trader* ("Canaan" in the original Hebrew), in whose hands are false balances, he loves to oppress."

[12] "Wail, O inhabitants of the Mortar! For *all the traders* ("all the people of Canaan" in the original Hebrew) are no more; all who weigh out silver are cut off."

[13] "and every pot in Jerusalem and Judah shall be sacred to the Lord of hosts, so that all who sacrifice may come and take of them and boil the flesh of the sacrifice in them. And there shall no longer be *a trader* ("Canaanite" in the original Hebrew) in the house of the Lord of hosts on that day."

The Parabolic Stories

Babylonians came to a crossroad between Jerusalem that lies west of the Jordan River and the Dead Sea, on the one hand, and Rabbah, the capital of Ammon that lies toward the east of these, on the other hand (vv.18-21). The first to be hit was Jerusalem (vv.22-27). However, just as Jerusalem scornfully derided Sodom when it was punished (16:56), the Ammonites will do the same at the sight of Jerusalem being chastised (21:28a). Since the Babylonians were on the other bank of the Dead Sea on their way south to subdue the mighty Egypt, the Ammonites thought that the Babylonians would not even think of crossing over to deal with the tiny kingdom of Ammon. But, lo and behold, the Ammonites were fooled and were punished (vv.28b-32) by divine judgment against their *mekurah* (v.30b). The striking lesson is that if a kingdom as tiny as Sodom paid for its sins, then surely Ammon would not be spared.

Still, the listener to Ezekiel has not heard the end of this matter. In its turn, Egypt will be equally held accountable for its arrogance (29:1-12). However, against the hearer's obvious expectation that its inhabitants would be forever "scattered among the nations and dispersed among the countries" (v.12), he will hear this prophetic utterance, "For thus says the Lord God: At the end of forty years I will gather the Egyptians from the peoples among whom they were scattered" (v.13). Nonetheless, what is even more perplexing is the purpose behind such divine decision:

> … and I will restore the fortunes of Egypt, and bring them back to the land of Pathros, the land of their origin (*mekurot*; self-serving dealings); and there they shall be a lowly kingdom. It shall be the most lowly of the kingdoms, and never again exalt itself above the nations; and I will make them so small that they will never again rule over the nations. And it shall never again be the reliance of the house of Israel, recalling their iniquity, when they turn to

them for aid. Then they will know that I am the Lord God." (vv. 14-16)

Egypt shall not be doomed to oblivion; rather it will be raised again on its own soil of *mekurot*, however, with a double twist of irony. The first is that the once mighty Egypt will be raised into "a lowly kingdom ... the most lowly of kingdoms" so that it may "never again exalt itself above the nations." God "will make them so small that they will never again rule over the nations." The second twist is even more unexpected; the lesson is not so much for Egypt as it is for "the house of Israel" who remains Ezekiel's primary addressee. The lesson for that house is to discard their self-confidence by recalling their own iniquity (*'awon*; punishable guilt) which lay in their king's having turned to Egypt for aid against the Babylonians (17:15). In turn, this lesson looks ahead to the time when the reverse will happen to that same "house of Israel"; from a "lowly" and insignificant heap of dry bones the Lord God will raise a living community (37:1-14), so strong that even the mighty Gog of Magog will not be able to prevail against it (chs. 38-39). However, that restored "house of Israel" is not to "exalt itself above the nations" or "rule over them" transforming itself in another Egypt and thus "returning there into bondage" under the leadership of a Pharaoh-type "king"—such was strictly forbidden in the "Book of the Law" (Deut 17:14-17). To the contrary, "the house of Israel" will prevail against Gog of Magog because it will be led by a shepherd-like king who will rule over the "house of Judah" together with the long forgotten "house of Joseph" as the one "house of Israel" (Ezek 37:15-28). In Ezekiel, majestic power, that is, *ge'ut* (prideful arrogance), befits solely the Lord God and no one else. Before him everyone and everything must lie in a full prostration, face to the ground. How could it be otherwise when his plenipotentiary assignee, Ezekiel, lay in that position before the Lord God (1:28; 3:23)? It is specifically through that "face" that God will be "acting" throughout the Ezekelian story.[14]

The terminology used to describe Jerusalem's birth is also functional within that story: "And as for your birth, on the day you were born your navel string was not cut, nor were you washed with water to cleanse you, nor rubbed with salt, nor swathed with bands. No eye pitied (*ḥasah*; from the root *ḥus*) you, to do any of these things to you out of compassion (*ḥumlah*; from the root *ḥamal*) for you; but you were cast out on the open field, for you were abhorred, on the day that you were born." (16:4-5) We have repeatedly encountered these two Hebrew roots, *ḥus* and *ḥamal*, in conjunction with God's withholding his mercy from Jerusalem in order to punish her: "my eye will not spare (*taḥus* from *ḥus*), and I will have no pity (*'eḥmol* from *ḥamal*)." (5:11; 7:4, 9; 8:18; 9:10) Consequently, God's punishment amounts to sending Jerusalem back to square one, that is, to the situation she was in before he had pity on her, when no one else cared. The corollary is that now he would not pity her and she would die in her own blood. This hyperbolic imagery of sending one back to the land from which one was taken is classic, as can be seen in the similar punishment threatening the people of Syria (Aram) to exile in Kir (Am 1:5) whence God had brought them out (9:7). This is tantamount to erasing the history of an entire people; it is as though they had never been, thus blotting out the memory of their existence! It is similar to what would have happened to our human race had God decided to proceed with his original decision:

---

[14] 3:8; 4:3, 7; 6:2; 13:17; 20:46; 21:2; 25:2; 28:21; 29:2; 35:2; 38:2.

The Lord saw that the wickedness of man was great in the earth, and that every imagination of the thoughts of his heart was only evil continually. And the Lord was sorry that he had made man on the earth, and it grieved him to his heart. So the Lord said, "I will blot out man whom I have created from the face of the ground, man and beast and creeping things and birds of the air, for I am sorry that I have made them." (Gen 6:5-7)

However, just as with the flood story where God ends by opting for a covenant in order to protect the human race from extinction (vv.18-21), here also he takes care of the new-born by "entering into a covenant" with her (Ezek 16:8).

Before leaving this passage concerning Jerusalem's birth it would be interesting to examine the occurrence of "field" in v.5 where we are told "you were cast out on the open field." God decided to grant life to the abandoned new-born in that same "field": "And when I passed by you, and saw you weltering in your blood, I said to you in your blood, 'Live, and grow up like a plant of the field.' And you grew up and became tall and arrived at full maidenhood; your breasts were formed, and your hair had grown; yet you were naked and bare." (v.6) The earlier occurrence of "field" found in chapter 7 describes the "end" of that city: "The sword is without, pestilence and famine are within; he that is in the field dies by the sword; and him that is in the city famine and pestilence devour." (v.15) In both cases the hearers are reminded of the sad end of the story that started with the same scenario, a "city" that is bloodied on the field.[15] One might ask why God didn't just leave her the way she was

---

[15] Earlier I discussed in detail the close link between the beginning of Ezekiel 16 and Genesis 23. It would be interesting to mention in this regard that the noun "field" occurs profusely—no less than six times—in Genesis 23. Delving here into this aspect of the connection between those two chapters would take us into an aside that would prove too lengthy for this commentary.

The Parabolic Stories

upon birth; why did he spare (*ḥus*) and pity (*ḥamal*) her (16:5) on the field only to end up saying to her on a similar field and twice in a row "my eye will not spare (*ḥus*), and I will have no pity (*ḥamal*)" (7:4, 9)? The answer lies in the following verses:

> When I passed by you again and looked upon you, behold, you were at the age for love; and I spread my skirt over you, and covered your nakedness: yea, I plighted my troth to you and entered into a covenant with you, says the Lord God, and you became mine. Then I bathed you with water and washed off your blood from you, and anointed you with oil. I clothed you also with embroidered cloth and shod you with leather, I swathed you in fine linen and covered you with silk. And I decked you with ornaments, and put bracelets on your arms, and a chain on your neck. And I put a ring on your nose, and earrings in your ears, and a beautiful crown upon your head. Thus you were decked with gold and silver; and your raiment was of fine linen, and silk, and embroidered cloth; you ate fine flour and honey and oil. You grew exceedingly beautiful, and came to regal estate. And your renown (*šem*; name, fame) went forth among the nations because of your beauty, for it was perfect through the splendor which I had bestowed upon you, says the Lord God. But you trusted in your beauty, and played the harlot because of your renown (*šem*; name, fame), and lavished your harlotries on any passer-by. (16:8-15)

The name (fame) bestowed upon her by God through sheer goodness was used by her to play the harlot, a subject which is detailed in the following 19 verses (vv.16-34). The hearer of Ezekiel cannot be but overwhelmed by this "harlotry" given that the noun *šem* in this book is used profusely to refer to God's "name." Instead of using the "name" bestowed upon her to have the "name" of the bestower praised among those nations, she used her renowned "name" to have his "name profaned in the sight of those same nations" (20:9, 14, 22), a statement that was already heard in chapter 13: "You have profaned me among my people for handfuls of barley and for pieces of bread, putting to death persons who should not die and keeping alive persons who should not live, by your lies to my people, who listen to lies." (v. 19) Put otherwise, instead of trusting in God who bestowed on her the beauty that secured her a "name among the nations" (16:14), she trusted in that beauty itself (v.15). Such is tantamount to self-righteousness as can be seen from the only other occurrence of the verb "trust" (*baṭaḥ*) in Ezekiel: "Though I say to the righteous that he shall surely live, yet if he trusts in his righteousness and commits iniquity, none of his righteous deeds shall be remembered; but in the iniquity that he has committed he shall die." (33:13) Notice the connection between the two instances since, in both, the divine will is for the addressee to "live" (16:6); the death that ensues is due to the addressee's own actions.

The culmination of Jerusalem's indictment is so demeaning to the modern ears that it sounds outlandish, if not totally unacceptable. We prefer to speak of a "slip," or a "mistake," or an "error of judgment." One should hear the hyperbole in its entirety in order to fathom the seriousness of the matter. No other text in the entire scripture comes even close to its description of the "scriptural sin," that is, betraying God and belittling him in the sight of outsiders. In Ezekiel, no one demeans God and profanes him in any way since doing so will provoke him to "act for the sake of my name" (20:9, 14, 22). Let us carefully listen to this hyperbole:

> How lovesick is your heart, says the Lord God, seeing you did all these things, the deeds of a brazen harlot; building your vaulted chamber at the head of every street, and making your lofty place in every square. Yet you were not like a harlot, because you scorned

hire. Adulterous wife, who receives strangers instead of her husband! Men give gifts to all harlots; but you gave your gifts to all your lovers, bribing them to come to you from every side for your harlotries. So you were different from other women in your harlotries: none solicited you to play the harlot; and you gave hire, while no hire was given to you; therefore you were different. (16:30-34)

The accusation sets the tone for the impending judgment: God will punish her with her own sin (vv.35-43). She will bear her *'awon* (guilt) by being condemned to proceed in her harlotry until she realizes that she was not fooling her lovers; rather they were fooling her all along by using her lewdness for their own satisfaction, and by spending her own money to do so! Indeed, "behold, I will requite your deeds upon your head, says the Lord God" (v.43). She will end where she started, "naked and bare" (v.39) as she was before God decked her (v.7). Even more, the parallelism between the two situations is sealed through blood: "when I passed by you, and saw you weltering in your blood, I said to you in your blood, 'Live, and grow up like a plant of the field.'" (vv.6-7). Instead of remembering God's goodness toward her, she betrayed him by allowing the blood of the children he gave her to be shed during the siege brought about by her misbehavior:

> Thus says the Lord God, Because your shame was laid bare and your nakedness uncovered in your harlotries with your lovers, and because of all your idols, and because of the blood of your children that you gave to them, therefore, behold, I will gather all your lovers, with whom you took pleasure, all those you loved and all those you loathed; I will gather them against you from every side, and will uncover your nakedness to them, that they may see all your nakedness. And I will judge you as women who break wedlock and shed blood are judged, and bring upon you the blood

of wrath and jealousy. And I will give you into the hand of your lovers, and they shall throw down your vaulted chamber and break down your lofty places; they shall strip you of your clothes and take your fair jewels, and leave you naked and bare. They shall bring up a host against you, and they shall stone you and cut you to pieces with their swords. (vv.36-40)

The concern with "blood" (through the enemies' swords; v.40) as punishment for the "shedding of blood" (of the children; v.36) along with "shaming bareness" (at God's hand; v.37) as punishment for the "shameful nakedness" (of Jerusalem; v.36) is intentional. The result is that the divine punishment is depicted as bringing Jerusalem back to her original situation in which she was "in the day of her youth" (vv.6-7) and whose memory she yearned to erase in her abominations: "And in all your abominations and your harlotries you did not remember the days of your youth, when you were naked and bare, weltering in your blood." (v.22). "Because you have not remembered the days of your youth, but have enraged me with all these things; therefore, behold, I will requite your deeds upon your head, says the Lord God. Have you not committed lewdness in addition to all your abominations?" (v. 43) On her own, *without* the caring God, Jerusalem is no better than how she was *before* he had compassion on her. Without God's—and only his—mercy, Jerusalem is just a pitiful harlot who "gave hire, while no hire was given to you" (v. 34).

A closer look at the vocabulary of the judgment will reveal a connection to what was said earlier. First and foremost, divine "jealousy" (*qin'ah*) is the underlying factor; it is mentioned twice in conjunction with divine fury (*ḥemah*) (vv.38 and 42). On the one hand, the punishment inflicted (*'awon*) corresponds to and is the result of the guilt committed (*'awon*): since Jerusalem shed blood, blood will be brought upon her by God in his wrath emanating from his jealousy (v.38). Indeed, the action of the lovers who "stone you and cut you to pieces with their swords" (v.40) is being brought about by the God who will gather those lovers (v.37) and give her to them (v.39). On the other hand, God's jealousy is related to his throne and thus his being judge as can be seen in the split between the pair fury and jealousy once the judgment has taken effect: "And they shall burn your houses and execute judgments upon you in the sight of many women; I will make you stop playing the harlot, and you shall also give hire no more. So will I satisfy my fury on you, and my jealousy shall depart from you; I will be calm, and will no more be angry." (vv.41-42) Notice that the divine fury will be satisfied to the extent that God will be calm and no longer angry (see also 5:13), whereas the divine jealousy will "depart" (*sarah*) from Jerusalem. Again, as usual in the wordplay of Ezekiel, there is more to this than meets the ear. The only other instance of the verb *sur* (depart) in the book is found in 6:9:

> And the slain shall fall in the midst of you, and you shall know that I am the Lord. Yet I will leave some of you alive. When you have among the nations some who escape the sword, and when you are scattered through the countries, then those of you who escape will remember me among the nations where they are carried captive, when I have broken their wanton (*zoneh*; playing the harlot, adulterous, fornicator) heart which has departed (*sar*) from me, and blinded their eyes which turn wantonly after their idols; and they will be loathsome in their own sight for the evils which they have committed, for all their abominations. And they shall know that I am the Lord; I have not said in vain that I would do this evil to them." (6:7-10)

The message is clear. By playing the harlot with other deities, the human heart "departed" from God, inciting his jealousy. He struck back at that heart and then "departed" from it, leaving it at the mercy of the lovers who turned into the aggressors.

The introduction of Jerusalem's two "sisters," Samaria and Sodom (16:44-58), is intended to amplify her sin. She did not listen to either of the two examples set before her, and thus proved to be heinous by committing more abominations than they. Instead of heeding the lessons and repenting, "you have committed more abominations than they, and have made your sisters appear righteous by all the abominations which you have committed. Bear your disgrace, you also, for you have made judgment favorable to your sisters; because of your sins in which you acted more abominably than they, they are more in the right than you. So be ashamed, you also, and bear your disgrace, for you have made your sisters appear righteous" (vv.51-52). Even more, instead of lamenting the loss of her younger sister and heeding the lesson that a young age does not matter before God's judgment, she actually mocked her sister unmercifully and pridefully: "Was not your sister Sodom a byword (šemu'ah) in your mouth in the day of your pride, before your wickedness was uncovered?" (vv.56-57a) The real irony lies in that the noun šemu'ah is found twice earlier (7:26) and once later (21:7) in conjunction with Jerusalem's indictment. Had Jerusalem hearkened to what was said to her earlier, "Disaster comes upon disaster, rumor (šemu'ah) follows rumor (šemu'ah); they seek a vision from the prophet, but the law perishes from the priest, and counsel from the elders" (7:26), in conjunction with her own "end" (ch.7), she would not have made a "demeaning rumor" (šemu'ah) of her sister's destruction. That is why, soon enough, her destruction at the Babylonians' hands will be made into a šemu'ah: "And when they say to you, 'Why do you sigh?' you shall say, 'Because of the tidings (šemu'ah). When *it comes*, every heart will melt and all hands will be feeble, every spirit will faint and all knees will be weak as water. Behold, *it comes* and it will be fulfilled,' says the Lord God." (21:7) The close connection between this verse and chapter 7 is sealed through the double occurrence of the verb *ba'* (come) that recurs profusely in chapter 7 as an exhausting refrain: vv.1, 5, 6 (thrice), 7 (twice), 10,[16] 12, 25, 26; in addition there is the similar metaphorical terminology between 21:7 and 7:17 (All hands are feeble, and all knees weak as water).

The passage 16:53-58 can be called "the equalizer" in that, at the restoration, all three sisters are put on par showing that, indeed, the Lord is the universal God.[17] It would be worthwhile for us to linger on that magisterially crafted passage:

> I will restore (*šabti* from the root *šub*; turn, turn around) their fortunes (*šebut* from the root *šabah*; captivity [in exile]), both the fortunes (*šebut*) of Sodom and her daughters, and the fortunes (*šebut*) of Samaria and her daughters, and I will restore your own fortunes (*šebut šebitayk* both from the root *šabah*; captivity [in exile] namely your captivity [in exile]) in the midst of them, that you may bear your disgrace (*kelimmah* from the root *kalam*; shame) and be ashamed (*niklamt* from the root *kalam*) of all that you have done, becoming a consolation (*niḥḥam*) to them. As for your sisters, Sodom and her daughters shall return (*tašobna* from the root *šub*; turn, turn around) to their former estate, and Samaria and her daughters shall return (*tašobna*) to their former estate; and you and your daughters shall return (*tešubenah* from the root *šub*; turn, turn around) to your former estate. Was not

---

[16] In the Hebrew the verb occurs only once. "Your doom has come" is "Your doom has gone forth (*ṣa'ah*)" in the original.

[17] Paul understood this lesson well and underscored it in his "universal" letter addressed to all Roman citizens, Gentiles as well as Jews: "Or is God the God of Jews only? Is he not the God of Gentiles also? Yes, of Gentiles also, since God is one; and he will justify the circumcised on the ground of their faith and the uncircumcised through their faith." (Rom 3:29-30).

your sister Sodom a byword (*šemu'ah*) in your mouth in the day of your pride, before your wickedness was uncovered (*tiggaleh*)? Now you have become like her an object of reproach (*ḥerpah*) for the daughters of Edom and all her neighbors, and for the daughters of the Philistines, those round about who despise you. You bear the penalty of your lewdness and your abominations, says the Lord. (vv. 53-58)

Several aspects are worthy of note. First and foremost is the wordplay on the sound *šb* that is repeated and covers both the idea of (being exiled into) captivity and returning thence, both of which apply to Samaria and Sodom as well as to Jerusalem. This is clearly in view of God's intervention at the end where the remnants of both Judah and Joseph will be reunited in one stock (37:15-28). Secondly, although Sodom is not in the full picture in that passage, she looms in the background and thus in the mind of the hearers, since it is she, and not Samaria, that is brought into the picture when the wanton behavior is detailed (16:48-50) and when Jerusalem's scornful pride is depicted in conjunction with that of Sodom (vv. 56-57). The cause behind Jerusalem's fate of being condemned as an object of reproach (*ḥerpah*) in 5:14-15 is explained here as the direct result of her having looked scornfully at her younger sister Sodom. Jerusalem would be the object of a similar reproach. That Sodom is in the background in the matter of restoration can also be seen in that, within this same context of comparison between the two, one hears the verb *tiggaleh* that means both "was uncovered" and "was taken into exile." Such corresponds completely to what was said before regarding the punishment of exile being the result of uncovering (stripping bare, revealing the nakedness of) the wickedness of Jerusalem; the wordplay also goes hand in hand with the previous wordplay on the sound *šb*, the former relating to punishment and the latter to restoration.

The Parabolic Stories 205

The third major feature of this passage is found in 16:54. After the fortunes of Samaria and Sodom are turned around individually, those of Jerusalem will follow suit "in the midst of them" (v.53) "so that (*lema'an*) you may bear your disgrace (*kelimmah* from the root *kalam*; shame) and be ashamed (*niklamt* from the root *kalam*) of all that you have done, becoming a consolation (*niḥam*) to them" (v.54). Verse 54 harks back to 14:22-23 where we have the previous two instances of the root *nḥm* (console) in Ezekiel: "Yet, if there should be left in it any survivors to lead out sons and daughters, when they come forth to you, and you see their ways and their doings, you will be consoled (*niḥam*) for the evil that I have brought upon Jerusalem, for all that I have brought upon it. They will console (*niḥam*) you, when you see their ways and their doings; and you shall know that I have not done without cause all that I have done in it, says the Lord God." The message the survivors are "bearing" is a forewarning to the others so that these may be given a chance to repent and be spared God's ire; thus the message is one of consolation. It is interesting to note that the chance for repentance is triggered by a similar "repentance" on the part of God as will be made clear later in the statement: "I the Lord have spoken; it shall come to pass, I will do it; I will not go back, I will not spare, I will not repent (*'ennaḥem*; and thus "console"); according to your ways and your doings I will judge you, says the Lord God." (24:14) However, the more important aspect lies in God's righteousness. It is only a righteous God who righteously *punishes* that offers hope that he would righteously *vindicate*. Hope would be vain if vindication would be decreed by an unrighteous judge since such vindication would be mere illusion and thus hope would be tantamount to self-righteousness. That is why the disgrace "borne" by Jerusalem in the midst of her sisters will prove to be a consolation for them (16:53-54).[18]

The parallel story to that of Jerusalem (vv.1-43) is that of Samaria and Sodom (vv.44-58), who are introduced as "sisters" of the same "mother" (vv.44-45). The intent behind this is to express *inclusiveness*. This is corroborated in that both sections have the same ending as a refrain: "therefore, behold, I will requite your deeds upon your head, says the Lord God. Have you not committed lewdness in addition to all your abominations?" (v.43b); "You bear the penalty of your lewdness and your abominations, says the Lord." (v.58) The universal God of chapter 1, as a just judge, punished not only Jerusalem (chs.2-15) and her forgotten sister Samaria, but also the long forgotten Sodom, sister of both, *in order to* give them a chance to repent and ultimately *to save them individually and all together.*

The conclusion in 16:59-63 will sound totally unexpected for someone who did not listen carefully to vv.54-58. The opening verse is masterly coined: "Yea, thus says the Lord God: I will deal with you as you have done, who have despised (*bazit*) the oath (*'alah*) in breaking the covenant." (v.59) First, as is usual in scripture,[19] a term is suddenly introduced to be picked up later in the book. Such is the case with the verb *bazah* and with the nouns *'alah* and covenant that are about to be used extensively in 17:13-19. Secondly, the thought of "despise" connects 16:59 to the previous vv.56-57. Thirdly, the verb *bazah* is homonymous

---

[18] This teaching is picked up by Paul, when dealing with Jews *and* Gentiles, and eloquently phrased by him in Galatians 3:33 and then, in an expanded manner, in Romans 11:29-32. Earlier, in Romans 9-11, Paul explains that the message of hope reached the Gentiles *because* the Jews refused it, a story line endorsed by Luke in his Acts.

[19] As I have repeatedly showed in my study of the Pauline epistles; see *C-Rom* 71, 110, 120, 134, 14; *C-1Cor* 47, 53, 74, 75, 92, 118, 225.

with *baz(az)* that means "to exile," which is the topic of vv.54-58; the noun *baz* (exile) occurred earlier in the chapter concerning "the end": "And I will give it into the hands of foreigners for a prey (*baz*; plunder), and to the wicked of the earth for a spoil; and they shall profane it." (7:21) Finally, this link is further underscored when one considers that *'alah* means "a curse associated with an oath" rather than simply an "oath." Hence one can hear obliquely the threat of the exile just as the verb *bazah* reflects the "sound" of punishment into exile. Thus, 16:59 not only prepares for chapter 17 but also forms a hinge between the passages 16:54-58 and 59-63.

Although Jerusalem broke the covenant with God (v.59; see further 17:19), God will salvage that covenant by recalling it and "will make it stand (as a lesson; [*haqimoti*]) *for* you [Jerusalem]"[20] and for the future. We shall hear later that, whenever God does so, it will be not because of Jerusalem, but rather "for the sake of my name, that it should not be profaned in the sight of the nations" (20:9, 14, 22). As for Jerusalem, such divine beneficence will trigger "shame" (16:61) on her part in place of the earlier "pride" (v.56). It would behoove us to linger on verse 61 which is pivotal to the Ezekelian message of universal *inclusiveness*. RSV is perniciously misleading; it smooths the English text in order to make the original easier on the ear of the modern hearer. Given that earlier the chapter spoke of two sisters to Jerusalem, RSV renders the original plural "your sisters, both your elder ones and your younger ones" into the singular: "Then you will remember your ways, and be ashamed when I take *your sisters, both your elder and your younger*, and give them to you as

---

[20] Translated in RSV as "establish with you." "Establish" is the rendering of the more common *karat* that is commonly used with *berit* (covenant). Here again RSV is rather loose, as it often is. See the following note.

daughters, but not on account of the covenant with you."²¹ (v.61) RSV and other translations, mainly those in English, appear to keep the covenant exclusive, "in the family," so to speak, of Abraham and his nephew Lot who "dwelt among the cities of the valley and moved his tent as far as Sodom" (Gen 13:12). The original, however, is actually inclusive since the many older sisters and the many younger sisters would encompass at least the Canaanites, the Amorites, and the Hittites and, by extension all the other nations, as many as they may be. God will make sure that his name shall not be profaned within them, in spite of Jerusalem, who is just one of the sisters,²² and as a lesson for her. Should Jerusalem accept the offer for repentance this time, she would become the "mother" of her sisters, both old and young, and they her "daughters" (Ezek 16:61). This is an obvious reference to the metaphoric city, "the Lord is there," of 48:35 or, according to Isaiah, the heavenly Zion that has many sons and daughters from among the nations (56:1-6; 60-1-4). The end of Ezekiel 16:61 "but not on account of the covenant with you" corroborates that Jerusalem is only an example, since Jerusalem's sisters are not bound by her, but by abiding by the divine covenant through which God "restores the fortunes of each of them *and her daughters*" (v.53) and "each of them *and*

---

[21] I am aware that, theoretically, one can defend the case that the English "both your elder and your younger" could also refer to many elder and many younger sisters. However, there is no way a hearer of RSV can deduce such meaning since the phrase can mean "one elder and one younger sisters," which fits more readily the immediate context. In these cases, if the language allows an equally good English translation that reflects the original, one is ethically as well as conscientiously bound to use it. The LXX and the Vulgate are unequivocal in this matter. As for other English translations, both the ERV (English Revised Version) and the ASV (American Standard Version) have "thy sisters, thine elder *sisters* and thy younger"; the Darby Bible has "thy sisters who are older than thou, together with those who are younger than thou."

[22] This is surely one of the intentions behind presenting Jerusalem as neither the eldest nor the youngest among the sisters.

The Parabolic Stories

her daughters shall return to their former estate" (v.55). The chapter ends with Jerusalem, and her sisters through her, being reminded that the corollary to her salvation, through God's everlasting covenant which reflects his forgiveness and not Jerusalem's intrinsic worth, is that she remember and carry *her shame* forever, lest she be proud again (v.56) and become once more an object of reproach for her neighbors (v.57): "I will establish (*haqimoti*; make stand) my covenant with you, and you shall know that I am the Lord, *that you may remember and be confounded, and never open your mouth again because of your shame*, when I forgive you all that you have done, says the Lord God." (vv.62-63)

The Parable of the Eagles and the Vine

The parable of chapter 17 picks up on the breaking of the covenant (16:59; 17:13-19) and describes the actual punishment that ensued. The introduction to the parable is worth investigating: "Son of man, propound (*ḥud*) a riddle (*ḥidah*), and speak (*mešol*) an allegory (*mašal*) to the house of Israel." (v.2) The Hebrew is striking in that we have a parallelism of two phrases each using a verb and a noun of the same root. So, a literal rendering would sound thus: "Son of man, 'riddle' a riddle and 'parable' a parable." The least one can say is that it is ear catching—the hearer cannot help but listen carefully. What is still more impressive concerning this introduction is that we find the same two nouns in parallel at the beginning of Psalm 78, which is also a lengthy story of Israel's saga of continual and stubborn disobedience:

> A Maskil of Asaph. Give ear, O my people, to my teaching (*torah*); incline your ears to the words of my mouth! I will open my mouth in a parable (*mašal*); I will utter dark sayings (*ḥidot*; plural of

ḥidah) from of old, things that we have heard and known, that our fathers have told us. (vv.1-3)

Since *maskil* means "a wise instructional teaching," the intention of the psalm is to communicate the divine *torah* (the Mosaic law) as the expression of God's will; thus we are to obey its instruction, even if the previous generations of "fathers" did not:

> He established a testimony in Jacob, and appointed a law in Israel, which he commanded our fathers to teach to their children; that the next generation might know them, the children yet unborn, and arise and tell them to their children, so that they should set their hope in God, and not forget the works of God, but *keep his commandments*. (vv. 5-7)

The similarity with Ezekiel 2-3 in tone and purpose is unmistakable. Ezekiel 17 is an invitation to the hearers not to do as "the king and the princes" (v.12) do. This, in turn, makes of this chapter a fitting prelude to the following one that underscores the individual accountability of each and every person.

Another interesting feature of chapter 17 is that it expounds a parable (vv.1-10) and then offers its explanation (vv.11-24).[23] One should not push the matter to the extreme by trying to find a difference in meaning between *ḥidah* (riddle, dark saying) and *mašal* (parable). In this case they are referring to one and the same story. A riddle would be a parable with the literary twist of a rhetorical question that will be answered by the narrator

---

[23] This prototype will be followed by Mark in dealing with his first parable, that of the sower (4:3-8 and 13-20). Such militates for the view I endorsed and defended, namely, that Jesus' appellation of "son of man" as authoritative teacher (2:10) was in view of his mission to teach in parables (4:1-13) just as his predecessor the "son of man" Ezekiel did.

The Parabolic Stories

himself. This is actually the case in Ezekiel 17: "Say, Thus says the Lord God: Will it thrive? Will he not pull up its roots and cut off its branches, so that all its fresh sprouting leaves wither? It will not take a strong arm or many people to pull it from its roots. Behold, when it is transplanted, will it thrive? Will it not utterly wither when the east wind strikes it—wither away on the bed where it grew?" (vv.9-10). Notice how actually RSV considers the answer to the questions in v.9a is given in v.9b and KJV does the same and also treats v.10b as an answer to the questions in v.10a: "Yea, behold, *being* planted, shall it prosper? shall it not utterly wither, when the east wind toucheth it? it shall wither in the furrows where it grew."[24] So, the question is not posed to engage the hearer in a debate over the answer as though it is a mind teaser; rather the question is an ear teaser requiring extra attention on the hearer's part. Whether the hearer will guess the answer is immaterial since the correct answer will be provided, given that the ḥidah is teaching material, not guesswork. A modern example would be the crossword puzzle (riddle). One could approach it as entertainment or as a teaching venue; if the latter, then if one does not solve the puzzle the answers are provided—very often in the same publication—and one can look them up to learn the usage of new words. The *maskil* (teaching material), which contains no rhetorical questions, is introduced simultaneously as ḥidot (riddles, dark sayings) and *mašal* (parable).

---

[24] JB reads v.9 as a series of two questions but, like KJV, considers v.10b as the answer to the questions in v.10a: "Say, 'The Lord Yahweh says this: Will it succeed? Will the eagle not tear out its roots and strip off its fruit, so that all the new leaves it puts out will wither, and no great strength is needed nor many people to pull it up by the roots? Planted it may be -- will it succeed? Will it not shrivel up when the east wind blows? It will wither in the bed where it was growing!'"

In chapter 17 two eagles are introduced, one much more majestic than the other. Compare the bland "there was another great eagle with great wings and much plumage" (v.7a) concerning Egypt to the very impressive and much more elaborate "A great eagle with great wings and long pinions, rich in plumage of many colors, came to Lebanon and took the top of the cedar; he broke off the topmost of its young twigs and carried it to a land of trade, and set it in a city of merchants" (vv.3-4) that describes Babylon. Moreover, it is the Babylonian eagle that transforms the fragile twig into a vine: "Then he took of the seed of the land and planted it in fertile soil; he placed it beside abundant waters. *He set it like a willow twig, and it sprouted and became a low spreading vine*, and its branches turned toward him, and its roots remained where it stood. *So it became a vine*, and brought forth branches and put forth foliage." (vv.5-6) In the parable's explanation we even hear that the king of Babylon was well intentioned in spite of being conqueror: "Behold, the king of Babylon came to Jerusalem, and took her king and her princes and brought them to him to Babylon. *And he took one of the seed*[25] *royal and made a covenant with him*, putting him under oath. (The chief men of the land he had taken away, that the kingdom might be humble and not lift itself up, and *that by keeping his covenant it might stand*.)" (vv.12b-14) The Egyptian eagle, on the other hand, cared for the already standing vine: "But there was another great eagle with great wings and much plumage; and behold, *this vine* bent its roots toward him." (v.7a) The intention of the vine bending its roots toward Egypt was to use Egypt as a buffer against the Babylonians; however, Egypt's power proved to be only a puff of smoke when compared to the might of Babylon (v.12).

---

[25] Notice the use of the same "seed" (*zera'*) that corresponds to the "seed" of the vine in v.5.

The Parabolic Stories

In Ezekiel, Babylon is a beneficent image because it is presented as being "God's hand," that is, Babylon is accomplishing his will. This is openly established in the second part of chapter 17 where Babylon is depicted as God's locum tenens; the actions of its king parallel those of God in the previous chapter. The actual texts show an amazing closeness in terminology and thought. The original divine punishment through the king of Babylon was intended not to destroy, but to belittle and shame Jerusalem (16:52, 54, 57; 17:14) in order to give her another chance; she was, in a sense, decapitated by the exile of her king (Jehoiachin) and princes (17:12); the assigned new king would be a vassal to the king of Babylon (v.13). Jerusalem, however, did not heed the warning and rebelled (v.15), which brought about her total destruction (vv.16-20). Even after her restoration she will always have to recall her shame in order to maintain herself in God's good pleasure and be safe from his ire (16:60-63).

The most important aspect of the parallelism between God and the king of Babylon lies in that the stand of "despising the oath and breaking the covenant" with God of which Jerusalem is accused in 16:59 corresponds to what Jerusalem does when her king "despises the oath and breaks the covenant" with the king of Babylon (17:16) as is clear from what we hear in v.19:

> Yea, thus says the Lord God: I will deal with you as you have done, who have despised the oath in breaking the covenant ... (16:59)

> As I live, says the Lord God, surely in the place where the king dwells who made him king, whose oath he despised, and whose covenant with him he broke, in Babylon he shall die ... Because he despised the oath and broke the covenant, because he gave his hand and yet did all these things, he shall not escape. Therefore

thus says the Lord God: As I live, surely my oath which he despised, and my covenant which he broke, I will requite upon his head. I will spread my net over him, and he shall be taken in my snare, and I will bring him to Babylon and enter into judgment with him there for the treason he has committed against me. (17:16-20)

Belittling through shaming is not a bad thing per se if its intention is to educate and ultimately to save the addressee from disaster that comes from the hand of the one who abhors arrogance. The terminology of 17:13-14 describes such: "And he took one of the seed royal and made a covenant with him, putting him under oath. The chief men of the land he had taken away, that the kingdom might be humble (*šephalah*) and not lift itself up (*hitnaśśeh*), and that by keeping his covenant it might stand." The restoration of that Egypt on which Jerusalem relied for help will be cast in similar terms:

> For thus says the Lord God: At the end of forty years I will gather the Egyptians from the peoples among whom they were scattered; and I will restore the fortunes of Egypt, and bring them back to the land of Pathros, the land of their origin; and there they shall be a lowly (*šephalah*) kingdom. It shall be the most lowly (*šephalah*) of the kingdoms, and never again exalt itself (*hitnaśśeh*) above the nations; and I will make them so small that they will never again rule over the nations. (29:13-15)

This aspect of lowliness is not passing thought but rather essential premise in Ezekiel as one can gather from an overview of all the occurrences of the root *šphl* in that book. Earlier in 17:6 we heard that the twig that was Jerusalem "sprouted and became a low (*šiphlat*) spreading vine" and should have remained so; indeed, when she grew arrogant, her judgment unto instruction was to bring her back to that lowly state (v.14).[26] The reason is given at the end of the chapter when, instead of the king of Babylon (vv.3-4), God will take off the lofty top of the cedar as the new Israel:

> Thus says the Lord God: I myself will take a sprig from the lofty top of the cedar, and will set it out; I will break off from the topmost of its young twigs a tender one, and I myself will plant it upon a high and lofty mountain; on the mountain height of Israel will I plant it, that it may bring forth boughs and bear fruit, and become a noble cedar; and under it will dwell all kinds of beasts; in the shade of its branches birds of every sort will nest. And all the trees of the field shall know that I the Lord bring low (*hišphalti*; abase) the high tree, and make high the low (*šaphal*) tree, dry up the green tree, and make the dry tree flourish. I the Lord have spoken, and I will do it. (vv.22-24)

Four chapters later we shall hear of the fate of the prince of Jerusalem cast in those similar terms:

> And you, O unhallowed wicked one, prince of Israel, whose day has come, the time of your final punishment, thus says the Lord God: Remove the turban, and take off the crown; things shall not remain as they are; exalt that which is low (*šaphalah*), and abase (*hašphil*; bring low) that which is high. (21:25-26)

---

[26] One can see the source behind all those instances of lowliness versus exaltation in the Gospels (Mt 11:23; 23:12; Lk 1:52; 10:15; 14:11; 18:14). It is further worthwhile to notice that the last instance of "exaltation," which is on its own, is directly linked to "abomination" that we encountered frequently in Ezekiel: "But he said to them, 'You are those who justify yourselves before men, but God knows your hearts; for what is exalted among men is an abomination (*bdelygma*) in the sight of God.'" (Lk 16:15) The Greek *bdelygma* is the usual LXX translation of the Hebrew *to'ebah*.

12
Individual Accountability

Earlier God endorsed a current proverb (Like mother, like daughter; 16:44) in order to indict Jerusalem. In chapter 18 he dismisses a proverb the exiles were circulating in order to vindicate themselves: "The fathers have eaten sour grapes, and the children's teeth are set on edge." (18:2) The exiles were complaining that they were punished into Babylon for the sins of their fathers, including those of the king and his retinue. They were pouting and acting as though the lesson of 14:22-23 and 16:60-62, namely, that the survivors are to be witnesses for God's righteousness *in the situation in which they are,* did not apply to them. Put otherwise, they should not be talking about themselves but of God who, precisely because he is righteous, is their only hope and the hope of all others as well. After reversing the false proverb, God offers a lengthy and inordinately detailed account to vindicate his righteousness. It is another version of 14:12-23, however, it is more impressive in that it clearly shows that divine justice is impartial and functions so regardless of the closest possible familial connection, even that of parent and child or grandchild (18:5, 10, 14). Everyone and anyone is righteous or wicked through his or her own actions.

As in chapter 16, the basic sin is that of "abomination" (18:12; see also vv.13 and 24[1]). That the author specifically has in mind chapter 16 is betrayed through the reference to the lack of care for "the poor and needy" in conjunction with the first mention of "abomination" in 18:12. Not caring for the poor and needy is

---

[1] In these last two verses RSV renders the same Hebrew *to'ebah* as "abominable thing."

an essential aspect of the sin of abomination; Sodom was found guilty of this sin in 16:49. The same pair "the poor and needy" is found once more in the invective against the misconduct of Jerusalem in chapter 22. Thus, whether it is Sodom and her daughters (ch.16), or Jerusalem (ch.22), or any individual (ch.18), care for the poor and the needy is a cornerstone in the divine indictment at judgment.[2]

Caring for the poor and needy is a matter of the Law. This can be gathered from the repeated use of the pair "statute (*ḥoq*) and ordinance (*mišpaṭ*)" in the passage dealing with the individual behavior of either the wicked or the righteous. "Ordinance" (*mišpaṭ*) is found four times in apposition to "righteousness" (*ṣedaqah*) and once independently. The terms occur as complements of the verbs "walk in," "keep (observe)," and "do (execute)" and are typically found in the books of the Law. The translations below, using a literal rendering of the Hebrew when necessary, allow the hearer to understand the overwhelming magnitude of the matter, since the RSV translations conceal the clear correspondence in the original:

> If a man is righteous (*ṣaddiq*; from the same root *ṣdq* as *ṣedaqah*) and *does* what is lawful (*mišpaṭ*; ordinance, what is ordained) and right (*ṣedaqah*; righteousness; what is righteous) ... (18:5)
>
> ... *executes* true justice (*mišpaṭ*; ordinance, what is ordained) between man and man ... *walks in* my statutes (*ḥuqqot*; plural of *ḥoq*), and is careful to *observe* my ordinances (*mišpaṭim*; plural of *mišpaṭ*) [in order to do justice (truth)][3]—he is righteous (*ṣaddiq*;

---

[2] This point will be enhanced to the extreme in Matthew 25:31-46.
[3] Omitted in RSV.

Individual Accountability

from the same root *ṣdq* as *ṣedaqah*), he shall surely live, says the Lord God. (vv. 8-9)

... observes my ordinances, and walks in my statutes ... (v.17)

... When the son has done what is lawful and right, and has been careful (has kept) to observe all my statutes, he shall surely live ... the righteousness of the righteous shall be upon himself ... But if a wicked man turns away from all his sins which he has committed and keeps all my statutes and does what is lawful and right, he shall surely live; he shall not die ... for (in, by) the righteousness which he has done he shall live. (vv.19-22)

But when a *righteous man* turns away from his *righteousness* and commits iniquity and does the same abominable things that the wicked man does, shall he live? None of the *righteous deeds* (*ṣedaqot*; plural of *ṣedaqah*) which he has done shall be remembered; for the treachery of which he is guilty and the sin he has committed, he shall die ... (v. 24)

When a *righteous man* turns away from his *righteousness* and commits iniquity, he shall die for it; for the iniquity which he has committed he shall die. Again, when a wicked man turns away from the wickedness he has committed and does what is *lawful and right*, he shall save his life. (26-27)

Therefore I will judge (*'ešpoṭ*; from the same root *špṭ* as *mišpaṭ*) you, O house of Israel ... (v.30)

Two conclusions ensue. First and most importantly, God is just *because* his judgment (*'ešpoṭ*) is not whimsical, but is based on the ordinances (*mišpaṭim*) of the Law (v.30). That is why we hear twice[4] the rhetorical question as an answer to the false

---

[4] Repetition at close range is a device of underscoring in an aural literature, written with the intention to be heard.

accusation by the house of Israel: "Yet you say, 'The way of the Lord is not just.' Hear now, O house of Israel: Is my way not just? Is it not your ways that are not just?" (v.25); "Yet the house of Israel says, 'The way of the Lord is not just.' O house of Israel, are my ways not just? Is it not your ways that are not just?" (v.29) The keen ear of someone who is cognizant of the Law will readily be struck by the repetition of the noun "way" (*derek*), which is again typical Law terminology; the way one walks is by doing or not doing God's bidding in his statutes and ordinances. That is why the Lord says immediately after v.29, "Therefore I will judge you, O house of Israel, every one according to *his ways*, says the Lord God. Repent and turn from all your transgressions, lest iniquity be your ruin" (v.30). This was stated earlier, "Have I any pleasure in the death of the wicked, says the Lord God, and not rather that he should turn from *his way* (*his ways* in Hebrew) and live?" (v.23) Indeed, since God is as much a good judge as he is, necessarily, a just judge, his *conditional* invitation to life *in his law* always stands, a teaching for which Leviticus 26 and Deuteronomy 28 are witnesses "until the fourth generation" (Ex 20:5; 34:7; Num 14:18; Deut 5:9), that is to say, for all upcoming generations given that the numeral four reflects universality. In turn this explains why God's proposition to his addressees is "get yourselves a new heart and a new spirit" (Ezek 18:31a) *in order to* walk in his statutes and ordinances. This point is so essential that we heard it earlier, and it will be repeated later:

> And I will give them one heart, and put a new spirit within them; I will take the stony heart out of their flesh and give them a heart of flesh, that they may walk in my statutes and keep my ordinances and obey them; and they shall be my people, and I will be their God. (11:19-20)

Individual Accountability

> A new heart I will give you, and a new spirit I will put within you; and I will take out of your flesh the heart of stone and give you a heart of flesh. And I will put my spirit within you, and cause you to walk in my statutes and be careful to observe my ordinances. (36:26-27)

It also explains why, after having invited them to get themselves a new heart and a new spirit, God's last call *as judge* ends on the positive note of hope: "Why will you die, O house of Israel? For I have no pleasure in the death of any one, says the Lord God; *so turn* (*hašibu*; make yourselves turn around)*, and live.*" (vv.31b-32)

The other conclusion is that care for the needy neighbor lies at the heart of the Law's requirements, and it applies to Sodom and Jerusalem and to every individual as well. In the last book of the Law one hears:

> All the commandment which I command you this day you shall be careful to do, that you may live and multiply, and go in and possess the land which the Lord swore to give to your fathers. And you shall remember all the way which the Lord your God has led you these forty years in the wilderness, *that he might humble you*, testing you to know what was in your heart, whether you would keep his commandments, or not. And *he humbled you* and let you hunger and fed you with manna, which you did not know, nor did your fathers know; that he might make you know that man (*ha'adam*; *the man*; human being in general; every human being) does not live by bread alone, but that [the] man (*ha'adam*; *the man*; the human being in general; every human being) lives by

everything that proceeds out of the mouth of the Lord. (Deut 8:1-3)[5]

---

[5] Paul the Apostle will share those teachings outright with the Gentiles. One can see where Paul is coming from when he considers that abiding by that rule, which is care for the neighbor, fulfills the Law (Gal 5:13-14 and Rom 13:8-10).

13
Lamentation for the Princes of Israel

The opening of chapter 19 speaks of the poem therein as a "lamentation" (*qinah*; dirge). The closing reiterates this assertion and adds that the "lamentation" poem has become a lamentation (dirge): "This is a lamentation (*qinah*), and has become a lamentation (*qinah*)." The same word *qinah* connotes both the reality of dirge as well as the poem that expresses it. However, in this particular case, *qinah* also refers to the literary form of the poem. When compared to prose, poetry uses verses that have a similar "sound" due to a given cadence that is repeated throughout the poem. The cadence is reflected through the same number of syllables, but also and more importantly, at least in Semitic poetry, through the same number of "beats" that are reflected in the "accents" or "accentuated syllables." When we speak in any language, not all the syllables in the sentence are equally accentuated at the same level. So every phrase or sentence has always a certain number of "beats." In Semitic poetry, the two halves of a verse have the same number of accents, the most common number being three and three since such cadence is most soothing, being neither too short (two and two) nor too long (four and four). Readers could actually try this by saying "one-two-three, one-two-three." In the *qinah* the cadence is broken in that the first half of the verse has three accents (one-two-three) followed by a second half that has two accents (one-two). The result is clearly unsettling rather than soothing; one feels a "brokenness" which is precisely what a dirge reflects. Readers cognizant of the Hebrew language can read aloud few verses of Ezekiel 19 in a row, and they will unmistakably get that feeling. Consequently, the closing verse of the chapter means:

"What you heard was a literary dirge that was actually translated into an actual dirge!" Put otherwise, "what God predicted took place," which goes hand in hand with the previously repeated "and they shall know that I, the Lord, have spoken in my jealousy, when I spend my fury upon them" (5:13); "I, the Lord, have spoken" (vv.15 and 17); "And they shall know that I am the Lord; I have not said in vain that I would do this evil to them" (6:10); "According to their way I will do to them, and according to their own judgments I will judge them; and they shall know that I am the Lord" (7:27); "And they shall know that I am the Lord, when I disperse them among the nations and scatter them through the countries" (12:15); "and you shall know that I, the Lord, have spoken" (17:21); "I the Lord have spoken, and I will do it" (v.24) besides all the other instances of "and you shall know that I am the Lord." The hearers of the book of Ezekiel could not have missed the "beat" of that bombardment with the same "shell" and now, in chapter 19, they can feel the calamitous collapse of Jerusalem as well as hear (and thus see) the rumbling of the fallen stones! Such is the power of the *qinah*. In this regard, it would behoove us to hear the classic as well as impressive *qinah* in one verse of Amos, which is also addressed to the "house of Israel": "Hear this word which I take up over you in lamentation (*qinah*; dirge), O house of Israel: '*Fa*llen, no *more* to *rise*, is the *vir*gin *Is*rael; for*sak*en *on* her *land*, with *none* to *raise* her up.'" (5:1-2)[1]

In Ezekiel the dirge is addressed specifically to the "princes of Israel." The previous parable of chapter 17 was aimed at their city Jerusalem. Just as the story of the three sister cities was cast into the mold of the parable, "Like mother, like daughter," in

---

[1] Since the English is close enough to the Hebrew, I took the liberty of underscoring the accents that correspond to the original Hebrew.

chapter 16, the dirge over two subsequent kings of Jerusalem is presented as that of two whelps of the same lioness, which is the city of Jerusalem itself. Such is evident in that "your mother," which was spoken of as lioness (19:2), is now "like a vine" (v.10); earlier the vine appeared as a metaphor for Jerusalem (15:2, 6; 17:6, 7, 8). The king as a citizen is the "son" of the city whose husband would be the deity. The king as a monarch would be the husband of his city and father of its citizens, and the son of its deity.

Clearly from the phraseology used to describe both whelps, their downfall was their arrogance in their own might: "And she brought up one of her whelps; he became a young lion, and he learned to catch prey; he devoured men" (19: 3); "… she took another of her whelps and made him a young lion. He prowled among the lions; he became a young lion, and he learned to catch prey; he devoured men." (vv.5b-6) Moreover, the city did not heed the first lesson when her first whelp was put down to shame: "The nations sounded an alarm against him; he was taken in their pit; and they brought him with hooks to the land of Egypt. When she saw that she was baffled, that her hope was lost, she took another of her whelps and made him a young lion." (vv.4-5) She even thought that, by bringing up her second whelp mightier than the first (He prowled among the lions … And he ravaged their strongholds, and laid waste their cities and the land was appalled and all who were in it at the sound of his roaring; vv.6a and 7) and thus more arrogant, she would succeed in making her second whelp mightiest of all. Her earlier arrogance bred more arrogance instead of contrition. This time, the Lord struck back and punished unto exile rather than unto survival in order to allow for another chance as he had done the first time. While the first king fell prey to the hooks of the already weakened Egypt (v.4), the second one was taken by the hooks of the mighty king of Babylon who "brought him into custody, that his voice should no more be heard upon the mountains of Israel" (v.9b), which mountains were specifically indicted for their arrogant haughtiness (ch.6). Corresponding scriptural information concerning the two kings is found in 2 Kings:

> Jehoahaz was twenty-three years old when he began to reign, and he reigned three months in Jerusalem. His mother's name was Hamutal the daughter of Jeremiah of Libnah. And he did what was evil in the sight of the Lord, according to all that his fathers had done. And Pharaoh Neco put him in bonds at Riblah in the land of Hamath, that he might not reign in Jerusalem, and laid upon the land a tribute of a hundred talents of silver and a talent of gold. And Pharaoh Neco made Eliakim the son of Josiah king in the place of Josiah his father, and changed his name to Jehoiakim. But he took Jehoahaz away; and he came to Egypt, and died there. (2 Kg 23:31-24)

> Jehoiachin[2] was eighteen years old when he became king, and he reigned three months in Jerusalem. His mother's name was Nehushta the daughter of Elnathan of Jerusalem. And he did what was evil in the sight of the Lord, according to all that his father had done. At that time the servants of Nebuchadnezzar king of Babylon came up to Jerusalem, and the city was besieged. And Nebuchadnezzar king of Babylon came to the city, while his servants were besieging it; and Jehoiachin the king of Judah gave himself up to the king of Babylon, himself, and his mother, and his servants, and his princes, and his palace officials. The king of Babylon took him prisoner in the eighth year of his reign, and carried off all the treasures of the house of the Lord, and the treasures of the king's house, and cut in pieces all the vessels of gold in the temple of the Lord, which Solomon king of Israel had

---

[2] This Jehoiachin should not be mistaken for his father Jehoiakim: "So Jehoiakim slept with his fathers, and Jehoiachin his son reigned in his stead." (2 Kg 24:6)

Lamentation for the Princes of Israel

made, as the Lord had foretold. He carried away all Jerusalem, and all the princes, and all the mighty men of valor, ten thousand captives, and all the craftsmen and the smiths; none remained, except the poorest people of the land. And he carried away Jehoiachin to Babylon; the king's mother, the king's wives, his officials, and the chief men of the land, he took into captivity from Jerusalem to Babylon. And the king of Babylon brought captive to Babylon all the men of valor, seven thousand, and the craftsmen and the smiths, one thousand, all of them strong and fit for war. And the king of Babylon made Mattaniah, Jehoiachin's uncle, king in his stead, and changed his name to Zedekiah. (2 Kg 24:8-17).

The metaphor of the vine (Ezek 19:10-14) is included for three reasons. The first is to link chapter 19 with chapters 15 and 17. The second is that it fits well with the total destruction through fire (19:12, 14) and being thrown into the wilderness (*midbar*), a notoriously dry and thirsty land with no water to support plant life (v.13). The third and most important reason is to prepare the way for the time of restoration that looms on the horizon; it is about to be mentioned at the end of the following chapter 20. Indeed, the entire passage about the vine is bracketed by a reference to the ruler's scepter as a stem that forms an *inclusio*: "Its strongest stem (*maṭṭot*; stems) became a ruler's scepter (*šibṭe mošelim*; scepters of rulers)" (v.11a); and "so that there remains in it no strong stem (*maṭṭeh*), no scepter for a ruler (*šebeṭ limšol*; scepter for ruling)." (v.14b) Add to this that the fire that consumes the vine originates in that stem itself, the royal scepter: "And fire has gone out from its stem (*maṭṭeh*), has consumed its branches and fruit." (v.14a) In 20:33 God takes over the kingship, and as King of Israel brings the exiles out into the "wilderness" (*midbar*) of the peoples (v.34a) and makes them pass under the rod (*maṭṭeh*), his scepter (v.35), with which he will judge equitably (vv.35b-36) in order to "purge out the rebels from among you, and those who transgress against me" (v.38a). In so doing, he will not be consuming the entire vine as King Jehoiachin did, but will be preserving some to "serve me in the land," "on my holy mountain, the mountain height of Israel" (v.40a), not on "the mountains of Israel" where only abominations took place (ch.6).

It is worth noting that the kingly rule is expressed in Hebrew with exactly the same verb *mašal* (19:14b) which also means "to strike a proverb (*mašal*)"; hence a "ruler" would be a *mošel*, someone who rules (v.11a). The close connection between the function of each lies in that the king, as father of his people, is supposed to be "ruling" them primarily through instruction, which implies using proverbs. Moreover, since the king is the "son of God," his instruction should be based in the *torah* (divine instruction) handed down to him upon his ascent to the throne as is evident in the directions of Deuteronomy:

> When you come to the land which the Lord your God gives you, and you possess it and dwell in it, and then say, 'I will set a king over me, like all the nations that are round about me'; ... And when he sits on the throne of his kingdom, he shall write for himself in a book a copy of this law, from that which is in the charge of the Levitical priests; and it shall be with him, and he shall read in it all the days of his life, that he may learn to fear the Lord his God, by keeping all the words of this law and these statutes, and doing them; that his heart may not be lifted up above his brethren, and that he may not turn aside from the commandment, either to the right hand or to the left; so that he may continue long in his kingdom, he and his children, in Israel. (Deut 17:14, 18-20)

That is why his scepter is a rod (*maṭṭeh*) with which he leads as well as gives a corrective nudge when necessary. This double understanding of *maṭṭeh* is taken from the Bedouin background where the patriarch is a shepherd who shepherds his children as well as his flock with the same "rod." The metaphor of the vine in Ezekiel 19:10-14 also looks ahead to chapter 34 where God criticizes the kings for not having been true shepherds, and he takes over as the shepherd and assigns the new David to shepherd his flock as *naśi'* (prince, leader) and not as *melek* (king) (vv.24-25). In this way the Lord God will remain sole king over his people (20:33).

14
The Abominations of the Fathers while in Egypt

The third parabolic story in chapter 20 is at the center of the section of lengthy parables (chs.16-24) which deal with the abominations of Jerusalem that led to its siege and the exile of its survivors. After this section the author will turn his attention to the nations (chs.25-32). Whereas chapters 16 and 23 detail the abominations of the fathers living in Samaria and Jerusalem, chapter 20 zeroes in on a subject that was not touched upon previously: the abominations of the fathers living *in Egypt*. The scene opens in a fashion similar to chapter 14 with "certain of the elders of Israel" coming to inquire from Ezekiel and "sitting" in his presence (14:1; 20:1). In chapter 14 the topic is the sins of Jerusalem; in chapter 20 the culprits are the "fathers" in the wilderness after the exodus from Egypt. Chapter 20 is also connected to chapter 8 in that both chapters begin with a dating sequence: "In the sixth year, in the sixth month, on the fifth day of the month, as I sat in my house, with the elders of Judah sitting before me, the hand of the Lord God fell there upon me" (8:1); "In the seventh year, in the fifth month, on the tenth day of the month, certain of the elders of Israel came to inquire of the Lord, and sat before me" (20:1). The intentionality of this linkage is evident in that these are the first references to a time frame after the introductory statement to the entire book: "On the fifth day of the month (it was the fifth year of the exile of King Jehoiachin), the word of the Lord came to Ezekiel the priest, the son of Buzi, in the land of the Chaldeans by the river Chebar; and the hand of the Lord was upon him there." (1:2-3)

Thus, chapter 20 seems to play a central role in the structure of the book in the following manner:

1. The ingenious phraseology of v.1 pulls together the entire content of the book up to this point by referring to chapters 1, 8, and 14, which content is so essential to Ezekiel's message that it is spread throughout the book at roughly equal intervals giving the impression that chapter 20 is a step forward in a crescendo culminating in chapter 24: "In the ninth year, in the tenth month, on the tenth day of the month, the word of the Lord came to me: 'Son of man, write down the name of this day, this very day. The king of Babylon has laid siege to Jerusalem this very day.'" (24:1-2)

2. Chapter 20 is also the center of the first part of the book (chs.1-39).

3. Its parabolic story is more overarching than that of either chapter 16 or 23. It encompasses the entire biblical story line starting with the "first exodus" (20:5-10) and ending with the "second" one from Babylon (v.33). Its special feature is the extensive lingering on the "first" wilderness episode (vv.11-26), when compared with the sojourn in the land of the promise (vv.27-31a), and in view of the "second" wilderness where the exiles are about to be led into judgment (vv.32-36). In this sense, chapter 20 is "aimed" at the exiles in a unique way. The situation of the "fathers" in the wilderness is more akin to that of

The Abominations of the Fathers while in Egypt 233

the exiles than to the story of the "fathers" in Samaria and Jerusalem. In turn, this explains why the hearers, two chapters back (ch.18), are faced with the lengthy teaching (32 verses) on the individual accountability that ends with the appeal "so turn, and live" (v.32b). Furthermore, this appeal ends a statement whose opening words (Therefore I will judge you, O house of Israel, every one according to his ways [v.30a]) prepare for the next instance of the verb "judge" occurring in 20:4a (Will you judge them, son of man, will you judge them?). Chapter 19 functions as a parenthetical reminder to the addressees of why they were exiled in the first place.

The most striking feature of chapter 20 is that the abominations are said to have started in Egypt and no less in conjunction with God's actions to free the people from their state of slavery. Even then the house of Jacob rebelled against God and preferred the idols of Egypt over him (vv.5-8). This view is found only here and in Hosea (11:1-2), the only other prophet who shares with Ezekiel the extensive use of the metaphor of harlotry to describe the behavior of Israel (chs.1, 2 and 4; see also 5:3, 4; 6:10; 9:1). In spite of its rarity, this teaching impacted scripture; one can detect it at the most important junctures in the biblical story as a whole. First, we have it in Exodus. Upon being sent with all assurance that God's plan will work, Moses expresses doubt regarding the people's reaction: "Then Moses answered, 'But behold, they will not believe me or listen to my voice, for they will say, The Lord did not appear to you.'" (4:1) Even the Lord's retort reflects that he also has his doubts and offers up three signs to be used by Moses in case the people are unconvinced (vv.2-9). The Lord was proven right since later, after having been saved from bondage, the people twice murmured in complaint wishing they would not have gone out of Egypt:

> And the whole congregation of the people of Israel murmured against Moses and Aaron in the wilderness, and said to them, "Would that we had died by the hand of the Lord in the land of Egypt, when we sat by the fleshpots and ate bread to the full; for you have brought us out into this wilderness to kill this whole assembly with hunger." (Ex 16:2-3)

> But the people thirsted there for water, and the people murmured against Moses, and said, "Why did you bring us up out of Egypt, to kill us and our children and our cattle with thirst?" (Ex 17:3)

Secondly, we hear at the end of Joshua the extremely incriminating passage:

> And Joshua said to all the people, "Thus says the Lord, the God of Israel, 'Your fathers lived of old beyond the Euphrates, Terah, the father of Abraham and of Nahor; and they served other gods...' Now therefore fear the Lord, and serve him in sincerity and in faithfulness; put away the gods which your fathers served beyond the River, *and in Egypt*, and serve the Lord." (24:2, 14)

Still what is even more impressive and found only in Ezekiel is that the Lord decided to pour his wrath on "the seed (*zera'*; progeny) of the house of Jacob" (Ezek 20:5), that is to say, eradicate that house, *in Egypt*:

> And I said to them, Cast away the detestable things your eyes feast on, every one of you, and do not defile yourselves with the idols of Egypt; I am the Lord your God. But they rebelled against me and would not listen to me; they did not every man cast away the detestable things their eyes feasted on, nor did they forsake the

idols of Egypt. Then I thought I would pour out my wrath upon them and spend my anger against them in the midst of the land of Egypt. (20:7-8)

However, had God implemented such, he could not have fulfilled his original oath to "bring them out of the land of Egypt into a land that I had searched out for them" (v.6). That in itself would not have been an issue if the oath remained between him and them. But the oath was taken "in the land of Egypt" (v.5) where he asked them not to "defile yourselves with the idols of Egypt" (v.7) which they did not forsake (v.8), thus siding openly for those idols against God. In this case, God's name would have been "profaned in the sight of the nations among whom they dwelt, in whose sight I made myself known to them in bringing them out of the land of Egypt" (v.9). That was the real issue. This is confirmed in that the Ezekelian God revealed himself at Chebar in Babylon, then the mightiest nation, as the deity whose throne was above the firmament and, therefore, was the God of all the nations that live under it. Reneging on his promise would have "deconstructed" him rather than the idols of Egypt and, by the same token, those of Babylon in the eyes of the exiles.

When God decided to "act" upon his promise, it was "for the sake of my name" (v.9). The repetition of this thought (vv.14, 22) seals the fact that it is central to the story and not just a passing whim. Such behavior might be viewed as "scandalous" nowadays, especially among Christians whose "thought" of God has been tainted with the notion of his sacrificial "love and care" for us, which is a projection of our contemporary view of "parenthood."[1] Yet, we have no qualms when we hear the flight

---

[1] One of the side effects of such a view is the widespread proclivity for the opposition between the "wrath" of God in the Old Testament and his "love" in the New

attendant announce at the beginning of a flight that, in case of sudden drop in cabin pressure, the adult is *first* to take care of himself by putting the oxygen mask and *then* take care of the child. God is first and foremost a deity, that is to say, a judge and secondarily a parent. The latter is his choice whereas the former is his basic function. Similarly, in our time, a judge who decides to marry and have children does not cease to be a judge. In fact being a judge is precisely how he is known to the world at large. Moreover, if such a person refrains from functioning as a judge and is unable to provide for his children the way a parent would and should, he then, by the same token, ceases to be a true parent. Let us extrapolate to the situation of the Ancient Near East. A city god is by definition a deity in the eyes of the surrounding nations even though he functions as such in his city and not necessarily in the neighboring cities; thus he is known as "the deity of a given city" and as such provides as a father would for his children who are exclusively the citizens of that city. However, in case of an empire, the god of the capital city is the honored deity and functions as such throughout the cities of the empire. Put otherwise, he would be a god and father not only to the citizens of the capital city, but also to the citizens of the empire and is recognized as such by all the different "nations" living within the boundaries of that empire. He would be "the god of all the nations" of the empire. This is not as strange as it might sound since the citizens of the United States of America today experience a similar situation. The president of the republic functions as the president of all the states and is honored as such in all of them. On the other hand, the governor of a given state is recognized as such by all the citizens of the United States, however, he *functions as governor* only for the

---

Testament, as though there were neither mention of his love in the Old Testament nor reference to "the wrath of the Lamb" in the New Testament (Rev 6:16).

citizens of his specific state. While a governor has in perspective his own state, the president has in his purview all fifty states. Since God introduced himself in Ezekiel as the universal deity, in all his actions his "horizon" encompasses not only Judah or the house of Jacob but all the nations or peoples; the corollary is that he is the judge of them all and the profanation of his name cannot be allowed to hamper this reality, that is to say, to belittle his "office." Should this happen, he would cease to be a respectable judge and, if so, then his eventual positive verdict of pardon and restoration unto a second chance would be null and void, and all would remain "forsaken on our ground, none to raise us up" (Am 5:2). Salvaging his name, that is, his fame as judge who does what his verdict ordains, secures assuredness that his promise to ultimately save those who will have lived righteously shall be implemented whatever the circumstances. Such will be confirmed at the end of the story when he will indeed take out his people *in order to* function as a judge this time *over them* rather than *for* them (Ezek 20:32-39).

For the time being and in order to justify this ultimate judgment against the house of Jacob both in their eyes and in those of the surrounding nations, we are told that he repeatedly gave the people he saved from slavery in Egypt chances to repent and correct their ways, but in vain. What is surprising is that the following two steps—giving the Law to the "fathers" (vv.11-12) and then issuing the same Law to their children (vv.18-20)—at the end of which the Lord reverses his decision (vv.13b-14; 21b-22) concern the Law "by whose observance man shall live" (vv.11 and 13a, 21a). Scholars spend too much time and energy trying to harmonize the data of this chapter with what is found in the Law and in the Prior Prophets, especially in the Books of Kings, and end up at an impasse. When one considers that the Latter Prophets are the earliest scriptural literature and form the basis for the rest of the Old Testament, then chapter 20 of Ezekiel begins to make sense on its own ground. It is built upon the "not only twice but thrice" structure, which is often used in scripture. By the time the hearers have reached v.14, they have already been faced twice with the fathers' rebellion, once while still in Egypt (vv.5-8) and once in the wilderness *after* the issuance of the Law (vv.10-13), which is a clear sign of obstinate recalcitrance. As to the children, they were specifically forewarned through the same Law (vv.18-20) and no less than *after* the unwarranted extra chance given to the fathers and, by the same token, to the children:

> Moreover I swore to them in the wilderness that I would not bring them into the land which I had given them, a land flowing with milk and honey, the most glorious of all lands, because they rejected my ordinances and did not walk in my statutes, and profaned my sabbaths; for their heart went after their idols. Nevertheless my eye spared them, and I did not destroy them or make a full end of them in the wilderness. (vv. 15-17)

Nevertheless, they rebelled, thus confirming the obstinacy that ran through "the seed of the house of Jacob" (v.21a). At this point, and especially after having gone through chapters 1-19, the hearers are expecting that God "will not spare" and "will have no pity" (5:11; 7:4, 9; 8:18; 9:10; see also 9:5), which actually did pass through the Lord's mind (20:21b). However, they are bewildered to hear for the third time: "But I withheld my hand, and acted for the sake of my name, that it should not be profaned in the sight of the nations, in whose sight I had brought them out." (v.22) Could such a just judge be so kind? Little did they know that he was preparing them for his justice that would be exacted on them, the hearers who are exiled in Babylon, "in the sight of the peoples" (v.35). Indeed, in the wilderness of Egypt, there would have been no witnesses; but

The Abominations of the Fathers while in Egypt

now the nations are witnesses and, in their turn, those nations had better heed the warning as will soon be evidenced in chapters 25-32. And the obstinate "elders of Israel" thought they were going to "inquire of" and "judge" the Lord (20:3)!

This reading not only fits the larger context of Ezekiel but also clarifies the function of "moreover" used twice in vv.23-26, after the third and final "But I withheld my hand, and acted for the sake of my name, that it should not be profaned in the sight of the nations, in whose sight I had brought them out" (v.22), and before the concluding "Therefore (*laken*), son of man, speak to the house of Israel and say to them, Thus says the Lord God" (v.27a):

> Moreover (*gam* [also; moreover]) I swore to them in the wilderness that I would scatter them among the nations and disperse them through the countries, because they had not executed my ordinances, but had rejected my statutes and profaned my sabbaths, and their eyes were set on their fathers' idols. (And) Moreover *(wegam* [and also, and moreover]) I gave them statutes that were not good and ordinances by which they could not have life; and I defiled them through their very gifts in making them offer by fire all their first-born, that I might horrify them; I did it that they might know that I am the Lord. (vv.23-26)

It is important to note the unity of the entire section vv.23-26 since this unity will help elucidate the function as well as meaning of these otherwise "scandalous" verses. In chapter 20 the conjunction "moreover" (*gam*) is found four times (vv.12, 15, 23, 25) within the divine indictment (vv.3-38). However, whereas the first three are independent in that they introduce independent statements in different sections separated by vv.14 and 22 that speak of God's refraining from striking and of his "acting for the sake of his name," the last two "moreover[s]" introduce statements made in a row and their connection is evident in that the last "moreover" is preceded by the conjunction "and" (*we*). This unity is further corroborated by that vv.23-26 immediately precede the concluding "Therefore" (*laken*) that is followed by "son of man, speak to the house of Israel and say to them, Thus says the Lord God" (v.27a) which forms an *inclusio* with the introductory verbatim formula (v.3) and thus is intended to wrap up the divine accusation and introduce the actual verdict of punishment through an exodus aimed at purging out the rebels (v.38).

Consequently, the function of vv.23-24 is to underscore to the hearers, the exiled elders of Israel, that the exile in Babylon, from which God was planning an exodus unto purging, was indeed *already* on his mind in the wilderness of Egypt and not simply an afterthought. Why? It is because Adam (man) contravened God's commandment and, beginning with Cain, the first "son of Adam," every "son of man" did the same, which explains why God assigned a "son of man" to deliver his *already* written message.[2] Moreover, the "fathers" of the "exiles" had *already* rebelled against God not only in Egypt (v.8), but also in the wilderness (v.13) right after he "gave them my statutes and showed them my ordinances" (v.11), thus revealing their obstinacy. This divine "plan" follows the scriptural literary device revolving around the numeral three. Just as in the case of God's three "actions for his name's sake" we have also three "oaths" in the same story. The first is to bring the seed of Jacob "into a land

---

[2] One can even add here a further point of similarity between Adam and Ezekiel. Adam was created in the image of God and thus "looked" like him as a son would his father; yet, when he thought that he was equal to God, he was forbidden to eat from the tree of life and was demoted to being "mere human." Ezekiel, who used to be a priest and thus a one of the "sons of God," was also demoted to the status of "mere human" to deliver the message to his peers.

The Abominations of the Fathers while in Egypt 241

that I had searched out for them, a land flowing with milk and honey, the most glorious of all lands" (vv.5-6). It is followed by another oath whose aim is to dismiss the first: "Moreover I swore to them in the wilderness that I would not bring them into the land which I had given them, a land flowing with milk and honey, the most glorious of all lands." (v.15) Although this second oath seems at first hearing to be discarded in vv.17 and 22, one gathers from the third oath that God has just postponed his decision until later: "Moreover I swore to them in the wilderness that I would scatter them among the nations and disperse them through the countries." (v.23) The reason given in v.24 is that the "children," who had been given an extra warning (vv.18-20) after their fathers' rejection of God's ordinances and statutes (v.16a), nevertheless also "rebelled against me" (v.21a).[3] Furthermore, the postponement itself is functional as can be seen from vv.27-29 where the children's disobedience is carried on in "the land which I swore to give them" (v.28). The parallelism in behavior is thus underscored: just as the "fathers" rebelled in both the land of Egypt and in the wilderness after having been forewarned, so too the "children," likewise having been warned, rebelled in both the wilderness and the land of Canaan. Consequently, God will be vindicated in his judgment when he will bring his people out of exile with the intention of purging them this time around (vv.33-38). The link of that action with his previous ones is corroborated in that, in conjunction with this upcoming purge, we hear for the last time of his original "oath": "And you shall know that I am the Lord, when I bring you into the land (*'adamah*; ground) of Israel, the country (*'ereṣ*; earth) which I swore to give to your fathers." (v.42) This promise

---

[3] Notice the tightness of the structure of the entire story of disobedience which is woven around two sets of "three[s]": three oaths and three "acting for the sake of my name."

will be realized at the end of the book when we encounter for the last time a reference to God's oath just before the tribal allotment:

> Thus says the Lord God: "These are the boundaries by which you shall divide the land (*'ereṣ*) for inheritance among the twelve tribes of Israel. Joseph shall have two portions. And you shall divide it equally; I swore to give it to your fathers, and this land (*'ereṣ*) shall fall to you as your inheritance." (47:13-14)

The close connection between all these instances of God's taking an oath is evident in the original Hebrew where, instead of the more common verb *nišba'* found in 16:8, we have the periphrastic "extend (put out) the hand" (*naśa' ['et]*[4] *yad*).[5] The importance of such usage becomes evident in that this divine control over all that might happen to either the house of Israel or the nations among whom that house would eventually be scattered, explains the hyperbole of 20:25-26 that is "scandalous" even by scriptural standards:

> Moreover I gave them statutes that were not good and ordinances by which they could not have life; and I defiled (*'aṭamme'*) them through their very gifts in making them offer by fire all their firstborn, that I might horrify them (*'ašimmem*; dismay them); I did it that they might know that I am the Lord. (vv.25-26)

---

[4] The Hebrew *'et* in this case is just a particle introducing the noun complement. It is not necessary as is clear from the presence in the same ch.20 of both phrases *naśi'ti yadi* (vv.5 [twice], 6, 15) and *naśi'ti 'et yadi* (vv.23, 8, 42) with the same meaning of "I extended my hand."

[5] It is interesting to note here that this use allowed the author to express God's reversal of his oath not to bring the people into the land in v.15 with the phrase *hašiboti 'et yadi* (I returned [took back] my hand) in v.22, which RSV renders into "I withheld my hand."

Verse 25 becomes understandable when one remembers that the Law imparted in the wilderness was intended to be fulfilled in the land of Canaan since there was no vegetation in the wilderness to support animal or cereal offerings. This, in turn, explains that the purpose of the Law was to secure life and its blessings in that land; conversely, any infraction of that same Law would bring curses, including the siege of a city and the scattering of the survivors (Lev 26; Deut 28). It is evident in Leviticus 26 and Deuteronomy 28 that it is the same God who is the source behind the infliction of the curses as well as the bestowal of the blessings. Put otherwise, Ezekiel 20:25 is tantamount to saying that, whenever the Law is disobeyed, the rebels are faced with the shattering reality that it is God who after all "gave them statutes that were not good and ordinances by which they could not have life." The explanation for this is that death as a verdict can be issued only by the judge who, in scripture, is exclusively God. Notice how the author circumvents saying that the divine statutes were outright "evil"; instead he refers to them as being "not good." He does the same with the ordinances, opting for "by which they could not have life" instead of "by which they would be condemned to death." The two negative phrases function as an oblique reminder to their hearer that the divine commandments are good and their basic purpose is to grant life. This is precisely how earlier in the chapter Ezekiel describes the issuance of those same statutes and ordinances: "So I led them out of the land of Egypt and brought them into the wilderness. I gave them my statutes and showed them my ordinances, *by whose observance man (ha'adam) shall live*" (vv.10-11); the original Hebrew underscores that basic purpose of the Law since it applies to *ha'adam*: the human being in general, any human being.[6]

Ezekiel 20:26 sounds even more "scandalous" than v.25 in that it depicts God as having "defiled them through their very gifts in making them offer by fire all their first-born." Again, as in the case of v.25, the solution lies in considering this statement against the background of a siege. A miscalculating king ends by dooming his city to a siege that includes its burning by the adversaries and, consequently, the fall of many to consuming fire. Since the king is the "father" of his city's dwellers, then his action is equivalent to "offering" his children as a senseless holocaust, especially since he, more often than not, ends in exile as the "honored" prisoner of the conqueror (17:12; 2 Kg 24:10-17; 25:27-30). Given that the siege in the Law is a direct punishment by God for the leaders' disregard for his statutes and ordinances, it looks as though it is God who is "defiling" those leaders by uncovering their cunning and "making" them offer the wrong sacrifices. The intention behind the defiling is undoubtedly one of shaming as is evident in the original Hebrew behind "I might horrify them," which is *'ašimmem* (dismay them; make them look and feel dismayed) from the root *šmm*, which was discussed earlier in comments on chapters 3, 4, and 6. One can find further corroboration for this reading in that the first incidences of both defilement and dismay in Ezekiel are

---

[6]This sheds light on what Paul boldly wrote to the Gentile Roman citizens: "I was once alive apart from the law, but when the commandment came, sin revived and I died; the very commandment which promised life proved to be death to me. For sin, finding opportunity in the commandment, deceived me and by it killed me. *So the law is holy, and the commandment is holy and just and good.*" (Rom 7:9-12)

found precisely conjoined in a passage describing an exile pursuant to a siege:

> And you shall set your face toward the siege of Jerusalem, with your arm bared; and you shall prophesy against the city. ... And you shall eat it as a barley cake, baking it in their sight on human dung. And the Lord said, "Thus shall the people of Israel eat their bread *unclean* (*ṭame'*; defiled), among the nations whither I will drive them. Then I said, "Ah Lord God! behold, *I have never defiled myself* (*meṭumma'ah*); from my youth up till now I have never eaten what died of itself or was torn by beasts, nor has foul flesh come into my mouth." Then he said to me, "See, I will let you have cow's dung instead of human dung, on which you may prepare your bread." Moreover he said to me, "Son of man, behold, I will break the staff of bread in Jerusalem; they shall eat bread by weight and with fearfulness; and they shall drink water by measure and in dismay (*šimmamon*; from the root *šmm*)." (4:7, 12-16)

What remains is to account for the sudden mention of "sabbaths" in conjunction with statutes and ordinances, which appears in Ezekiel for the first time in chapter 20. Before the second part of the book (chs.40-48), the sabbath is restricted to chapters 20 (6 times), 22 (twice) and 23 (once). It is chapter 20 that sets the tone with its coinage of the phrase "profane my sabbaths" (vv.13, 16, 21, 24) that is found verbatim in 22:8 and 23:38 and obliquely in 22:26: "and they have disregarded my sabbaths, so that I am profaned among them." The question that immediately comes to mind is, "Why is there not an indictment against the profanation of the sabbaths before chapter 20, especially in chapter 16 whose content closely parallels that of chapter 23?" One can ask the same question regarding chapters 5 and 6 which echo the accusations against Jerusalem in chapter

22.⁷ The question is quite pertinent since, according to chapter 20, the institution of the sabbath is ascribed to the period of the post-exodus trek through the wilderness of Egypt.

A cursory look at a Bible concordance will readily show that "keeping the sabbath" is a major concern in the Law (Ex; Lev; Num; Deut), but is virtually absent in the Former Prophets (Josh; Judg; 1-2 Sam; 1-2 Kg).⁸ It reappears several times in Nehemiah whose context is post-exilic and then in the later Books of 1 and 2 Maccabees where we have several references to profanation of the sabbath (1 Macc 1:43, 45; 2:34) as well as to keeping it (2 Macc 6:6; 8:27; 12:38; 15:3). The conclusion is that, although the sabbath is a concern of the Law, it actually becomes functional only with the exile. However, a more plausible explanation is that it was conceived during the exile as a special day. The exiles had lost their temple; even the priest Ezekiel could not function as a priest; instead he was a prophet who would utter the words already written down on the scroll handed to him. It stands to reason then that the "sabbath rest from manual work" was intended to be dedicated to listening to that scroll. Ezekiel was structured so that chapter 16 was meant to address the inhabitants of Judah before the fall of Jerusalem, and chapter 23 was intended to address the exiles in Babylon.

---

⁷ Compare 22:4a (Therefore I have made you *a reproach [ḥerpah] to the nations*, and a mocking to all the countries) to 5.14 (Moreover I will make you a desolation and *an object of reproach [ḥerpah] among the nations* round about you and in the sight of all that pass by) and 22.13 (Behold, therefore, *I strike my hands together [hikketi kappi]* at the dishonest gain which you have made, and at the blood which has been in the midst of you) to 6.11(Thus says the Lord God: "*Clap your hands [hakkeh bekappeka]*, and stamp your foot, and say, Alas! because of all the evil abominations of the house of Israel; for they shall fall by the sword, by famine, and by pestilence"). Also there is reference to "the princes of Israel" in 22:6.

⁸ The five instances in 2 Kg (4:23; 11:5, 7, 9; 16:18) do not deal with the "keeping" of the sabbath.

Chapter 20 looks ahead to chapter 23 and thus makes "keeping the sabbath" a divine ordinance, and relocates the institution of the sabbath in the "wilderness of Egypt" which was a stand-in for the exilic "wilderness of the peoples" as witnessed by the text itself:

> I will bring you out from the peoples and gather you out of the countries where you are scattered, with a mighty hand and an outstretched arm, and with wrath poured out; and I will bring you into the wilderness of the peoples, and there I will enter into judgment with you face to face. As I entered into judgment with your fathers in the wilderness of the land of Egypt, so I will enter into judgment with you, says the Lord God. (Ezek 20:34-36)

In turn, this explains the reference to profanation of the sabbath in chapter 23 and its absence in chapter 16.

Why is there no explicit mention of what one is supposed to be doing on a sabbath day regarding listening to the reading of the Law? Only the assumption that Ezekiel is launching this tradition can be the answer. But then the question becomes, "Are there any indications in chapter 20 that would reflect Ezekiel's intention?" There is in the phraseology he uses to speak of the sabbath. It is indeed strange that, although he speaks of walking in statutes and observing ordinances, he declares that the sabbaths are to be hallowed or sanctified (considered holy), which is a literal translation of the Hebrew *qiddeš*. Conversely, by not walking in the statutes and rejecting the ordinances, Ezekiel's God says "they profaned (*ḥillelu*; rendered common and thus unholy) my sabbaths." The root of these two words in Hebrew occurs repeatedly in conjunction with God's name in chapter 20. After having acted thrice "for the sake of my name, that it should not be profaned (*heḥel*, from the same root *ḥillel* as *ḥillelu*) in the sight of the nations" (vv.9, 14, 22) God will finally act, still *in the sight of the nations*, in a manner that will reverse the profaning dealings of the people after his purging intervention (v.38):

> As for you, O house of Israel, thus says the Lord God: Go serve every one of you his idols, now and hereafter, if you will not listen to me; *but my holy name you shall no more profane* with your gifts and your idols. For on my *holy* mountain, the mountain height of Israel, says the Lord God, there all the house of Israel, all of them, shall serve me in the land; there I will accept them, and there I will require your contributions and the choicest of your gifts, with all your *sacred offerings (holy things)*. As a pleasing odor I will accept you, when I bring you out from the peoples, and gather you out of the countries where you have been scattered; and I will *manifest my holiness among you in the sight of the nations*. And you shall know that I am the Lord, when I bring you into the land of Israel, the country which I swore to give to your fathers. And there you shall remember your ways and all the doings with which you have polluted yourselves; and you shall loathe yourselves for all the evils that you have committed. And you shall know that I am the Lord, when I deal with you *for my name's sake*, not according to your evil ways, nor according to your corrupt doings, O house of Israel, says the Lord God. (vv. 39-44)

As mentioned earlier, the "name" has the connotation of "fame" and thus indicates one's renown, that is, the way one is known to the outside world. By recalling or uttering a name that person or object becomes "real," and the bearer of the name "appears" to us. Since the God of Ezekiel has no tangible reality except his voice, his "presence" is reflected in the written scroll he handed to the prophet, which included his statutes and ordinances that the hearers have to obey should they want to become "his people and he their God" (37:39), and to have his "*sanctuary (holy place)* in the midst of them for evermore" (v.40). If the scroll is his presence among them, then the sabbath gathering is his "sanctuary" and, if so, then the sabbath (gathering) is to be hallowed (sanctified).

The aspect of holiness linked to the sabbath is sealed through its being "a sign between God and the people," a point of importance that is underscored through repetition: "I gave them my statutes and showed them my ordinances, by whose observance man shall live. Moreover I gave them my sabbaths, as a sign between me and them, that they might know that I the Lord sanctify them" (20:11-12); "I the Lord am your God; walk in my statutes, and be careful to observe my ordinances, and hallow my sabbaths that they may be a sign between me and you, that you may know that I the Lord am your God." (vv.19-20) Notice how in both cases, the author is careful to put the sabbath in a different category than the other statutes and ordinances, the first time through the conjunction "moreover" and the second time through the verb "hallow." This intent is at its clearest in Nehemiah where mention of the sabbath is sandwiched between two parallel statements referring to statutes and ordinances (commandments): "Thou didst come down upon Mount Sinai, and speak with them from heaven and give them right ordinances and true laws, good statutes and commandments, and thou didst make known to them thy holy sabbath and command them commandments and statutes and a law by Moses thy servant." (Neh 9:13-14) In other words, the sabbath is not simply another item among the statutes and ordinances of the Law. When one recalls that the first two covenants, the Noachic and Abrahamic, were also sealed through "a sign between God and human beings" (Gen 9:12, 13, 17; 17:11), then one realizes the special value accorded the sabbath in Ezekiel. The importance, if not centrality, of Ezekiel is that the only passage in the entire Law—Exodus through Deuteronomy—that speaks of "sign" in conjunction with "covenant" is thoroughly impregnated with terminology found in chapter 20 of his book:

> And the Lord said to Moses, "Say to the people of Israel, 'You shall keep my sabbaths, for *this is a sign between me and you* throughout your generations, that you may know that I, the Lord, sanctify you. You shall keep the sabbath, *because it is holy for you; every one who profanes it shall be put to death*; whoever does any work on it, that soul shall be cut off from among his people. Six days shall work be done, but the seventh day is a sabbath of solemn rest, holy to the Lord; whoever does any work on the sabbath day shall be put to death. Therefore the people of Israel shall keep the sabbath, observing the sabbath throughout their generations, *as a perpetual covenant.* It is a sign for ever between me and the people of Israel that in six days the Lord made heaven and earth, and on the seventh day he rested, and was refreshed.'" (Ex 31:12-17)

By using the phrase "a perpetual (*'olam*) covenant," Exodus is putting the sabbath on an equal footing with the two previous covenants that are also introduced as "everlasting (*'olam*)" (Gen 9:16; 17:7, 13, 19). Even more, by linking the rest on the sabbath to that of God himself in Genesis 2:2-3, the author was giving "precedence" to the sign of the sabbath over those of the rainbow and circumcision! On the other hand, since the sign of the sabbath covenant is none other than the Mosaic covenant whose expression is the Law, it stands to reason to understand that the sabbath functions as a sign in conjunction with that Law and its divine statutes and ordinances. If this is the case, then the sabbath is a sign in the sense that it would be the day when the Law is read to the congregated people; put otherwise, it is the sign through which the Mosaic covenant would be "visible" or rather "audible" to the people. Indeed, "the Law was read to the congregated people" not "read individually by the people." Since precious few copies of official literature were available, it was read aloud to congregations, a tradition that survived until the advent of the printing press. In Deuteronomy, we have a text that reflects this reality in conjunction with the Mosaic Law:

> And when he sits on the throne of his kingdom, he shall write for himself in a book *a copy* of this law, from that which is in the charge of the Levitical priests; and it shall be with him, and he shall read in it all the days of his life, that he may learn to fear the Lord his God, by keeping all the words of this law and these statutes, and doing them. (17:18-19)

"Binding them [all the words of the Law] as a sign upon your hand, and having them as frontlets between your eyes" (Deut 11:18b; see also 6:8) cannot be adduced as a counter argument since it is obviously a metaphor intended to say that the words ought to be on your mind (between the eyes) in order to do them (with your hand) as is clear from the parallel statement that precedes it, "You shall therefore lay up these words of mine in your heart and in your soul" (11:18a). Still, what is interesting in both 11:18b and 6:8 is the addition "as a sign," which accounts for the only two instances of "sign" in conjunction with the Law in Deuteronomy, "the Book of this Law" (17:18; 28:61) or "this Book of the Law" (29:21; 30:10; 31:26). Such becomes important since the context in both cases is the communication of that Law to others:

> And these words which I command you this day shall be upon your heart; and *you shall teach them diligently to your children*, and *shall talk of them* when you sit in your house, and when you walk by the way, and when you lie down, and when you rise. And you shall bind them as a sign upon your hand, and they shall be as

frontlets between your eyes. And *you shall write them on the doorposts of your house and on your gates*. (Deut 6:6-9)

You shall therefore lay up these words of mine in your heart and in your soul; and you shall bind them as a sign upon your hand, and they shall be as frontlets between your eyes. And *you shall teach them to your children, talking of them* when you are sitting in your house, and when you are walking by the way, and when you lie down, and when you rise. And *you shall write them upon the doorposts of your house and upon your gates*, that your days *and the days of your children* may be multiplied in the land which the Lord swore to your fathers to give them, as long as the heavens are above the earth. (Deut 11:18-21)

A passage in chapter 23 of Leviticus will corroborate that this Ezekelian view of the sabbath has impacted the phraseology of the Law itself. Leviticus 23 is the only chapter in scripture dedicated to all the "appointed feasts" throughout the year, although the individual feasts are mentioned in different locations and in the different books throughout scripture. This chapter, which otherwise deals with yearly festivities, makes an exception for the sabbath, which in turn explains the odd double introduction:

The Lord said to Moses, "Say to the people of Israel, *The appointed feasts of the Lord* which you shall proclaim as holy convocations, *my appointed feasts, are these*. Six days shall work be done; but on the seventh day is a sabbath of solemn rest, a holy convocation; you shall do no work; it is a sabbath to the Lord in all your dwellings. *These are the appointed feasts of the Lord*, the holy convocations, which you shall proclaim at the time appointed for them." (23:1-4)

A weekly "appointed feast," during which one is not supposed to do anything, at the head of a series of yearly "appointed feasts," during which one is supposed to do something, is definitely strange, unless the sabbath is the day to listen to the Law that is precisely describing as well as prescribing those other yearly gatherings. Otherwise, when would one hear the proclamation (announcement) of the appointed time of the feast (v.4), especially if one lives away from Jerusalem where at least two of the feasts were held since they involved an offering through the priest (vv.10-11 and 20) who was a servant of the temple? Actually, the feast of unleavened bread (v.6) and that of booths (vv.34, 39, 41) are each referred to as *ḥag*[9] (pilgrimage feast). Since the "appointed feasts" are to be announced, they are also referred to as "holy convocations" (vv.2 and 4), the Hebrew original being *miqra'e qodeš* (convocations [callings] of holiness). It is important to notice that these convocations are to be proclaimed (*tiqra'u*) as such (vv.2 and 4). Consequently, when hearing the Hebrew the ear is hit with the root *qara'* (proclaim; call out; *read out*; *read aloud*) twice in each case: "which you shall proclaim [*tiqra'u*] as holy convocations [*miqra'e qodeš*]" (v.2); "the holy convocations [*miqra'e qodeš*], which you shall proclaim [*tiqra'u*]." (v.4) What is striking in this regard is that the sabbath, which is a day of "solemn rest," is nevertheless a "holy convocation" (*miqra' qodeš*; v.3), that is to say, a "meeting" which the people are "called out" to attend. Since nothing is to be "done" at that meeting, it is safe to assume that the people are "called out" (*qara'*) to that meeting in order to have the Law "read aloud" (*qara'*) in their hearing. Put otherwise, the sabbath is a *miqra'* on two counts: a meeting that is called for and, at the same time, a meeting where a text is read aloud. Moreover, since nothing is "done," then it is the "action" of hearing that makes both the convocation and the people attending it "holy." Finally,

---

[9] This is the same word as the Arabic "hajj" that is used to refer to the pilgrimage to Mecca and also, among the Arab Christians, to describe their pilgrimage to Jerusalem.

given that what is to be read are the divine "statutes and ordinances," then ultimately the holiness of the people is to be expressed through the "action" of "doing" what those statutes and ordinances command; any "non-action" in this matter is equivalent to "profaning" the sabbath.

Of note in Ezekiel 20 is verse 37 that is rendered in RSV as "I will make you pass under the rod, and I will let you go in by number." RSV recognized in its footnote this translation of the LXX over the Hebrew translation, "I will make you pass under the rod, and I will bring you into the bond of the covenant." The original Hebrew for verse 37b is "and I will bring you *bemasoret habberit*." The LXX ignored the word *habberit*, which means "of the covenant." In doing so it understood *bemasoret* (by the measure, [in] according to a rule) as meaning *en arithmō* (by number), which makes sense just before the verse "I will purge out the rebels from among you, and those who transgress against me; I will bring them out of the land where they sojourn, but they shall not enter the land of Israel" (v.38). "Covenant" is used profusely in chapters 16 and 17, then disappears until the two parallel statements of 34:25 and 37:26 where we hear of "the covenant of peace" as an "everlasting covenant," *if one disregards* 20:37.[10] In chapter 16 we hear exclusively about the original covenant (v.8) which, in spite of its being broken (v.59), is remembered at the end and made into an "everlasting covenant" (vv.60). All the instances of covenant in chapter 17 refer to the breaking of the covenant since the story covered therein is that detailed in 16:8-60. Thus these two chapters deal with the covenant that was broken by the people, then reestablished by God to stand undisturbed forever. The ending of the story in

---

[10] I am not counting 30:5 where the *berit* refers to a political league between countries or peoples.

16:60 (yet I will remember my covenant with you in the days of your youth, and I will establish with you an *everlasting covenant*) looks ahead to its ultimate fulfillment in 37:26 (I will make a covenant of peace with them; it shall be an *everlasting covenant* with them; and I will bless them and multiply them, and will set my sanctuary in the midst of them for evermore) after the raising of the dry bones (vv.1-14) and the reunification of Ephraim and Judah under the new David (vv.15-25). From this perspective, it looks odd that, in between, one would hear of a covenant that is implemented with a "(restrictive) measure," which is the meaning of *masoret* (20:37b),[11] especially at the end of a chapter whose content parallels that of chapter 16. However, it is precisely the link between these two chapters that helps us defuse the dilemma. The "everlasting covenant" of 16:60 includes the shaming of those with whom it is established, and is the concluding note of the chapter: "I will establish my covenant with you, and you shall know that I am the Lord, that you may remember and be confounded, and never open your mouth again because of your shame, when I forgive you all that you have done, says the Lord God." (vv.62-63) The concluding remarks of the "story" in chapter 20 are precisely of the same tenor:

> And you shall know that I am the Lord, when I bring you into the land of Israel, the country which I swore to give to your fathers. And there you shall remember your ways and all the doings with which you have polluted yourselves; and you shall loathe

---

[11] As is clear from its cognate *moser*, a (binding) band that encircles an object or holds together several objects. See, e.g., Jer 2:20 (For long ago you broke your yoke and burst your bonds [*moserot*; plural of *moser*]; and you said, "I will not serve." Yea, upon every high hill and under every green tree you bowed down as a harlot) and Nah 1:13 (And now I will break his yoke from off you and will burst your bonds [*moserot*] asunder).

yourselves for all the evils that you have committed. And you shall know that I am the Lord, when I deal with you for my name's sake, not according to your evil ways, nor according to your corrupt doings, O house of Israel, says the Lord God. (vv.42-44)

This line of thought, that one will carry one's own shame at the end, is so essential in Ezekiel that one finds it again at the end of the first section of the book:

> They shall carry/bear (*naśu*) their shame, and all the treachery they have practiced against me, when they dwell securely in their land with none to make them afraid, when I have brought them back from the peoples and gathered them from their enemies' lands, and through them have vindicated my holiness in the sight of many nations. Then they shall know that I am the Lord their God because I sent them into exile among the nations, and then gathered them into their own land. I will leave none of them remaining among the nations any more; and I will not hide my face any more from them, when I pour out my Spirit upon the house of Israel, says the Lord God. (39:26-29)

But, here again, the "scandal" of such thought made RSV and many other modern translations including the JB, the New American Standard Bible, the French TOB (Ecumenical Translation of the Bible), the Romanian Bible (Cornilescu Version), and the German Schlachter Version, translate *naśu* into "shall forget." The bias is so evident that even the LXX uses *lēmpsontai* (shall receive) while the Vulgate has *portabunt* (shall carry). The basis for "shall forget" goes back in the unwarranted emendation of *naśu* into *našu* (from the verb *našah* meaning forget) that was launched by the German scholar F. Hitzig in his 1847 Commentary on Ezekiel.[12] The verb *našah* (in the *qal*

---

[12] Zimmerli, W. *Ezekiel 1: A Commentary on the Book of the Prophet Ezekiel, Chapters 1-24*. Hermeneia. Philadelphia: Fortress Press, 1979, p.295.

form) is never found in Ezekiel and occurs only once in scripture (Lam 3:17). The idea of carrying one's shame in order never to forget it acts as a powerful reminder that God's ultimate intervention for the good of the human beings is rooted in the fact that he always acts "for his name's sake," and not through any merit on the part of mankind. His action is taken "not according to your evil ways, nor according to your corrupt doings, O house of Israel" (20:44). That thought is precisely the crimson thread that holds together chapter 20 starting with verse 9.

15
The Wrath of the Lord

The long passage of 20:45 through 22:31 (Hebrew 21:1-22:31) is bracketed with a reference to fire that is sent by God to consume the entire land (*'adamah*) of Israel:

> And the word of the Lord came to me: "Son of man, set your face toward the south, preach against the south, and prophesy against the forest land in the Negeb; say to the forest of the Negeb, Hear the word of the Lord: Thus says the Lord God, Behold, I will kindle a fire in you, and it shall devour every green tree in you and every dry tree; the blazing flame shall not be quenched, and all faces from south to north shall be scorched by it. All flesh shall see that I the Lord have kindled it; it shall not be quenched." (20:45-48)

> Therefore I have poured out my indignation upon them; I have consumed them with the fire of my wrath; their way have I requited upon their heads, says the Lord God. (22:31)

This last verse of chapter 22 is specifically addressed to Jerusalem, the "bloody city" (v.2). Fire will consume all vegetation from south to north (20:47) with a special concentration on Jerusalem (22:19-20, 31). The breadth of the devastation is underscored in that the punishing fire will be so powerful that it will overflow from Judah west of the Jordan into Ammon (21:28-32). As overwhelming as this fire seems, it is the "sword" that steals the show. It occurs 15 times in chapter 21 and is repeated twice in two cadences and four times in another:

> Son of man, prophesy and say, Thus says the Lord, Say: A sword, a sword is sharpened and also polished, (21:9)

> Prophesy therefore, son of man; clap your hands and let the sword come down twice, yea thrice, the sword for those to be slain; it is the sword for the great slaughter, which encompasses them, that their hearts may melt, and many fall at all their gates. I have given the glittering sword; ah! it is made like lightning, it is polished for slaughter. (vv.14-15)
>
> And you, son of man, prophesy, and say, Thus says the Lord God concerning the Ammonites, and concerning their reproach; say, A sword, a sword is drawn for the slaughter, it is polished to glitter and to flash like lightning. (v.28)

Moreover, at the outset and three times in a row this sword is introduced as God's so that there would not be a shred of doubt in the hearer's mind as to who is behind the entire utter destruction, even when one hears later of "the sword of the king of Babylon" (v.19):

> ... and say to the land of Israel, Thus says the Lord: Behold, I am against you, and will draw forth my sword out of its sheath, and will cut off from you both righteous and wicked. Because I will cut off from you both righteous and wicked, therefore my sword shall go out of its sheath against all flesh from south to north; and all flesh shall know that I the Lord have drawn my sword out of its sheath; it shall not be sheathed again. (vv. 3-5)

So, the hearer has no choice but to perceive that fire and sword are two avenues of God's one hand. The fire will burn down all vegetation (it shall devour every green tree in you and every dry tree; 20:47), and the sword will "cut off from you both righteous and wicked" (21:3). This brings to mind the planned total end in Genesis 6: "So the Lord said, 'I will blot out man whom I have created from the face of the ground, man and beast and creeping things and birds of the air, for I am sorry that I have made them.'" (v.7) This destruction was also aimed at the

The Wrath of the Lord

vegetation that is meant to support those beings (1:29-30), as will be made clear at the termination of the flood when it will take a lengthy time for the vegetation to grow anew (8:6-12).

On the other hand, this complete "end" by fire and sword parallels the announcement of the "end" in Ezekiel 7 on the formal level and includes:

1. The repetition of both nouns "end" (five times in ch.7; twice [in Hebrew] in ch.21)[1] and "sword" (twice in ch.7; thirteen times in ch.21).

2. The doubling of each noun twice (7:2, 6; 21:9, 28).

3. The sword "comes" (21:19, 20) just as the end does (7:2, 6).[2]

4. The "day" that is coming (7:7, 10, 12; 21:25, 29).

5. In 7:17 "All hands are feeble, and all knees weak as water"; in 21:7 "every heart will melt and all hands will be feeble, every spirit will faint and all knees will be weak as water."

6. The "prince" is individually targeted (7:27; 21:25; see also v.12).

7. The prince's indictment in 21:25 (And you, O unhallowed wicked one, prince of Israel, whose *day* has come, the *time* (*'et*) of your final

---

[1] In 7:24 "end" is not in the original.
[2] Counting the original Hebrew verb *ba'*.

punishment) is cast in the phraseology of 7:7 (the time [*'et*] has come, the day is near) and 7:12 (The time [*'et*] has come, the day draws near).

8. The accusation of Jerusalem as a city of bloodshed and violence is paramount in both chapters:

> Violence (*ḥamas*) has grown up into a rod of wickedness ... the land is full of bloody crimes (*mišphat damim*; bloodshed worthy of judgment) and the city is full of violence (*ḥamas*). (7:11a, 23b)

> And you, son of man, will you judge (*tišphot*), will you judge (*tišphot*) the bloody city (*'ir haddamim*; city of bloodshed)? Then declare to her all her abominable deeds. You shall say, Thus says the Lord God: A city *that sheds blood* in the midst of her, that her time may come, and that makes idols to defile herself! You have become guilty by the *blood* which you have *shed*, and defiled by the idols which you have made ... Her priests *have done violence* (*ḥamesu*) to my law and have profaned my holy things. (22:2-4, 26a)

9. Ezekiel is asked to "*judge* (*tišphot*) the *bloody city* (*'ir haddamim*; city of bloodshed)" (22:2) because earlier the accusation was that "the land is full of

bloody crimes and the city is full of violence" (7:23).

The terminology of chapters 21-22 harks back to several earlier chapters. The princes of Israel (21:12, 25; 22:6, 27) were indicted in chapters 11, 12, 17, and 19. Reference to eating on the mountains (22:9) is found thrice in chapter 18 (vv.6, 11, 15). The Lord's intervention through his prophet's clapping of hands (21:14) was encountered in 6:11. So chapters 21-22 function as a recapitulation of the previous chapters in view of the strong caveat that will be expressed to the exiles in chapter 23, which is followed by their last reminder in chapter 24 that details the fate of the "bloody city" (*'ir haddamim*; vv.6 and 9) for her stubborn recalcitrance. Then in order to stress to the same exiles God's righteousness and the justice of his verdict (18:25, 29), what follows is God's judgment of the surrounding nations, great and small, thus proving that he is indeed the universal God of all nations (chs. 25-32). That this aim was already on the author's mind is evident in the otherwise unexplainable inclusion of God's verdict against the Ammonites (21:28-32) immediately after that of Judah (vv.1-27). The mention of the Ammonites piques the hearers' curiosity that will be soon satisfied when they realize that the Ammonites are featured at the head of the list of indicted nations (25:1-7). In other words, the passage of 21:28-32 is meant to be a foretaste of chapters 25-32. The Ammonites mistakenly thought that "at the parting of the way" (21:21), the king of Babylon would choose to go west instead of east, and they would be spared. They forgot that no matter how tiny a kingdom may be, it will not be missed by God's keen eye. Even more, they thought they were entitled to look down at Judah and mocked her as an "(object of) reproach" (*ḥerpah*; v.28). Indeed, they will be punished for their attitude: "Say to the Ammonites, Hear the word of the Lord God: Thus says the Lord God, Because you said, 'Aha!' over my sanctuary (*miqdaš*) when it was profaned, and over the land of Israel (*'admat yisra'el*) when it was made desolate, and over the house of Judah when it went into exile." (25:3) The link to chapter 21 is unmistakable in that there we heard, "Son of man, set your face toward Jerusalem and preach against the sanctuaries (*miqdašim*); prophesy against the land of Israel (*'admat yisra'el*)" (v.2). Moreover, the punishment implemented in 25:4 (therefore I am handing you over to the people of the East for a possession, and they shall set their encampments among you and make their dwellings in your midst; they shall eat your fruit, and they shall drink your milk) was predicted in 21:30-31 (In the place where you were created, in the land of your origin [*'ereṣ mekurotayk*], I will judge you. And I will pour out my indignation upon you; I will blow upon you with the fire of my wrath; and I will deliver you into the hands of brutal men, skilful to destroy). Finally, for the keen ear, the use of "the land of origin" is intended as reverse mockery—tit for tat—against Ammon since it corresponds to "the land of origin" of Jerusalem: "Your origin (*mekurotayk*) and your birth are of the land (*'ereṣ*) of the Canaanites" (16:3)

The content of chapter 22 prepares in a specific way for chapter 23 where the sisters Samaria and Jerusalem are accused of contravening God's will. Up to this point Ezekiel has been referring intensively as well as extensively to "statutes and ordinances," which is unambiguously Law terminology. One will readily notice that in comparison with the other books of the Prophets, the incidence of statutes and ordinances in Ezekiel is unusually high: *ḥuqqot* (statutes) occurs 22 times in Ezekiel compared to 6 times in Jeremiah and once in Micah, while *mišpaṭim* (ordinances; judgments) is found 24 times in Ezekiel compared to five times in Isaiah, five times in Jeremiah, once in Hosea and once in Zephaniah. As for the sabbath, it is mentioned twice in Ezekiel 22 (vv.8 and 26); in the second instance, it appears in conjunction with the priests who are presented in the Pentateuch as the official guardians of the Law and its requirements, including the sabbath: "Her [Jerusalem's] priests have done violence to my law and have profaned my holy things; they have made no distinction between the holy and the common, neither have they taught the difference between the unclean and the clean, and they have disregarded my sabbaths, so that I am profaned among them." On the other hand, virtually all the shortcomings which Jerusalem or its leaders are accused of are found predominantly in Leviticus, but also in Deuteronomy. One can then safely assume that since it was Ezekiel who launched the sabbath gatherings, he must also have been behind the Pentateuchal Law.

Finally, it would behoove us to notice that the indictment of the bloody city in chapter 22 begins and ends on the same note and thus forms an *inclusio*. After having referred to "all the princes of Israel" as perpetrators of bloodshed (v.6), the first item on the agenda, before the profanation of the sabbath (v.8), is the disregard for father and mother (v.7a), followed immediately with the accusation that "the sojourner (*ger*) suffers extortion (*'ošeq*) in your midst, and that the fatherless and the widow are wronged in you [Jerusalem]" (v.7b). In the last item on the list, again after reference is made to the leaders of the land (vv.24-28), the entire "people of the land" are accused in the following terms: "The people of the land have practiced extortion (*'ašequ 'ošeq*; extorted through extortion) and committed robbery; they have oppressed the poor and needy, and have extorted (*'ašequ*) from the sojourner (*ger*) without redress." (v.29) Such confirms that it was not just a passing thought on the part of the author that the abominations of which Sodom and her daughters were accused of in 16:49 (she and her daughters had pride, surfeit of food, and prosperous ease, but did not aid the poor and needy) fade in comparison to those committed by Jerusalem and her daughters (v.48).

16
The Parable of Oholah and Oholibah

Chapter 16 speaks mainly of Jerusalem, but introduces Samaria and Sodom as her sisters. Chapter 20 relates from the beginning the story of the two sisters, Samaria and Jerusalem, and maintains this coupling until the concluding verses 46-48. This is done in view of 37:15-28 when they again will be joined at the restoration. In chapter 23 they are referred to as Oholah (*'oholah*) and Oholibah (*'oholibah*), two metaphoric feminine names that are constructed from the noun *'ohel* (tent), which relates to the eschatological shepherd David, under whose leadership both restored sisters will be preserved (34:23; 37:24). This reading finds corroboration in the earlier discussion of the connection between the introduction to chapter 17 (Son of man, propound [*ḥud*] a riddle [*ḥidah*], and speak [*mešol*] an allegory [*mašal*] to the house of Israel"; v.2) and Psalm 78 (I will open my mouth in a parable [*mašal*]; I will utter dark sayings [*ḥidot*; plural of *ḥidah*] from of old; v.2), which ends on a note combining the punishment spoken of in Ezekiel 23 against Samaria and the ultimate restoration predicted in Ezekiel 34 and 37:

> Then he led forth his people like *sheep*, and guided them in the wilderness like a *flock* ... He drove out nations before them; he apportioned them for a possession and settled the tribes of Israel in their *tents*. Yet they tested and rebelled against the Most High God, and did not observe his testimonies ... For they provoked him to anger with their high places; they moved him to jealousy with their graven images. When God heard, he was full of wrath, and he utterly rejected Israel. He forsook his dwelling at Shiloh, the *tent* where he dwelt among men ... He rejected the *tent* of Joseph, he did not choose the tribe of Ephraim ... He chose

David his servant, and took him from the *sheepfolds*; from tending the ewes that had young he brought him to be the *shepherd* of Jacob his people, of Israel his inheritance. With upright heart he tended (*shepherded* in Hebrew) them, and guided them with skilful hand. (Ps 78:52, 55-56, 58-60, 67, 70-72)

David is said to be the shepherd of Jacob, who is the father of both Judah and Joseph (Ephraim). The name Israel encompasses both Judah and Ephraim as is clear from Ezekiel 37:16-17: "Son of man, take a stick and write on it, 'For Judah, and the children of Israel associated with him'; then take another stick and write upon it, 'For Joseph (the stick of Ephraim) and all the house of Israel associated with him'; and join them together into one stick, that they may become one in your hand."

Thus, the choice of the metaphorical names Oholah and Oholibah that recall the tent is intended to remind the hearers of their humble origin. By the same token, those names function as sarcasm against their proclivity for being mesmerized with anything and everything that looks impressive and then easily falling prey to manipulative cajoling. As in chapter 16, such proclivity started at a young age when the two sisters were still in Egypt (23:3, 8, 19-20). It is no wonder then that Samaria had fallen for the dashingly majestic Assyrians (vv.9-10) and that Jerusalem also would be attracted to them and even more so to the imposing Chaldeans (vv.11-18).

Furthermore, since Samaria is the elder of the two, the sin of Jerusalem becomes even more flagrant given that she witnessed her older sister's catastrophic experience and should have learned from it (v.11a). Instead, she acted as the consummate unfaithful wife by enlisting the Chaldeans' help against the Assyrians (v.16) and when the Chaldeans, who had taken advantage of Jerusalem against the Assyrians, came to conquer her, she remembered her youthful years and tried to solicit Egypt's support against them (vv.19-21).[1] That is why her chastisement will be of the same nature as that of Samaria, but exceedingly greater (vv.32-34)

Jerusalem is punished by the Lord God, her protector, as both father and husband, whose hand is forced to act in accordance with his essential function as judge of all, including deities as well as humans. God summons the Chaldeans to raze her; the irony is that his decision was made easier by Jerusalem herself: all he had to do is to let the Chaldeans pursue what they had already started when taking advantage of Jerusalem's proclivity for lewdness. This is actually God's approach to sin: he lets it take its own course. The people pay for their guilt (*'awon*) with its own punishment (*'awon*): "Therefore thus says the Lord God: Because you have forgotten me and cast me behind your back, therefore bear the consequences of your lewdness and harlotry." (v.35)

The phraseology and vocabulary of verses 35-49 betray that we have reached the end of the part of the book dealing with Jerusalem and Judah (chs.3-24). The next part of the book (chs.25-32) will deal with the nations. So chapter 23 looks both back and ahead. On the one hand, it recapitulates what was said in the previous chapters and, on the other hand, it harks back to the very beginning of the book where it was made clear that Ezekiel's foremost addressees, and thus the culprits, are not so much the past or present residents of Jerusalem, but rather the exiles themselves.

"Son of man, will you judge Oholah and Oholibah?" (v.36a) recalls the same wording in 20:4 and 22:2. Indeed, 23:37a (For they have committed adultery, and blood is upon their hands;

---

[1] See Ezek 17:15.

with their idols they have committed adultery; and they have even offered up to them for food the sons whom they had borne to me) is a carbon copy of 22:3-4a: "You shall say, Thus says the Lord God: A city that sheds blood in the midst of her, that her time may come, and that makes idols to defile herself! You have become guilty by the blood which you have shed, and defiled by the idols which you have made." The reference to sons being sacrificed in 23:37b and 39a (and they have even offered up to them for food the sons whom they had borne to me... For when they had slaughtered their children in sacrifice to their idols) is found in 20:31a: "When you offer your gifts and sacrifice your sons by fire, you defile yourselves with all your idols to this day."[2] Furthermore, the defilement with idols in this last verse (20:31a) occurs again in chapter 23 in the same context: "Moreover this they have done to me: they have defiled my sanctuary on the same day and profaned my sabbaths. For when they had slaughtered their children in sacrifice to their idols, on the same day they came into my sanctuary to profane it. And lo, this is what they did in my house." (vv.38-39) The reference to the sabbath (v. 38), especially in conjunction with its profanation, is of prime importance since sabbath was encountered earlier in chapters 20 and 22.

A review of 23:38-39 will reveal a unique feature in Ezekiel: not only is it the only instance where sabbaths and sanctuary are mentioned in the same breath, but more importantly they both appear as noun complements of the verb "profane." Moreover, the disregard for both takes place "on the same day" on which "they had slaughtered their children in sacrifice to their idols." The three actions are interconnected in that, as discussed earlier,

---

[2] The LXX actually makes explicit this connection by adding "by fire" (*di' empyrōn*; through burning) after "offered up" in 23:37b.

the metaphor of sacrificing one's children is linked to the imagery of siege, which usually ends with the destruction of the city and the defilement of its temple through its trampling by the conquering army, and its profanation through the installation of the conquering army's deity inside it. But what about the profanation of the sabbaths? When one considers that, ultimately, in scripture the siege itself is God's punishment for contravening his statutes and ordinances which are communicated to the people during the "sabbath" gatherings, at least from the perspective of the exiles, one can see in which sense the sabbaths also are profaned by the people. The striking vocabulary peculiarity in the description of the Babylonians' invasion of Jerusalem in chapter 23 confirms this. Thrice the conquerors are referred to with the Hebrew *qahal* translated as "host":

> And they shall come against you from the north with chariots and wagons and a *host* [*qahal*] of peoples; they shall set themselves against you on every side with buckler, shield, and helmet, and I will commit the judgment to them, and they shall judge you according to their judgments. (v.24)

> For thus says the Lord God: Bring up a *host* [*qahal*] against them, and make them an object of terror and a spoil. And the *host* [*qahal*] shall stone them and dispatch them with their swords; they shall slay their sons and their daughters, and burn up their houses. (vv.46-47)

In scripture *qahal* (LXX *ekklēsia*) is the basic noun that designates Israel as God's congregation. The punishment for a member of the congregation who disregards God's commands is death by stoning, especially in the case of idolatry (Lev 20:2-5; Deut 13:6-10; 17:2-5), blasphemy against God (Lev 24:16), and contravention of the sabbath rule (Num 15:32-36).

Consequently, the choice of *qahal* in Ezekiel 23:24, 46-47 cannot possibly be happenstance, particularly when one considers that the parallel statement in 16:40 also speaks of stoning by the *qahal*: "They shall bring up a host [*qahal*] against you, and they shall stone you and cut you to pieces with their swords." This understanding is verified in that these are the sole instances of stoning in Ezekiel and are unwarranted since they seem an unnecessary parallel to the reference to death by the sword, which is a staple of the book.

Thus, the divine punishment in chapters 16 and 23 of death by stoning is to expel the contravening persons from the *qahal*. Still chapter 23 does three more things when compared with chapter 16. First, it underscores the message of chapter 16 by referring to the *qahal* three times. Secondly, it expands the punishment intended for Jerusalem (16:40 and 23:24) to include both sisters (23:47-48) in view of the restoration of both (37:15-28). Finally, and most importantly, reference to the sabbaths (23:38), which is not in chapter 16, is clearly aimed at the exiles. The corollary is that for the exiles expulsion is from the sabbatical *qahal*, wherever that might be gathered, since Jerusalem is only a ghost from the past. Furthermore, such expulsion would be the result of a righteous judgment by the *qahal* itself, reflecting no less than God's justice:

> They shall bring up a host (*qahal*) against you, and they shall stone you and cut you to pieces with their swords. And they shall burn your houses and execute judgments upon you in the sight of many women; I will make you stop playing the harlot, and you shall also give hire no more. (16:40-41)

> And they shall come against you from the north with chariots and wagons and a host (*qahal*) of peoples; they shall set themselves against you on every side with buckler, shield, and helmet, and I

The Parable of Oholah and Oholibah 273

will commit the judgment to them, and they shall judge you according to their judgments. (23:24)

But righteous men shall pass judgment on them with the sentence of adulteresses, and with the sentence of women that shed blood; because they are adulteresses, and blood is upon their hands. For thus says the Lord God: Bring up a host (*qahal*) against them, and make them an object of terror and a spoil. And the host (*qahal*) shall stone them and dispatch them with their swords; they shall slay their sons and their daughters, and burn up their houses. (23:45-47)[3]

On the other hand, the fact that *qahal* is used in reference to the Babylonians again confirms that, in Ezekiel, Babylon fulfills the role of God's representative.

As previously noted, there is a functional importance linked to the proper names used in scripture. Such is the case in chapter 23 with "Pekod and Shoa and Koa" (v.23). More often "scholarship" tends de facto to be dismissive of the *scriptural* text, very often making out of it simply an *informational* rather than authoritative text.[4] Quoted below are comments about verse 23 by an eminent Old Testament German scholar, Walther Zimmerli, who wrote a two-volume eleven hundred page

---

[3] Paul will follow suit in 1 Corinthians: "For though absent in body I am present in spirit, and as if present, I have already pronounced judgment in the name of the Lord Jesus on the man who has done such a thing. When you are assembled, and my spirit is present, with the power of our Lord Jesus, you are to deliver this man to Satan for the destruction of the flesh, that his spirit may be saved in the day of the Lord Jesus." (5:3-5)

[4] I would not even bother with "theologians" who are interested in scripture merely as a collection of key words or passages (the like of "creation," "salvation," "in Christ," "in the Spirit") for their own "structured thoughts" whose reality is already formulated in their minds. In other words, they use scripture as proof-text rather than a text reflecting a flowing "story."

commentary in its English translation, published in the world famous *Hermeneia* series:

> Three further groups of people, the names of which with their thick 'O' sounds are undoubtedly deliberately quoted for their sound, are then listed in order. פְּקוֹד[5] mentioned again in Jer 50:21 in connection with an oracle against Babylon, denotes an important Aramean tribe *puqudu* in east Babylonia. It is not only mentioned by Tiglath-pileser III, but also in the inscription of Sargon II in a list of those conquered by Marduk-apal-iddin. [Av,[6] mentioned again in Is 22:5, has mostly been connected with the Sutaeans, who are known from Mari, from the Amarna letters, and from Assyrian royal inscriptions. They were a nomadic group of the Syro-Arabian desert, which was later to be found east of *diyāla*. However, this identification remains very uncertain. This is even more true of the identification of the [Aq,[7] which stands alongside [Av to rhyme with it, with the *qutu* (so Delitzsch, otherwise Zimmern), which would be located in the same east-*diyāla* territory.[8]

The real issue remains unsolved. *Why* would Ezekiel bother mentioning those three groups when they are unnecessary for his point, which the reading of vv.22-23 with their omission will readily prove: "Therefore, O Oholibah, thus says the Lord God: 'Behold, I will rouse against you your lovers from whom you turned in disgust, and I will bring them against you from every side: the Babylonians and all the Chaldeans, ... and all the Assyrians with them, desirable young men, governors and commanders all of them, officers and warriors, all of them riding on horses." No hearer will have missed the omission, especially

---

[5] Peqod.
[6] Shoa.
[7] Koa.
[8] Zimmerli, W. *Ezekiel 1: A Commentary on the Book of the Prophet Ezekiel, Chapters 1-24*. Hermeneia. Philadelphia: Fortress Press, 1979, p.488.

The Parable of Oholah and Oholibah

when the rest of the chapter speaks essentially of the Babylonians, Chaldeans, and Assyrians as the "lovers."[9] Words in a text that is written with the intention to be heard by secondary as well as primary recipients must carry an immediate meaning and intention readily understood by the common hearers of the time.[10]

The trouble with Zimmerli's comments is that though they do contain some important elements, unfortunately he does not elaborate upon them: "the names ... are *undoubtedly deliberately quoted for their sound*"; "the identification of the [Aq, which stands alongside [Av *to rhyme with it*." That is to say, he recognizes these features of the text but does not deem them functional in its actual "message." If Ezekiel chose those names over many other possibilities, it is because they helped carry his message more pointedly to his *hearer*. The Hebrew *peqod* is from the verb *paqad* that is used in the Prophets to speak of God's visitation of the people in order to judge them for their sins. The Hebrew *šoa'* is from a root meaning "crying for help" and is found profusely in the Old Testament. In Isaiah 22:5 *šoa'* is translated as "shouting" in RSV, "cries for help" in JB, "crying"

---

[9] My contention is that one should give importance to those seemingly unnecessary asides if one gives credence, even with a grain of salt, to the Lord's statement in Matthew 5:17-18: "Think not that I have come to abolish the law and the prophets; I have come not to abolish them but to fulfil them. For truly, I say to you, till heaven and earth pass away, not an iota, not a dot, will pass from the law until all is accomplished."

[10] Indeed, the Apostle ordained that his letters be "read (aloud)," not explained, let alone commented upon: "And when this letter has been read among you, have it read also in the church of the Laodiceans; and see that you read also the letter from Laodicea." (Col 4:16). The original meaning of the Greek *anaginōskō* is "read aloud"—rather than "read for oneself"—as is reflected in that (1) it is the scriptural translation of the Hebrew *qara'* and (2) refers to the action of the congregational reader: "Blessed is he who reads aloud the words of the prophecy, and blessed are those who hear, and who keep what is written therein; for the time is near." (Rev 1:3)

in KJV; and these translations *fit the context*: "For the Lord God of hosts has a day of tumult and trampling and confusion in the valley of vision, a battering down of walls and a shouting (*šoaʾ*) to the mountains." It could not have meant something else *here*. As Zimmerli remarked, *qoaʿ* is intended to rhyme with *šoaʿ*. The assonance is usually used to underscore a similar or corresponding meaning. In that case, the best educated guess is to surmise that *qoaʿ* is intended to recall the root *taqaʿ* (strike, thrust)[11] which occurs thrice in Ezekiel in conjunction with the context of battle: "They have blown (*taqeʿu*) the trumpet (*hattaqoaʿ*; the [trumpet] blast) and made all ready; but none goes to battle, for my wrath is upon all their multitude" (7:14); "and if he [the watchman] sees the sword coming upon the land and blows (*taqaʾ*) the trumpet (*šophar*) and warns the people ... But if the watchman sees the sword coming and does not blow (*taqaʾ*) the trumpet (*šophar*), so that the people are not warned, and the sword comes, and takes any one of them." (33:3, 6) Consequently, *qoaʿ* in 23:23 is reminiscent, for the hearer, of the earlier instance of *taqoaʿ* (trumpet blast). The result is that, *to the ear*, when heard in sequence in the context of 23:22-24 that speaks of the Babylonians coming to Jerusalem to destroy her in judgment for her sins, the three nouns *peqod*, *šoaʿ*, and *qoaʿ* sound as though God is coming to "visit" his people, among the clamor of their cries and the trumpet sound, in order to judge them, as he did in 20:33-35, rather than save them as he did in 20:6-9.

---

[11] My readers should not be surprised by the extra consonant *t*. The Semitic languages are consonantal and most of the roots are trilateral (tri-consonantal). So the root *qoʿ* and *tqʿ* are closer than meets the eye since the *o* in *qoʿ* is actually the consonant *w*; thus *qoʿ* is actually *qwʿ*. And, as I showed earlier in the case of the verbs *yšb* and *šub/šwb*, the assonance is secured through two out of three identical consonants.

17
A Review of the Story

Chapter 24 serves as the conclusion to the section of the book that is mainly concerned with Jerusalem and Judah. So it is only fitting that it speaks of the siege of that city (vv.1-14) and the subsequent exile of the survivors (vv.15-27), and does so using a vocabulary reminiscent of previous chapters. Since the following section, chapters 25-32, deals with the "oracle against the nations," chapter 24 functions as a recapitulation of the preceding chapters. Yet, in the same manner as chapters 1-23, it looks ahead to the final restoration described in chapter 37. Thus, it would be fruitful as well as interesting to study some of the vocabulary and phraseology in the chapter.

The chapter starts by harking back to the introduction of the book. Besides the use of the priestly device of dating to the day when "the word of the Lord came to" Ezekiel (24:1; see 1:1, 3), one hears that Ezekiel is summoned not only to "say" to the people what God asks of him (24:3; see also 2:4) but also to "write down" (24:2), a unique instance in the book. Such is evidently intended to recall the written scroll of 2:9-10 whose mention comes in conjunction with a repeated reference to the "rebellious house" (2:5, 6, 8),[1] which is precisely whom Ezekiel is addressing in 24:3; add to this that "writing" occurs practically only in these two instances in the book.[2] A further indication

---

[1] Also in v.7 in RSV that follows the LXX; the Hebrew has "rebels."
[2] The root *ktb* (write) is also found in 13:9: "My hand will be against the prophets who see delusive visions and who give lying divinations; they shall not be in the council of my people, nor be enrolled (*yikkatebu*; written) in the register (*ketab*; written document) of the house of Israel, nor shall they enter the land of Israel; and you shall know that I am the Lord God."

that chapter 24 is recalling chapter 2 can be seen in the use of the phrase "this very day" *('eṣem hayyom*; the bone [hard center] of this day; 2:5; 24:2 [twice]) which occurs only once more in Ezekiel (40:1) where it is found also in conjunction with the fall of Jerusalem. As discussed earlier, the use of "bone" looks ahead to the raising to the dry bones in 37:1-14. However, the link between chapters 24 and 37 through the mention of "bone" is more impressive than that between chapter 2 and 37 in that this noun is functional in the immediate context where one hears of "bones" in 24:4, 5, and 10:

> Set on the pot, set it on, pour in water also; put in it the pieces of flesh, all the good pieces, the thigh and the shoulder; fill it with choice bones. Take the choicest one of the flock, pile the logs under it; boil its pieces, seethe also its bones in it ... Heap on the logs, kindle the fire, boil well the flesh, and empty out the broth, and let the bones be burned up. (vv.3b-5, 10)

The "burned" bones here are the prelude to the "very dry" bones of 37:1-2. A further indication that chapter 24 forms a bridge between the previous and the following chapters is detected in the mention of "flock" (*ṣo'n*) which, on the one hand, is not found earlier and, on the other hand, will reappear in chapter 34, the ending of which parallels that of chapter 37.

On the other hand, the burning of the bones is brought up in the context of a pot whose content is brought to boil by fire (24:3-11), which is precisely the metaphor used earlier in 11:3-12 in conjunction with the punishment of Jerusalem at the Babylonians' hands, as is the case here. In chapter 11 we hear of flesh (vv.3, 7, 11) as in 24:10,³ but not of bones, which further confirms the intention of looking ahead to chapter 37.

The phraseology of "bloody city" (24:6, 9) is clearly reminiscent of 7:23 (the land is full of bloody crimes and the city is full of violence) and more so of 22:2 (And you, son of man, will you judge, will you judge the bloody city?). "I shall not spare" (24:14) brings immediately and unmistakably to mind the previously repeated "my eye shall not spare" (5:11; 7:4, 9; 8:18; 9:10). In 24:13 one hears the last instance of "lewdness" (*zimmah*) after a long series of such in chapters 16, 22, and 23. Similarly, God's "satisfying his fury" (24:13) is the last such instance in the book after being used three previous times (5:13; 16:42; 21:17). As for "fire" (24:10, 12), it is a pervading metaphor in the book. Finally, those castigating "words of the Lord" (vv. 3b-14) are introduced with "utter an allegory" (*mešol mašal*; strike a parable, v.3a), mimicking the beginning of chapter 17 (v.2) which deals with the destruction of Jerusalem at the Babylonians' hand, the same subject matter of chapter 24.

An overview of the second part of chapter 24 will confirm that, all in all, it is a recapitulation of all the preceding up to this point and looks ahead to the following chapters as well. Verses 15-27 are a reprise of 12:1-20 where Ezekiel is presented as a prototype of the exiles and thus a "sign" (*mophet*) for them (vv.24, 27; see 12:6). Moreover, the exile who is addressed by Ezekiel is referred to as *paliṭ* (fugitive; 24:26, 27) a noun that was used in the plural both earlier in the book (6:8, 9; 7:16;⁴ see also 14:22⁵) to

---

³ In 24:4 the original for RSV's "pieces of flesh" is simply "pieces."
⁴ The original Hebrew reads "And if any fugitives (*paliṭim*; escapees) escape" for RSV's "And if any survivors escape."
⁵ The reference in the original is to "a remainder that has escaped" for RSV's "if there should be left in it any survivors."

describe the exiles and later in chapter 33, which is the continuation of 24:26-27:

> And you, son of man, on the day when I take from them their stronghold, their joy and glory, the delight of their eyes and their heart's desire, and also their sons and daughters, on that day a *fugitive* (*paliṭ*) will come to you to report to you the news. On that day your mouth will be opened to the *fugitive* (*paliṭ*), and you shall speak and be no longer dumb. So you will be a sign to them; and they will know that I am the Lord. (24:25-27)

> In the twelfth year of our exile, in the tenth month, on the fifth day of the month, *a man who had escaped* (*paliṭ*) from Jerusalem came to me and said, "The city has fallen." Now the hand of the Lord had been upon me the evening before *the fugitive* (*paliṭ*) came; and he had opened my mouth by the time the man came to me in the morning; so my mouth was opened, and I was no longer dumb. (33:21-22)

In a unique way, chapter 24 functions as a conclusion to the previous chapter. This is detected in the play on the root *ḥmd* used to describe the divine punishment resulting from the people's behavior as underscored in 24:14b: "… according to your ways and your doings I will judge you, says the Lord God." Following this statement we hear thrice the phrase "delight (*maḥmad*) of the eyes" (vv.16, 21, 25) to correspond to the thrice mentioned "desirability" (*ḥemed*) of the Assyrians and Babylonians to those same eyes in chapter 23:

> … warriors clothed in purple, governors and commanders, all of them [the Assyrians] desirable (*ḥemed*) young men, horsemen riding on horses … She doted upon the Assyrians, governors and commanders, warriors clothed in full armor, horsemen riding on horses, all of them desirable (*ḥemed*) young men … the

A Review of the Story

> Babylonians and all the Chaldeans, Pekod and Shoa and Koa, and all the Assyrians with them, desirable (*ḥemed*) young men, governors and commanders all of them, officers and warriors, all of them riding on horses. (23:6, 12, 23)

> Son of man, behold, I am about to take the delight (*maḥmad*) of your eyes away from you at a stroke; yet you shall not mourn or weep nor shall your tears run down ... Say to the house of Israel, Thus says the Lord God: Behold, I will profane my sanctuary, the pride of your power, the delight (*maḥmad*) of your eyes, and the desire of your soul; and your sons and your daughters whom you left behind shall fall by the sword ... And you, son of man, on the day when I take from them their stronghold, their joy and glory, the delight (*maḥmad*) of their eyes and their heart's desire, and also their sons and daughters, on that day a fugitive will come to you to report to you the news. (24:16, 21, 25-26)

As usual in scripture, the guilt (*'awon*) of the people is their own punishment (*'awon*). All that God has to do is just to show them the ultimate outcome of their desire. They have defiled God's sanctuary (23:38) by desiring the beauty of other deities and their cronies. However, God will foil their actions by profaning his own sanctuary himself (24:21) before their own wanton (practicing harlotry) eyes, as he has earlier promised:

> Behold, I, even I, will bring a sword upon you, and I will destroy your high places. Your altars shall become desolate, and your incense altars shall be broken; and I will cast down your slain before your idols ... Yet I will leave some of you alive. When you have among the nations some who escape (*peliṭim*; plural of *paliṭ*) the sword, and when you are scattered through the countries, then those of you who escape (*peliṭim*; plural of *paliṭ*) will remember me among the nations where they are carried captive, when I have broken their wanton (*zoneh*; harlot) heart which has departed from me, and blinded their eyes which *turn wantonly* (*zonot*; [are]

harlots) after their idols; and they will be loathsome in their own sight for the evils which they have committed, for all their abominations. And they shall know that I am the Lord; I have not said in vain that I would do this evil to them. (6:3-4, 8-10)

At the beginning of the story, Ezekiel was "dumb and unable to reprove them; for they are a rebellious house" (3:26), yet God assured him: "But when I speak with you, I will open your mouth, and you shall say to them, 'Thus says the Lord God'; he that will hear, let him hear; and he that will refuse to hear, let him refuse; for they are a rebellious house" (v.27). Finally in chapter 24 his mouth is opened:

And you, son of man, on the day when I take from them their stronghold, their joy and glory, the delight of their eyes and their heart's desire, and also their sons and daughters, on that day a fugitive will come to you to report to you the news. On that day your mouth will be opened to the fugitive, and you shall speak and be no longer dumb. So you will be a sign to them; and they will know that I am the Lord. (vv.25-27)

18
Oracles against the Nations

Before moving to the period of restoration alluded to several times previously, the author goes on an aside to include the surrounding nations in the divine indictment (chs. 25-32). Chapters 25-28 deal with Israel's neighboring nations; chapters 29-32 are dedicated to Egypt and its Pharaoh in whom the leaders of Jerusalem had put their hope (17:15-18).

The overall function of the "oracles against the nations" in all the prophetic books is to remind Samaria and Jerusalem, especially the surviving exiles of those cities, that the punishing God lords over all nations. The exiles are never to imagine that they could hide from God under the protection of another nation's deity. In Ezekiel, the message is even more potent since he just bombarded the exiles with the abominations committed by their "fathers" in Jerusalem, which consisted of following other "idols." That message was at its clearest in chapter 20: "What is in your mind shall never happen—the thought, 'Let us be like the nations, like the tribes of the countries, and worship wood and stone.' As I live, says the Lord God, surely with a mighty hand and an outstretched arm, and with wrath poured out, I will be king over you." (vv.32-33)

The indictments begin with Ammon (25:1-7), which was protractedly introduced in 21:28-32. Next is Moab (25:8-11), then Edom (vv.12-14), and Philistia (vv.15-17). The choice of Ammon is dictated by its geographical proximity (21:24-26). Its capital city Rabbah means "great, populous" in Hebrew. It is the only capital city that is singled out in chapter 25. However, and perhaps more importantly, it was presented earlier as "fortified" (*beṣurah*; fortress-like, impregnable) city, in parallel with Jerusalem (21:20). So the intention is to underscore that, in spite of their apparent strength, both cities are easily overcome. Such is corroborated in that later, at the time of restoration, we hear the only other instance of *beṣurah* in Ezekiel:

> Thus says the Lord God: On the day that I cleanse you from all your iniquities, I will cause the cities to be inhabited, and the waste places shall be rebuilt. And the land that was desolate shall be tilled, instead of being the desolation that it was in the sight of all who passed by. And they will say, 'This land that was desolate has become like the garden of Eden; and the waste and desolate and ruined cities are now inhabited and fortified (*beṣurot*; plural of *beṣurah*).' (36:33-35)

Still, as is clear from the actual indictment, it is the arrogance of Ammon, expressed in its derision of Judah's punishment (25:3, 6, 8, 15; 26:2), that brings about its doom. This will be confirmed in the conclusion to chapters 25-28:

> And for the house of Israel there shall be no more a brier to prick or a thorn to hurt them among all their neighbors who have treated them with *contempt*. Then they will know that I am the Lord God. Thus says the Lord God: When I gather the house of Israel from the peoples among whom they are scattered, and manifest my holiness in them in the sight of the nations, then they shall dwell in their own land which I gave to my servant Jacob. And they shall dwell securely in it, and they shall build houses and plant vineyards. They shall dwell securely, when I execute judgments upon all their neighbors who have treated them with *contempt*. (28:24-26)

In dealing with the surrounding nations, Ezekiel is acknowledging that they too are within the final purview of

God's everlasting covenant of peace. Isaiah makes this point very ostensibly (66:18-21); Ezekiel does it deftly. As pointed out earlier, Ezekiel prefers *'adamah* (ground) over *'ereṣ* to speak of the "land" of Israel in order to include *'adam* (every human being, all human beings) in the divine plan. He does the same here in his description of the Ammonites' plight: "I will make Rabbah a pasture (*naweh*) for camels and the cities of the Ammonites a fold (*mirbaṣ*; from the root *rbṣ*) for flocks (*ṣo'n*; flock). Then you will know that I am the Lord." (25:5) Later, within the context of restoration and a few verses before the mention of the "covenant of peace' (34:25) we hear:

> As a shepherd seeks out his flock (*ṣo'n*) when some of his sheep have been scattered abroad, so will I seek out my sheep; and I will rescue them from all places where they have been scattered on a day of clouds and thick darkness. And I will bring them out from the peoples, and gather them from the countries, and will bring them into their own land (*'adamah*); and I will feed them on the mountains of Israel, by the fountains, and in all the inhabited places of the country. I will feed them with good pasture (*mir'eh*), and upon the mountain heights of Israel shall be their pasture (*naweh*); there they shall lie down (*tirbaṣnah*; from the root *rbṣ*) in good grazing land (*naweh*), and on fat pasture (*mir'eh*) they shall feed on the mountains of Israel. I myself will be the shepherd of my sheep (*ṣo'n*), and I will make them lie down (*'arbiṣ*; from the root *rbṣ*), says the Lord God. (34:12-15)

The intentional link between those two passages is unmistakable; in them we find the only occurrences of *naweh* in Ezekiel and the only two instances in the entire scripture where one hears the combination of flock, *naweh*, and the root *rbṣ*. Although misled by their own shepherds, God gives hope for the future to the

Ammonites and the other nations he punished (25:10) by including them as "sheep of a flock in a pasture."

Among the nations surrounding Judah, prominence is given to Tyre, long known for its hegemony over the Mediterranean Sea commerce as can be seen in the long list of cities and nations with whom she trafficked (ch. 27). The oracle against her covers three chapters and comprises two addresses to the city itself (chs. 26 and 27) and two to its ruler (28:1-10 and vv.11-19). Although Egypt surpasses her in attention, Tyre's importance is still evident in that the spoils of Egypt were given to Nebuchadrezzar, king of Babylon, as wages for the pain his army endured during the sack of Tyre (29:18-20)! However, there is a special ring to the name Tyre that strikes the hearers' ears even if they have no inkling of her historical significance. The Hebrew, and the general Semitic, for Tyre is *ṣor* both with a short "o" (*ṣor*; צֹר) as in 26:2 and with a long "o" (*ṣōr*; צוֹר) as in v.15. The latter tri-literal form, when vocalized as *ṣūr* (צוּר), means "rock." Consequently, the naming of Tyre corresponds to its description as an island offshore and thus a "rock" in "the midst of the sea" (26:5; 27:32).[1] The author, aware of this consonance, plays on that meaning from the beginning: "Behold, I am against you, O Tyre, and will bring up many nations against you, *as the sea brings up its waves*. They shall destroy the walls of Tyre, and break down her towers; and I will scrape her soil from her, and make her a *bare rock (ṣeḥiaḥ selaʿ)*" (26:3-4), which is repeated in v.14 (I will make you a *bare rock*).

---

[1] See also for its offshore location 26:18 (Now the isles tremble on the day of your fall; yea, *the isles that are in the sea are dismayed at your passing*); 27:3 (and say to Tyre, who dwells *at the entrance to the sea*); 27:29b-30a (The mariners and all the pilots of the sea *stand on the shore* and wail aloud over you, and cry bitterly).

Just as the text betrays a parallelism between the fates of Ammon and Judah in order to underscore the universality of Ezekiel's God, the hearer can detect a similar parallelism between Tyre, the prototype of the surrounding "nations," and Judah. The exact same phrase "bare rock" (*ṣeḥiaḥ selaʻ*), used twice to describe Tyre's punishment, has already been heard, also twice, in the indictment against Jerusalem: "For the blood she has shed is still in the midst of her; she put it on the bare rock, she did not pour it upon the ground to cover it with dust. To rouse my wrath, to take vengeance, I have set on the bare rock the blood she has shed, that it may not be covered." (24:7-8) Just as God pronounced a lamentation on Jerusalem in chapter 19 (vv.1, 14), he also proclaims "lamentations" (dirges) on Tyre (26:17; 27:2, 32; 28:12). Except for Egypt (32:2, 16), no other kingdom is addressed with a "lamentation" (*qinah*). In the scroll of "lamentations (*qinnim*; plural of *qinah*) and mourning and woe"[2] (2:10) handed to Ezekiel and addressed to the "house of Israel," there is only one "lamentation" directed at "the princes of Israel" (19:1). Thus, the use of the plural "lamentations"—especially that it stands in contrast to the two singulars "mourning" and "woe"—is intentional and has in view the two "pairings," Ammon and Judah, and Tyre and Judah, which in turn reflect that the "nations" were included within the message of woe against the "house of Israel." This was adroitly done in order to integrate them into the final restoration of that house.[3] Such an "inclusion" can be detected further in that the "king (*melek*) of Tyre" who is the object of a "lamentation" (28:12) has been

---

[2] RSV has "words of lamentation and mourning and woe," obscuring thus that, in the original, only "lamentations" is in the plural while "mourning" and "woe" are in the singular.

[3] I covered that point already at the beginning when dealing with chapters 1-3 where I showed that the ultimate addressee is each and every person that is "hearing" the Book of Ezekiel being read aloud.

addressed in the previous invective as "prince (*nagid*) of Tyre" (v.2) which corresponds to how the leaders of Israel were addressed in 19:1 (And you, take up a lamentation for the princes [*neśi'im*; plural of *naśi'*] of Israel). Since *nagid* and *naśi'* are practically equivalent in meaning, the choice of *nagid* to speak of the king of Tyre is aimed at differentiating between him and the "leaders" (*neśi'im*; 26:16 and 27:21) of nations trading with Tyre who were of lesser importance.

Four chapters are dedicated to Egypt and its Pharaoh, who is also called a "prince" (30:13) in spite of his being "king" (29:2, 3; 30:21, 22; 31:2; 32:2). Egypt is especially noted among the nations who are named in 32:22-30 since the Judahites turned to Egypt thinking that it would be mighty enough to eschew their divine punishment at the hand of the Babylonians. Egypt, instead, proved to be a paper tiger. Thus, the author wanted his Judahite hearers exiled at Chebar to remember that it is Egypt, and not Babylon, that is their real "oppressor" liable for a dirge (32:2-16) because of its arrogance. Babylon is nowhere to be found among the nations (32:22-30) punished by God because it submitted to God's design by acting as his instrument of retribution against Judah. Yet, in spite of their being punished by God, the exiled Egyptians will be brought back to their land of origin and their fortunes will be restored:

> And I will make the land of Egypt a desolation in the midst of desolated countries; and her cities shall be a desolation forty years among cities that are laid waste. I will scatter the Egyptians among the nations, and disperse them among the countries. For thus says the Lord God: At the end of forty years I will gather the Egyptians from the peoples among whom they were scattered; and I will restore the fortunes of Egypt, and bring them back to the land of Pathros, the land of their origin; and there they shall be a lowly kingdom. It shall be the most lowly of the kingdoms, and never

again exalt itself above the nations; and I will make them so small that they will never again rule over the nations. And it shall never again be the reliance of the house of Israel, recalling their iniquity, when they turn to them for aid. Then they will know that I am the Lord God. (29:12-16)

Thus, more clearly than in the case of Ammon and Tyre, Egypt is "included"—even terminology wise—in the story that would culminate with the restoration at the punishing God's hand when he would act through his sheer beneficence. Furthermore, along with Egypt, those also included will be Assyria (32:22), Elam (v.24), and even "Meshech and Tubal and all their multitude" (v.26) whose chief "prince" (*nasi*) is none less than God's archenemy, Gog of the land of Magog (38:2, 3; 39:1). Here again, the vocabulary of "consolation" that is used in conjunction with the "inclusion" of all those nations (32:31) harks back to that describing the role of the Judahites in "consoling" others through the divine punishment endured by them:

> For thus says the Lord God: How much more when I send upon Jerusalem my four sore acts of judgment, sword, famine, evil beasts, and pestilence, to cut off from it man and beast! Yet, if there should be left in it any survivors to lead out (*musa'im*; from the verb *yasa'*) sons and daughters, when they come forth (*yose'im*; from the verb *yasa'*) to you, and you see their ways and their doings, you will be consoled (*nihamtem*) for the evil that I have brought upon Jerusalem, for all that I have brought upon it. They will console (*nihamu*) you, when you see their ways and their doings; and you shall know that I have not done without cause all that I have done in it, says the Lord God. (14:21-23)

In the same way, the punished Assyria, Elam, and Meshech and Tubal will prove to be a consolation for Egypt that was punished for doing the same deeds:

> When Pharaoh sees them, he will comfort himself (*niḥam*) for all his multitude, Pharaoh and all his army, slain by the sword, says the Lord God. For he spread terror in the land of the living; therefore he shall be laid among the uncircumcised, with those who are slain by the sword, Pharaoh and all his multitude, says the Lord God. (32:31-32)

Part III

The Restoration

19
The Offer for Repentance

Chapter 33 begins with a passage that introduces Ezekiel as a watchman (33:1-9), a position he was assigned to at the start of his activity (3:17-21). This is done to reaffirm that his mission is no more but definitely no less than relaying God's words as written in the scroll. The object of the mission is to invite the surviving exiles to understand that God's instructive punishment is unto life, not death (33:10-20), and that this divine beneficence is intentional and not merely an aside. This is evident in that the main addressee is the wicked, rather than the righteous:

> And you, son of man, say to the house of Israel, Thus have you said: "Our transgressions and our sins are upon us, and we waste away because of them; how then can we live?" Say to them, As I live, says the Lord God, *I have no pleasure in the death of the wicked*, but that the wicked turn from his way and live; turn back, turn back from your evil ways; *for why will you die, O house of Israel?* (vv.10-11)

However, life is granted on the condition of repentance, which is not to be merely lip service, but an actual change from disobedience to submission to God's will (33:12-20). This is the central facet of Ezekiel's message, and it resounds here for the third time after having been heard in 14:1-20 and in 18:21-30. Indeed, "O house of Israel, I will judge each of you *according to his ways*" (33:20b), ways which each will have followed *after* the offer of repentance (vv.12-16).

Keeping God's will is not a matter of feelings or assumptions. It is to be realized through "walking in [God's] statutes *of life*," which confirms that his purpose when issuing his statutes was life, not death, even for the wicked: "if the wicked restores the pledge, gives back what he has taken by robbery, and walks in the statutes of life, committing no iniquity; he shall surely live, he shall not die." (v.15). This is precisely and clearly stated in the concluding remarks after the issuance of the Law to the "second generation of survivors" in Deuteronomy:

> See, I have set before you this day life and good, death and evil. If you obey the commandments of the Lord your God which I command you this day, by loving the Lord your God, by walking in his ways, and by keeping his commandments and his statutes and his ordinances, then you shall live and multiply, and the Lord your God will bless you in the land which you are entering to take possession of it. But if your heart turns away, and you will not hear, but are drawn away to worship other gods and serve them, I declare to you this day, that you shall perish; you shall not live long in the land which you are going over the Jordan to enter and possess. I call heaven and earth to witness against you this day, that I have set before you life and death, blessing and curse; *therefore choose life, that you and your descendants may live, loving the Lord your God, obeying his voice, and cleaving to him; for that means life to you and length of days, that you may dwell in the land which the Lord swore to your fathers, to Abraham, to Isaac, and to Jacob, to give them.* (30:15-20)

Nonetheless, and in order to underscore that the ultimate divine judgment is a matter of rightfulness and thus not appealable once issued, Ezekiel stresses the legal aspect of God's will. He does so, beyond his referring to it as "statutes" (33:15), by stating no less than three times that implementing God's will is equivalent to "doing what is lawful (*mišpaṭ*; what is ordained, ordinance) and right (*ṣedaqah*; righteousness)" (vv.14, 16, 19). What one is supposed to be doing is obeying the divine "ordinance" (*mišpaṭ*) in order to be considered "orderly." In practicing "righteousness" (*ṣedaqah*) one comes to be considered "righteous" (*ṣaddiq*; vv.12, 13, 18). That is why, "when the wicked turns from his wickedness, and does what is lawful and right (*ṣedaqah*; righteousness), he shall live by it" (v.19); conversely, "when the righteous turns from his righteousness, and commits iniquity, he shall die for it" (18).

Having clarified this matter, Ezekiel once more reminds his hearers of the fall of Jerusalem. Verses 21-33 are magisterially crafted. The entire message covered previously in numerous chapters filled with repetitions is compressed into these few verses. The first two verses (21-22) build a bridge that spans over the "oracles against the nations" (chs.25-32) and connects it to the first part of the book dealing with Jerusalem and Judah (chs.4-24). Indeed, the fugitive appearing at the end of chapter 24 (vv. 25-27) reappears here:

> In the twelfth year of our exile, in the tenth month, on the fifth day of the month, *a man who had escaped* (*paliṭ*) from Jerusalem came to me and said, "The city has fallen." Now the hand of the Lord had been upon me the evening before *the fugitive* (*paliṭ*) came; and he had opened my mouth by the time the man came to me in the morning; so my mouth was opened, and I was no longer dumb. (33:21-22)

Ezekiel builds his message (vv. 23-29) on elements taken from previous chapters:

> **33:24** (Son of man, the inhabitants of these waste places in the land of Israel [*'admat yisra'el*] keep saying, "Abraham was only one

man, yet he got possession of [*yiraš*; inherited from the root *yaraš*][1] the land [*ha'areṣ*]; but we are many; the land is surely given us to possess [*lanu nitnah ha'areṣ lemorašah*—for an inheritance; from the root *yaraš*]) harks back to 11:15 (Son of man, your brethren, even your brethren, your fellow exiles, the whole house of Israel, all of them, are those of whom the inhabitants of Jerusalem have said, "They have gone far from the Lord; to us this land is given for a possession [*lanu nitnah ha'areṣ lemorašah*—for an inheritance]").

33:25 refers to shedding of (innocent) blood and honoring the idols spoken of throughout the previous chapters.

33:26 that speaks of abominations and defilement of the neighbor's wife harks back to 22:11: "One commits abomination with his neighbor's wife."

33:27 is a brief description of the aftermath of a siege: "As I live, surely those who are in the waste places shall fall by the sword; and him that is in the open field I will give to the beasts to be devoured; and those who are in strongholds and in caves shall die by pestilence."

33:28-29 are filled with Ezekelian terms underscoring the sin of arrogance: "And I will make the land a desolation (*šemamah*) and a waste (*mešammah*); and her proud (*ge'on*) might (*'oz*) shall come to an end; and the *mountains of Israel* shall be so desolate (*šamemu*) that none will pass through. Then they will know that I am the Lord, when I have made the land a desolation (*šemamah*) and a waste (*mešammah*) because of all their abominations (*to'abot*) which they have committed."

---

[1] Here again RSV, as it often does in the Book of Joshua, misleadingly renders "inheritance" into "possession."

The Offer for Repentance

The chapter ends with a divine address to Ezekiel that underscores the people's obstinate recalcitrance to his message. It begins by describing their stand as one of mockery. Although they invite one another to "Come, and hear what the word is that comes forth from the Lord" (v.30b), "they sit before you" (v.31), just as the elders did, with the intention of inquiring in order to assess (8:1; 14:1; 20:1) rather than to listen, which is clear from the repeated "they hear what you say but they will not do it" (33:31 and 32). But what the people are unaware of is that God's strategy shall not be thwarted by their attitude; his last words "they will know that a prophet has been among them" (33b) are only an echo of what he had planned from the start: "And whether they hear or refuse to hear (for they are a rebellious house) they will know that there has been a prophet among them." (2:5) This is a fitting end to the cycle that began in chapter 2. It comes just before the invective against "the shepherds of Israel" (ch.34) so that the hearers would not be able to find in their mental repertoire any shred of an excuse for their rebellious behavior.

20
God the Shepherd and his Flock

The most noticeable aspect of chapter 34 is the monotonous repetition of the noun *ṣo'n* (flock)—used 20 times—and words based on the root *ra'ah*, connoting both grazing and shepherding—used 38 times. Even those with no knowledge of Hebrew will be struck by this and be able to figure out the message, especially after hearing the name David, the shepherd who became a king. The versatility associated with *ra'ah* is due to the following features:

1. The verb means both "graze" and "shepherd" and thus, in the first case, can have the sheep as the subject, or, in the latter case, the shepherd is the subject.

2. The English "pasture" is the rendering of the Hebrew *mir'eh* (vv.14 [twice], 18) or *mar'it* (v.31) from the same root *ra'ah*; it is a verbal noun formed through the addition of the consonant *m* at the beginning of the verbal root, which is a feature of Semitic languages. So *mir'eh* is a place where sheep graze and thus where shepherds tend their flock.

3. Finally, and most importantly, in Hebrew the active participle functions also as a noun referring to the person performing the action; thus, the active participle *ro'eh* can function either verbally, thus pointing out the action performed by the "one who is shepherding," or nominally, thus

referring to a "shepherd." The Hebrew *'ani ro'eh* translates into either "I am a shepherd" or "I am shepherding." In the latter case, it corresponds to the English verbal present tense "I shepherd." Technically speaking, in Hebrew one cannot be emeritus; either one is actually shepherding and thus is a shepherd, or one is not shepherding, and thus is *not* a shepherd. One cannot be a shepherd "on a break," so to speak. It is precisely this reality in Ezekiel 34 that allows God to castigate the kings in the following versatile manner:

> Son of man, prophesy against the *shepherds* of Israel, prophesy, and say to them, even to the *shepherds*, Thus says the Lord God: Ho, *shepherds* of Israel who have been feeding (*ro'im*, participle plural of *ra'ah*; shepherding) yourselves! Should not *shepherds* feed (*yir'u*, verbal form of *ra'ah*; shepherd) the sheep? You eat the fat, you clothe yourselves with the wool, you slaughter the fatlings; but you do not feed (*tir'u*, verbal form of *ra'ah* shepherd) the sheep[1]... My sheep were scattered, they wandered over all the mountains and on every high hill; my sheep were scattered over all the face of the earth, *with none to search or seek for them*. Therefore, you *shepherds*, hear the word

---

[1] Actually "the sheep" is not in the Hebrew, corroborating thus what I said earlier that the verb *ra'ah* means "to shepherd," the complement being assumed in the verb; after all one shepherds sheep!

of the Lord: As I live, says the Lord God, because my sheep have become a prey, and my sheep have become food for all the wild beasts, since there was no shepherd (*one shepherding*); and because my *shepherds* have not searched for my sheep, but the *shepherds* have fed (*yir'u*; shepherded) themselves, and have not fed (*ra'u*, verbal form of *ra'ah*; shepherded) my sheep; therefore, you shepherds, hear the word of the Lord: Thus says the Lord God, Behold, I am against the shepherds; and I will require my sheep at their hand, and put a stop to their feeding (*re'ot*, verbal form of *ra'ah*; shepherding) the sheep; no longer shall the shepherds feed (*yir'u*; shepherd) themselves. I will rescue my sheep from their mouths, that they may not be food for them. (vv.2-3, 6-10)

It is no wonder then that God, as the sole true King of Israel (20:33), decides to take over the function of shepherd, and will implement this through his "beloved" (David)[2] whom he will establish as shepherd forever (34:11-31). His action will culminate in the sheep being gathered as his people and he their God: "And they shall know that I, the Lord their God, am with them, and that they, the house of Israel, are my people, says the Lord God. And you are my sheep (*ṣo'ni*; my flock), the sheep (*ṣo'n*) of my pasture (*mar'it*), and I am your God, says the Lord God." (vv.30-31)

---

[2] This is the meaning of the Hebrew consonantal *dwd* vocalized as *dod* except in the case of David where it is vocalized as *dawid*.

This passage is an obvious strike at arrogance since the divine pasture will spread over "the mountains of Israel" that will be subdued to God's will: "And I will bring them out from the peoples, and gather them from the countries, and will bring them into their own land (*'adamah*; ground); and I will feed (*re'iti*; I will shepherd) them on *the mountains of Israel*, by the fountains,³ and in all the inhabited places of the country. I will feed (*'er'eh*; shepherd) them with good pasture (*mir'eh*), and upon *the mountain heights of Israel*⁴ shall be their pasture (*naweh*); there they shall lie down in good grazing land (*naweh*), and on fat pasture (*mir'eh*) they shall feed (*tir'enah*; graze) on *the mountains of Israel*." (vv.13-14) Further corroboration is that "my holy mountain, *the mountain height of Israel*" (20:40) is referred to simply as "my hill" around which the divine blessing of peace shall be secured: "I will make with them a covenant of peace and banish wild beasts from the land, so that they may dwell securely in the wilderness and sleep in the woods. And I will make them and the places round about my hill a blessing; and I will send down the showers in their season; they shall be showers of blessing." (34:25-26)

Nevertheless, this caring shepherding will be *divine* shepherding since God will not cease to don his mantle of judgment: "I will seek the lost, and I will bring back the strayed, and I will bind up the crippled, and I will strengthen the weak, and the fat and the strong I will watch over; I will feed (*'er'eh*; shepherd) them *in justice* (*bemišpaṭ*; according to ordinance)." (v.16) This corresponds fully to what God himself had

---

³ This is the Hebrew *'aphiqim* (ravines) that was used in conjunction with "the mountains of Israel" (6:3) in the harsh invective against these (ch.6).

⁴ Notice how the second reference to mountains adds "heights" to underscore their arrogance.

announced from the beginning in conjunction with his gathering in his scattered people:

> Therefore say, Thus says the Lord God: I will gather you from the peoples, and assemble you out of the countries where you have been scattered, and I will give you the land of Israel. And when they come there, they will remove from it all its detestable things and all its abominations. And I will give them one heart, and put a new spirit within them; I will take the stony heart out of their flesh and give them a heart of flesh, (*in order*) *that they may* walk in my statutes and *keep my ordinances and obey them*; and they shall be my people, and I will be their God. *But as for those whose heart goes after their detestable things and their abominations, I will requite their deeds upon their own heads, says the Lord God.* (11:17-21)

Such, in turn, explains the tone of the following verses after 34:16. Although the people are "his flock," nevertheless he will judge each sheep individually and the judgment will be based on the behavior of one sheep toward the others:[5]

> As for you, my flock, thus says the Lord God: Behold, *I judge between sheep and sheep, rams and he-goats.* Is it not enough for you to feed on the good pasture, that you must tread down with your feet the rest of your pasture; and to drink of clear water, that you must foul the rest with your feet? And must my sheep eat what you have trodden with your feet, and drink what you have fouled with your feet? Therefore, thus says the Lord God to them: Behold, I, I myself will judge between the fat sheep and the lean sheep. Because you push with side and shoulder, and thrust at all the weak with your horns, till you have scattered them abroad, I will save my flock, they shall no longer be a prey; *and I will judge between sheep and sheep.* (vv.17-22)

---

[5] Matthew 25:31-46 will build upon this premise as is evident in his use of "sheep and goats" that is reminiscent of "rams and he-goats" (Ezek 34:17).

Put otherwise, the covenant of peace (v.25) does not preclude divine judgment.

The Mountain of God

Before dealing with the restoration of "the mountains of Israel" (ch.36) that were heavily castigated at the start of the divine invective (ch.6) immediately after coverage of the siege of Jerusalem (chs.4-5), the author speaks against "Mount Seir" (ch.35). It is clear that Mount Seir is connected with Edom: "As you rejoiced over the inheritance of the house of Israel, because it was desolate, so I will deal with you; you shall be desolate, Mount Seir, and all Edom, all of it. Then they will know that I am the Lord." (v.15) Since Edom is reprimanded for the same sin of gloating (36:2) which was covered in 25:12-14, the only possible explanation for its use here is its function within chapter 35.

From the following two passages it is clear that Mount Seir is related to the divine mountain in Sinai where the Lord revealed himself:

> This is the blessing with which Moses the man of God blessed the children of Israel before his death. He said, "The Lord came from Sinai, and dawned from Seir upon us; he shone forth from Mount Paran, he came from the ten thousands of holy ones, with flaming fire at his right hand. Yea, he loved his people; all those consecrated to him were in his hand; so they followed in thy steps, receiving direction from thee, when Moses commanded us a law, as a possession for the assembly of Jacob..." (Deut 33:1-4)

> Hear, O kings; give ear, O princes; to the Lord I will sing, I will make melody to the Lord, the God of Israel. Lord, when thou didst go forth from Seir, when thou didst march from the region of Edom, the earth trembled, and the heavens dropped, yea, the

clouds dropped water. The mountains quaked before the Lord, yon Sinai before the Lord, the God of Israel. (Judg 5:3-5)

Given the parallelism between Seir and Paran in Deuteronomy 33:2, and what one learns from Habakkuk, Seir remains through scripture the traditional mount of divine epiphany:

> A prayer of Habakkuk the prophet, according to Shigionoth. O Lord, I have heard the report of thee, and thy work, O Lord, do I fear. In the midst of the years renew it; in the midst of the years make it known; in wrath remember mercy. God came from Teman, and the Holy One from Mount Paran. His glory covered the heavens, and the earth was full of his praise. Selah. His brightness was like the light, rays flashed from his hand; and there he veiled his power. Before him went pestilence, and plague followed close behind. He stood and measured the earth; he looked and shook the nations; then the eternal mountains were scattered, the everlasting hills sank low. His ways were as of old. (Hab 3:1-6)

An overview of the etymology of the named places will readily show that, except for Teman, all are associated with divine epiphany. The Hebrew *teman* means south and thus has a geographical connotation. It was used previously in Ezekiel with such meaning: "Son of man, set your face toward the south (*temanah*), preach against the south (*darom*), and prophesy against the forest land in the Negeb." (Ezek 20:46)[6]

The Hebrew *se'ir* is from the root *sa'ar* that connotes a dreadfulness causing trembling: "All the inhabitants of the

---

[6] See also later Ezek 47:19 (On the south side [*temanah*], it shall run from Tamar as far as the waters of Meribathkadesh, thence along the Brook of Egypt to the Great Sea. This shall be the south side [*temanah*]) and 48:28 (And adjoining the territory of Gad to the south [*temanah*], the boundary shall run from Tamar to the waters of Meribathkadesh, thence along the Brook of Egypt to the Great Sea).

coastlands are appalled at you; and their kings are horribly afraid (*sa'aru sa'ar*), their faces are convulsed" (27:35); "I will make many peoples appalled at you, and their kings shall shudder (*yis'aru sa'ar*) because of you, when I brandish my sword before them; they shall tremble every moment, every one for his own life, on the day of your downfall." (32:10) The Hebrew *pa'ran* is from *pa'ar* connoting glory; from that comes the noun *pe'er* which refers to an ornate headdress: "Sigh, but not aloud; make no mourning for the dead. Bind on your turban (*pe'er*), and put your shoes on your feet; do not cover your lips, nor eat the bread of mourners" … "Your turbans (*pe'erim*) shall be on your heads and your shoes on your feet; you shall not mourn or weep, but you shall pine away in your iniquities and groan to one another."[7] (24:17, 23)

The Hebrew *'edom* (*'adom*) is from the root *'dm* connoting the redness of the soil of the ground (*'adamah*). The classic text is found in Genesis:

> And the Lord said to her, "Two nations are in your womb, and two peoples, born of you, shall be divided; the one shall be stronger than the other, the elder shall serve the younger." When her days to be delivered were fulfilled, behold, there were twins in her womb. The first came forth red (*'admoni*), all his body like a hairy[8] mantle; so they called his name Esau. Afterward his brother came forth, and his hand had taken hold of Esau's heel; so his name was called Jacob. Isaac was sixty years old when she bore them. When the boys grew up, Esau was a skilful hunter, *a man of*

---

[7] See also later 44:18 (They shall have linen turbans [*pe'erim*] upon their heads, and linen breeches upon their loins; they shall not gird themselves with anything that causes sweat).

[8] The Hebrew for "hairy" is "of hair (*se'ar*)." In turn *se'ar* is from the same trilateral root *s'r* as *se'ir* (Seir), which further corroborates the intended scriptural connection between Esau/Edom and Mount Edom/Seir/Paran.

the field,⁹ while Jacob was a quiet man, dwelling in tents. Isaac loved Esau, because he ate of his game; but Rebekah loved Jacob. Once when Jacob was boiling pottage, Esau came in *from the field*, and he was famished. And Esau said to Jacob, "Let me eat some of that red pottage (*ha'adom ha'adom hazzeh*; the red, this red), for I am famished!" (Therefore his name was called Edom [*'edom*].) Jacob said, "First sell me your birthright." Esau said, "I am about to die; of what use is a birthright to me?" Jacob said, "Swear to me first." So he swore to him, and sold his birthright to Jacob. Then Jacob gave Esau bread and pottage of lentils,¹⁰ and he ate and drank, and rose and went his way. Thus Esau despised his birthright. (Gen 25:23-34)

The color red brings to mind both fire, mentioned in Deuteronomy 33:2, and blood/bloodshed which brings about death that is reflected in the reference to pestilence and plague in Habakkuk 3:5. All these features are linked to the situation of siege. In other words, whenever God appears, he does so as judge. By recalling that Esau and Jacob were twins, one can see the scriptural association between Edom and Israel—more specifically the mount of Seir and the mountains of Israel (Ezek 35 and 36)—when it comes to the divine final judgment. However, the same God, who comes in the "redness" of his wrath and fury to chastise his people, can also come in his gracefulness to put an end to that same "redness" by making "desolate, Mount Seir, and all Edom, *all of it* (*kullah*)" (35:15) in order to reestablish "the mountains of Israel" (ch.36:1-8) and, upon them, "the whole house of Israel, *all of it* (*kulloh*)" (v.10).

---

⁹ The "field" brings to mind the ground (*'adamah*): "... when no plant of the *field* was yet in the earth and no herb of the *field* had yet sprung up -- for the Lord God had not caused it to rain upon the earth, and there was no man (*'adam*) to till the ground (*'adamah*)." (Gen 2:5)

¹⁰ Consequently, the "red" Esau was referring to in v.30 is nothing else than the product of the "ground" (*'adamah*), bread and lentils (v.34).

One is not, however, to understand that Ezekiel is referring to the same "old" mountains on which abominations were perpetrated (ch.6), but rather God's "new" and "one" mountain:

> As for you, O house of Israel, thus says the Lord God: Go serve every one of you his idols, now and hereafter, if you will not listen to me; but my holy name you shall no more profane with your gifts and your idols. For on my holy mountain, the mountain height of Israel, says the Lord God, there all the house of Israel, *all of them* (*kulloh*; all of it), shall serve me in the land; there I will accept them, and there I will require your contributions and the choicest of your gifts, with all your sacred offerings. (20:39-40)

Such is evident not only in the reminder of the previous sins of the house of Israel described in 36:16-23, but also in that the terminology of these verses is reminiscent of chapter 20:

> So I poured out my wrath upon them for the blood which they had shed in the land, for the idols with which they had defiled it. I scattered them among the nations, and they were dispersed through the countries; in accordance with their conduct and their deeds I judged them. But when they came to the nations, wherever they came, they profaned my holy name, in that men said of them, "These are the people of the Lord, and yet they had to go out of his land." But I had concern for my holy name, which the house of Israel caused to be profaned among the nations to which they came. Therefore say to the house of Israel, Thus says the Lord God: It is not for your sake, O house of Israel, that I am about to act, but for the sake of my holy name, which you have profaned among the nations to which you came. And I will vindicate the holiness of my great name, which has been profaned among the nations, and which you have profaned among them; and the nations will know that I am the Lord, says the Lord God, when through you I vindicate my holiness before their eyes. (36:18-23)

The ultimate aim of the divine mercy is to shame the house of Israel, which is a refrain in Ezekiel: "It is not for your sake that I will act, says the Lord God; let that be known to you. Be ashamed and confounded for your ways, O house of Israel." (v.32)

It is precisely this scriptural approach to the "graceful end" that explains the reference to Mount Seir (ch.35) as a preamble to the restoration of the mountain of Israel (ch.36). This is corroborated in that immediately following these two chapters we hear of the raising of the dry bones and the reunification of Samaria and Jerusalem under the leadership of the new David, which recalls the ending of chapter 34. The following extra features confirm that chapters 35 and 36 are fittingly inserted between chapters 34 and 37:

1. In his chastening of Edom God refers to two wronged nations instead of one (35:10-11) in preparation for 37:15-28.

2. The repeated reference to animal as well as agricultural fruitfulness (36:8, 11, 30) is reflective of the divine blessing mentioned in both 34:26-27 and 37:26.

3. In spite of the mention of deserted cities (36:4) and those inhabited anew (36:10, 33, 35, 38), the concluding verses reference "flock" three times, and the passage ends with a fourth instance underscoring that the urban dwellers themselves will be a "flock": "Thus says the Lord God: This also I will let the house of Israel ask me to do for them: to increase their men like a flock. Like the flock for sacrifices, like the flock at

Jerusalem during her appointed feasts, so shall the waste cities be filled with flocks[11] of men. Then they will know that I am the Lord." (vv.37-38) One cannot miss the intended link to chapters 34 and 37.

---

[11] The Hebrew has the singular *ṣo'n 'adam* (human flock) preserving the connotation of oneness. RSV's "flocks of men" reflect merely the quantity, glossing over the oneness, and is thus misleading.

21
God and Gog of Magog

The Ezekelian story culminates in chapter 37. Israel is restored out of dry bones (vv.1-14),[1] and both its houses are handed over to the care of the "shepherd" David (vv.15-28).[2] At this point one would expect the book to move to the description of the new Jerusalem and its temple (chs.40-48); however, Ezekiel takes another aside in chapters 38 and 39. Since these two chapters are "appended" to the preceding one, all three chapters are to be read in tandem.

The function of chapter 37 is to reverse the Davidic story in the Books of Samuel (1 Sam 16-2 Sam 24). There David, a humble shepherd and the youngest of his siblings, used a sling, a shepherd's weapon, to slay the Philistine champion Goliath and brought victory to his people (1 Sam 17). Later when he became a king, he tried to consolidate a kingdom through endless intrigues and wars. His dream of a peaceful kingdom would never be fulfilled due to his own sins and those of his progeny. It is precisely those kings who are the object of God's harsh judgment in Ezekiel 34. In chapters 34 and 37, God reverses the trajectory by eliminating kingship altogether. Through the "shepherd" David (37:24), he re-establishes his rule over his people under a divine covenant of peace (v.26). The confirmation that a shepherd would be ruler is reflected in that God's sanctuary (*miqdaš*; vv.26, 28, a term connoting a building) will be a simple dwelling place (*miškan*, from the verb *šakan*

---

[1] See pp.46-47 and 79-81.
[2] See pp.146-47, 229, and 267.

[abide, dwell, reside];³ v.27) reflecting a shepherd's abode. Notice how the divine sanctuary is said to be "in the midst of them" (vv.26, 28) while the same abode as "dwelling place" will be "over them *('alehem)*"⁴ (v.27a) as a tent covering. Moreover, it is precisely in this context that we are told "and I will be their God, and they shall be my people" (v.27b). God will establish his "everlasting covenant" of peace (v.26) in the domain of the new David which will be an open pasture with no defensive walls. A lexical overview of chapters 38-39 will show that they are filled with terms that recapitulate Ezekiel's message and bring the Ezekelian story to its conclusion. The hearers are then invited to enter, through Ezekiel's "visions of God" (40:2), into the new Jerusalem around God's new "house" rather than "temple" (chs.40-48).⁵

In order to validate his point, the author devises an Iliad style showdown in chapters 38-39. It functions as "proof" that God's power, which appears to be tenuous at best, is actually mightier than the ominous armies of Gog. After this show of might, God the judge of all will be recognized by all the nations (39:21). The hearers can "see" through their ears that God's design will pass the final test with flying colors, just as he had made the shepherd David win the battle against the consummate warrior Goliath. Although David's name appears meteorically in chapters 34 (vv.23, 24) and 37 (vv.24, 25), it will not show up again in the book. The ultimate battle is God's alone and, in Ezekiel, glory belongs exclusively to God.

---

³ This root was taken over by Greek to refer to a tent (the noun *skēnē*) as well as to pitching a tent (the verb *skēnō*).
⁴ And not "with them" as in RSV.
⁵ See my comments below on those chapters.

The three geographical areas Magog, Meshech, and Tubal mentioned in 38:2 occur together in the twin texts Genesis 10:2 and 1 Chronicles 1:5, where they are presented as "sons of Japheth": "The sons of Japheth: Gomer, Magog, Madai, Javan (Heb *yawan*), Tubal, Meshech, and Tiras." That Ezekiel 38:2 had in mind "sons of Japheth" is evident since a few verses later he refers to Gomer and his son Togarmah's "house"[6] (v.6), and Tarshish (v.13) who is a son of Javan (Gen 10:4). In an earlier invective against Tyre, the queen city of the Mediterranean, we heard of Tarshish (27:12) and the triad of "Javan, Tubal, and Meshech" (v.13) just as it appears in Genesis 10:2, and of Togarmah's "house" (Ezek 27:14). Given the commercial link of all these names with Tyre, one can deduce that they refer to Mediterranean Sea nations or cities, especially that later Magog is linked with the "coastlands" (39:6) that were repeatedly referred to in conjunction with Tyre (26:15; 27:3, 15, 35). In the LXX, Javan, the central name in the list of the seven "sons of Japheth" (Gen 10:2), is associated with the Greeks (Hellenes); in the LXX translation of Ezekiel 27:13 Javan is translated into "Greece" (*hē Hellas*).[7] Such fits with the express qualification of Meshech and Tubal, Javan's "brothers," as "uncircumcised" in Ezekiel 32:26. The "Hellenes" (*Hellēnes*; Greeks) in 1 and 2 Maccabees[8] and in the New Testament are the uncircumcised Gentiles par excellence. So the universal onslaught against God's people is purposely presented as run by the "uncircumcised" in view of the

---

[6] I purposely kept the literal translation of the Hebrew *bet togarmah* in lieu of RSV's Bethtogarmah in order to show the connection intended in the original with Genesis and 1 Chronicles where Togarmah is one of Gomer's sons: "The sons of Gomer: Ashkenaz, Riphath, and Togarmah." (Gen 10:3; 1 Chr 1:6)

[7] The same translation occurs also in Isaiah 66:19. In Joel 4.6, Zech 9:13, and Dan 8:21; 10:20; 11:2 we have *Hellēnes* (Hellenes, Greeks) for the Hebrew *yawan* (Javan).

[8] 1 Macc 1:15, 48, 60-61; 2:46 ; 2 Macc 6:10.

upcoming harsh comments concerning the "uncircumcised in heart and flesh":

> And say to the rebellious house, to the house of Israel, Thus says the Lord God: O house of Israel, let there be an end to all your abominations, in admitting foreigners, uncircumcised in heart and flesh, to be in my sanctuary, profaning it, when you offer to me my food, the fat and the blood. *You have broken my covenant*, in addition to all your abominations. And you have not kept charge of my holy things; but you have set foreigners to keep my charge in my sanctuary. Therefore thus says the Lord God: No foreigner, uncircumcised in heart and flesh, of all the foreigners who are among the people of Israel, shall enter my sanctuary. (Ezek 44:6-8)

The reference to "covenant" in 44:7 is its only instance after that in 37:26 which introduced the universal battle described in chapters 38-39. Consequently, by defending his new "dwelling" against the "uncircumcised" God is upholding his everlasting covenant.

This, in turn, explains in part why the chief enemy is introduced thrice as "chief prince of Meshech and Tubal" (38:2, 3; 39:1). The question that remains is why the author chose the two names Meshech and Tubal over the names of the other "sons of Japheth," particularly that of Javan. Furthermore, why are they not put in the order found in Genesis 10:2 or 1 Chronicles 1:5 where Tubal precedes Meshech, particularly since Ezekiel did use "Javan, Tubal, and Meshech" in 27:13, which is precisely the order found in Genesis and 1 Chronicles? Why did he switch to "Meshech and Tubal" in Ezekiel 32:26, at the end of the oracles against the nations, and continue to use this sequence in the following section (chs.33-39)? Add to this the phrase "chief prince" (*neśi' ro'š*) that occurs in scripture only in

Ezekiel 38:2-3 and 39:1. One should include in the same debate the oddity "the land of Magog," which in the original Hebrew is "the land of *the* Magog" (*'ereṣ hammagog*). This phrase appears in 38:2 in conjunction with "Meshech and Tubal" then disappears totally, although Magog is one of "the sons of Japheth," and in spite of the fact that (1) it is assonant with Gog that reoccurs with "Meshech and Tubal" in 38:3 and 39:1 and (2) it is brought up again in 38:6.

The best point of departure for understanding these peculiarities is "the land of *the* Magog," chiefly because of its apparent incongruence; indeed, it *seems* an afterthought when one considers that it intervenes between "Gog" and "chief prince of Meshech and Tubal" (38:2) that occur in immediate sequence in 38:3 and 39:1. Due to its "intervening" position, many translations, including the LXX and the Vulgate, assumed it is appositional to Gog and thus considered that the prophetic address was aimed at Gog *and* the land of Magog. On the other hand, even the translations that take it as a noun complement to Gog ("Gog, of the land of Magog" as in RSV) do not account either for the definite article "the" before Magog or for the fact that nowhere else in scripture do we find the name of a monarch or leader followed by the name of his "land" as noun complement. Other than in the lists of Genesis and 1 Chronicles in the Old Testament, Magog is encountered only in Ezekiel 38:2 and 39:6, and its occurrence in 39:6 is concomitant with the only instance of "coastlands" in Ezekiel outside chapters 26 and 27.

When listening to 38:2, the hearer is immediately aware of the assonance of Magog with Gog, the main character in the next two chapters (eight instances). Magog's unexpected introduction may well be behind the equally unexpected addition of the definite article before the name since it draws attention to the intended link between Gog and Magog. In the Old Testament, except for 1 Chronicles 5:4 where it appears in a lengthy genealogy (vv.4-6), the name "Gog" is restricted to Ezekiel 38 and 39. If one hears the name Gog (*gog*) as a wordplay on its Hebrew root *gag* meaning roof or top slab, then the rest of the unusual Ezekiel 38:2 begins to make sense. Such a connection is not farfetched since that noun is not unknown to Ezekiel who uses it twice in 40:13: "Then he measured the gate from the back (*gag*; roof) of the one side room to the back (*gag*; roof) of the other, a breadth of five and twenty cubits, from door to door." Gog is someone whose rule "covers," as a roof, not only the entire realm of the "sons of Japheth" represented by Gog, Meshech and Tubal (38:2), Gomer and Togarmah's "house" (v.6), Tarshish (v. 13), but also that of the sons of Ham represented by Cush and Put (v.5; see Gen 10:6), and Sheba and Dedan (Ezek 38:13), Cush's grandsons (Gen 10:7), and even the sons of Shem if one considers Persia (Ezek 38:5) as equivalent to Elam, as may well be the case since the latter is mentioned in 27:10 together with Lud, both of whom are "sons of Ham" (Gen 10:22). Be that as it may, the general impression is that Gog's rule "covers" the universal realm of the human being (*'adam*). This functional understanding of the name Gog is corroborated in that the specific choice of the pair Meshech and Tubal from the list of the sons of Japheth is meant to be a shortened reference for the entire realm of Gog. The verb *mašak* (from the same root *mšk* as *mešek* [Meshech]) means "draw out, stretch out" and *tubal* (Tubal) is from the same root *tbl* as the noun *tebel* that means "inhabited earth, habitation." To the hearer's ear, taken together they fit the context perfectly: Gog's rule stretches over the entire human realm. Just as *gag*, the verb *mašak* is part of Ezekiel's vocabulary: "But I the Lord will speak the word which I will speak, and it will be performed. It will no longer be delayed (*timmašek*), but in your days, O rebellious house, I will speak the word and perform it, says the Lord God ... Therefore say to them, Thus says the Lord God: None of my words will be delayed (*timmašek*) any longer, but the word which I speak will be performed, says the Lord God" (12:25, 28); "They shall fall amid those who are slain by the sword, and with her shall lie (*mašeku*) all her multitudes." (32:20) The broad expanse of Gog's rule over the entire orb explains why he is called the "chief prince" (38:2; 39:1), which is a unique instance in scripture. The original Hebrew is even more impressive since *neśi' ro'š* means "the prince of the head" lending thus to the entire phrase *neśi' ro'š mešek wetubal* the denotation of "the prince of the leader[s] of Meshech and Tubal," that is, the "overlord of all earthly leaders."

Obviously the choice of the made up name Gog was intended to be consonant with Magog in order to draw the hearer's attention to the wordplay. But then one might ask why not opt for Gomer, the name of Japheth's first son, and make up a corresponding name. The first part of the answer to such a question is, "This is the text we have and we need to explain what we have." The question then becomes, "Why did the author do what he did?" There is a reason for choosing Magog over Gomer, although Gomer was definitely in the author's purview since a few verses later he and his youngest son Togarmah[9] are brought into the picture: "Gomer and all his hordes; Bethtogarmah from the uttermost parts of the north with all his hordes—many peoples are with you." (38:6). In order to create assonance with Gomer, the author would have had to name the leader *mer* which has the connotation of

---

[9] See fn. 6 above.

"bitterness." This would not have fit the context of the message, nor would it have allowed the author to use the two other brothers, Meshech and Tubal, to form an interrelated triad. Using Gog allowed him to bring a third brother, Magog, into the picture. Since the numeral three reflects plurality and thus totality, having three brothers brings to mind the totality of Japheth's progeny. The addition of the definite article before the personal name Magog makes out of it a generic name of a people and allowed the author to introduce before *hammagog* (the Magog[ite]) *'ereṣ* (the land [earth] of), expressing thus the idea of a realm (Gog of the land of the Magog[ite]) encompassing all Magogites, that is, those pertaining to the family of Magog and, by extension, Japheth. This, in turn, corroborates the understanding of *gog* in conjunction with *mešek* and *tubal*. Thus "Gog, of the land of [the] Magog, the chief prince of Meshech and Tubal," which in the original is very strange at face value, does make sense.

In spite of all his might Gog is referred to as a prince rather than king (38:2, 3; 39:9) and so are his chief allies (39:18), thus reminding the hearer that God is sole king. Still Gog's might is impressive since his hordes are likened twice to a "cloud" (38:9, 16) analogous to the divine cloud in chapter 1. However, Gog's scheme is evil (v.10)—he is coming to destroy the people (v.16) whom the Lord had just made his (37:27). The link between these two events is confirmed in that God will destroy Gog's armies with the same *ra'aš* (shaking: 38:19) he used to raise the dry bones (*ra'aš*; rattling, 37:7) and turn them into his people. These instances are the last occurrences of *ra'aš* in Ezekiel. It is further interesting to note that the terminology of 38:10 in Hebrew is identical to that of Genesis 6:

> The Lord saw that the wickedness (*ra'ah*) of man (*ha'adam*) was great in the earth, and that every imagination of the thoughts (*maḥšebot*; plural of *maḥašabah*) of his heart (*leb*) was only evil (*ra'*) continually. (Gen 6:5)
>
> Thus says the Lord God: On that day thoughts will come into your mind (*leb*; heart), and you will devise (*ḥašabta*) an evil (*ra'ah*) scheme (*maḥašabah*). (Ezek 38:10)

One cannot miss the intended connection. In both cases, it is the universalism of the evil that is underscored, which explains the radical divine response. Furthermore, God's equity is reflected in his evenhandedness when requiting the ill doers, whether it is his own city Jerusalem or the hordes of Gog; in either case it is the same punishment:

> Thus shall my anger spend itself, and I will vent my fury (*ḥemah*) upon them and satisfy myself; and they shall know that I, the Lord, have spoken in my jealousy (*qin'ah*), when I spend my fury (*ḥemah*) upon them ... I will send famine and wild beasts against you, and they will rob you of your children; pestilence (*deber*) and blood (*dam*) shall pass through you; and I will bring the sword upon you ... There will be a deluge of rain (*gešem šoṭeph*), great hailstones (*'abne 'elgabiš*) will fall, and a stormy wind break out; (5:13, 17; 13:11)
>
> But on that day, when Gog shall come against the land of Israel, says the Lord God, my wrath (*ḥemah*) will be roused. For in my jealousy (*qin'ah*) and in my blazing wrath I declare, On that day there shall be a great shaking in the land of Israel ... With pestilence (*deber*) and bloodshed (*dam*) I will enter into judgment with him; and I will rain upon him and his hordes and the many

peoples that are with him, torrential rains (*gešem šoṭeph*) and hailstones (*'abne 'elgabiš*), fire and brimstone.[10] (38:18-19, 22)

In all that, God has total control over the situation. Not only does he send Ezekiel to speak to Gog face to face (v.14), but Gog's plans had been foreseen long ago by God's prophets (v.17). And, once more, the ultimate object is that all nations would recognize God as the sole monarch: "So I will show my greatness and my holiness and make myself known in the eyes of many nations. Then they will know that I am the Lord." (v.23)

Chapter 39 describes the universal peace (vv.7-10) that will be established after the destruction of all the forces opposing God's plans (vv.1-6). The terminology here parallels that of Isaiah:

> He shall judge between the nations, and shall decide for many peoples; and they shall beat their swords into plowshares, and their spears into pruning hooks; nation shall not lift up sword against nation, neither shall they learn war any more. (Is 2:4)

> Then those who dwell in the cities of Israel will go forth and make fires of the weapons and burn them, shields and bucklers, bows and arrows, handpikes and spears, and they will make fires of them for seven years; so that they will not need to take wood out of the field or cut down any out of the forests, for they will make their fires of the weapons; they will despoil those who despoiled them, and plunder those who plundered them, says the Lord God. (Ezek 39:9-10)

As we have seen all along in this odyssey, Ezekiel plays on important terms. Since the "mountains of Israel" have center stage in God's victory over Gog (vv.2, 4), the author revisits a

---

[10] "Fire and brimstone" denotes total destruction as in the case of Sodom (19:24).

noun he used in his invective against those mountains in chapter 6: "On that day I will give to Gog a place for burial in Israel, the Valley (*gay'*) of the Travelers (*'oberim*) east of the sea; it will block the travelers, for there Gog and all his multitude (*hamon*) will be buried; it will be called the Valley (*gay'*) of Hamon-gog." (39:11). One sees here how the noun *gay'* that means "valley" and whose root also connotes "arrogance," which was introduced in chapter 6 in the diatribe against the mountains of Israel,[11] is brought into the picture through its double use in 39:11. It appears once more in v.15, to speak of a valley (*gay'*) that is filled with the dead bodies of Gog's warriors. Both of the valley's names are functional. *hamon gog* means the multitude of Gog, reflecting the size of his hordes; indeed, it would take seven months to bury their corpses (vv.12-13); *'oberim* (passers through, travelers) identifies any one passing through, and should a traveler find an exposed corpse, after the initial seven months of burying corpses, he would have to report it in order for it to be buried (vv.14-15). The rationale is given twice: the land is to be cleansed (vv.12 and 16) from the dead bodies that are "impure" (e.g. Lev 21:11: Num 6:6). The burial city would be known as *hamonah* (Ezek 39:16), the city of the *hamon* (multitude).

This lengthy dealing with the corpses of Gog's armies prepares for 43:7-9 where we shall hear that the bodies of the dead kings of Judah would defile God's land. In Ezekiel, any king, whether Judahite or Gentile, is an object of loathing. As was stressed in Deuteronomy 17:14-20 the scriptural Israel is not to be ruled by kings but by God's law, and what applies to Israel applies equally to the nations. That is why the goal of God's action of cleansing is double pronged:

---

[11] See earlier my comments on chapter 6.

The house of Israel shall know that I am the Lord their God, from that day forward. *And the nations shall know* that the house of Israel went into captivity for their iniquity, because they dealt so treacherously with me that I hid my face from them and gave them into the hand of their adversaries, and they all fell by the sword. I dealt with them according to their uncleanness and their transgressions, and hid my face from them. (Ezek 39:22-24)

This knowledge is the outcome of the implementation of God's *mišpaṭ*, justice through his judgment imbedded in his ordinance, which is to be found in his law made of statutes and ordinances: "And I will set my glory among the nations; and all the nations shall see my judgment (*mišpaṭ*) which I have executed, and my hand which I have laid on them." (v.21) This statement rejoins the book's overture in chapters 1-3 where the glory of God expressed in the written scroll handed to Ezekiel will prove to be greater than its stony place (3:12)[12] and God will move away from it (v.13) in order to settle at Chebar (ch.10) "among the nations."[13]

The closing statement of the first part of the book (39:25-29) is, the least to say, unexpected to the ears of those living in our contemporary Western society as well as to the ears trained in classical theology. So it would be worth covering these verses in some detail:

Therefore thus says the Lord God: Now I will restore (*'ašib*; from the root *šub* [turn, return]) the fortunes (*šebut*) of Jacob, and have mercy upon (*riḥamti*) the whole house of Israel; and I will be jealous (*qinne'ti*) for my holy name. They shall carry[14] (*wenasu*)

---

[12] See my comments on this verse that is mistranslated in RSV.
[13] Later Paul will follow suit by planting Christ among the nations (Col 1:27) through his communicating to them the teachings of the Law (Rom 1:1-2).
[14] RSV and other translations have "forget."

their shame, and all the treachery they have practiced against me, when they dwell securely (*labeṭaḥ*; trustfully, confidently) in their land (*'adamah*; ground) with none to make them afraid, when I have brought them back (*šobebi*; from the root *šub* [turn, return]) from the peoples and gathered them from their enemies' lands (*'arṣot* [plural of *'ereṣ*]; earths), and through them have vindicated my holiness (*niqdašti*; have been sanctified) in the sight of many nations. Then they shall know that I am the Lord their God because I sent them into exile among the nations, and then gathered them into their[15] land (*'adamah*; ground). I will leave none of them remaining among the nations there[16] (*šam*); and I will not hide my face any more (*'od*; again) from them, when I pour out my Spirit (*ruaḥ*) upon the house of Israel, says the Lord God. (Ezek 39:25-29)

The phrase "restore fortunes" (v. 25a) is not reserved to the three sisters, Samaria, Sodom, and Jerusalem, since it applies as well to Egypt (29:14). However what is remarkable here is the second part of 39:25 "[I will] have mercy upon (*riḥamti*) the whole house of Israel; and I will be jealous (*qinne'ti*) for my holy name" which links in one breath two contradicting statements by our standards—one of total "altruism" and the other of extreme "self-centeredness." In this verse 25 we have the only instance of mercy[17] in Ezekiel, and in order to understand the "paradox" of this verse one would have to follow the itinerary of God's jealousy to see how it becomes the source of his mercy. The

---

[15] RSV adds here an unwarranted "own."
[16] RSV has "anymore" instead.
[17] The only apparent exception is *reḥem* in Ezek 20:26 where it means "womb." RSV's "first-born" is the translation of the original *peṭer raḥam* that literally means "opener of the womb." My readers should not worry about the difference in sound between *reḥem* and *raḥam* since, as I often remind them, in Hebrew it is the consonants that count. A close parallel in English would be the triad "break, broke, broken" that are connected through the consonantal root *b-r-k*.

intent of the people's disregard of God's "seat of jealousy," that is, his throne of judgment (8:3), is to drive him away (vv.5-6) from such position. This disregard will result in his releasing his wrath upon them (5:13; 16:38) through the nations (23:25). Furthermore, he will make his "jealousy depart" from them (16:42) and settle at Chebar, "among the nations." There he will be able to watch those nations and through his jealousy will produce a *ra'aš* (quaking; 38:19) to punish their arrogance (35:11-12; 36:5-6) just as he did with the house of Israel (12:18). It is through the same "jealousy" that he will "restore the fortunes of Jacob," which is the expression of his "mercy upon the whole house of Israel" (39:25).

It is God's scattering (*šebut*) his people as punishment for their obstinacy that allowed him to turn around (*'ašib*) their misfortune and bring them back (*šobebi*) *in his mercy* from the "earths" of the nations to the "ground" where he will pasture them (vv.26, 28). By so doing, all the nations will know that God's plan was unfolding all along and that he never lost his "grip" (*ḥazaq*), thus vindicating his holiness before their eyes (v.27). In the meantime, that whole house of Israel will have learned to *carry* its "shame" (v.26)[18] before those same eyes. In order to secure that such a horrendous "burden" not be cast off by them, God will pour his spirit (v.29) upon them this time round instead of his wrath (9:8; 14:19; 20:8, 13, 21; 22:22). However, this pouring of the spirit is not an end in itself as, unfortunately, it is usually taken to mean. Rather its goal is to "control" for good, *with the same divine "grip,"* the house of Israel "so that they may walk in my statutes and keep my ordinances and obey them; and they shall be my people, and I

---

[18] Translations try to smooth out this difficulty by opting for "forget" instead of "carry," a matter I discussed earlier on pp.256-7.

will be their God." (11:20). This makes perfect sense in the Ezekelian scheme of things given that the pouring of the divine wrath was actually *loosening* that same grip and letting go of the people, "departing" from them (16:42). That the spirit is indeed a controlling, rather than "liberating," factor is corroborated in 40:1-2 that throw the hearers back to where the book started:

> In the thirtieth year, in the fourth month, on the fifth day of the month, as I was among the exiles by the river Chebar, the heavens were opened, and I saw *visions of God*. On the fifth day of the month (it was the fifth year of the exile of King Jehoiachin), the word of the Lord came to Ezekiel the priest, the son of Buzi, in the land of the Chaldeans by the river Chebar; and *the hand of the Lord was upon him* there. (1:1-3)

> In the twenty-fifth year of our exile, at the beginning of the year, on the tenth day of the month, in the fourteenth year after the city was conquered, on that very day, *the hand of the Lord was upon me*, and brought me in the *visions of God* into the land of Israel, and set me down upon a very high mountain, on which was a structure like a city opposite me. (40:1-2)

That the ending of chapter 39 and the beginning of chapter 40 are to be heard in tandem is evident in the original Hebrew through the adverb "there" (*šam[mah]*) which, on the one hand, is reminiscent of the start of the book and, on the other hand, looks ahead to its closure:

> … the word of the Lord came to Ezekiel the priest, the son of Buzi, in the land of the Chaldeans by the river Chebar; and the hand of the Lord was upon him *there* (*šam*). (1:3)

> Then they shall know that I am the Lord their God because I sent them into exile among the nations, and then gathered them into

their land. I will leave none of them remaining among the nations *there* (*šam*). (39:28)

In the twenty-fifth year of our exile, at the beginning of the year, on the tenth day of the month, in the fourteenth year after the city was conquered, on that very day, the hand of the Lord was upon me *there* (*šammah*).[19] (40:1)

And the name of the city henceforth shall be, The Lord is *there* (*šammah*). (48:35b)

---

[19] Which is omitted in RSV.

Part IV

The New Jerusalem

22
The New Jerusalem

Chapters 40-48 describing the new Jerusalem that is restored according to God's will opens with a precise dating (40:1). All of the previous instances of dating in the book were done in conjunction with an announcement of divine punishment against Israel (1:1-2; 8:1; 20:1; 24:1; 33:21) or against the nations (26:1; 29:1, 17; 30:20; 31:1; 32:1, 17). Here we have the first dating that inaugurates the new era, and picks up where the previous one left off:

> In the twelfth year of *our exile*, in the tenth month, on the fifth day of the month, a man who had escaped from Jerusalem came to me and said, "*The city has fallen* (*hukketah ha'ir*; the city was struck down)." (33:21)

> In the twenty-fifth year of *our exile*, at the beginning of the year, on the tenth day of the month, in the fourteenth year after *the city was conquered* (*hukketah ha'ir*; the city was struck down), on that very day, the hand of the Lord was upon me, and brought me in the visions of God into the land of Israel, and set me down upon a very high mountain, on which was a structure like a city opposite me. (40:1-2)

However, beyond this connection with the previous section (chs.33-39), Ezekiel 40:1-2 harks back to the beginning of the book itself, again through the use of similar phraseology:

> In the thirtieth year, in the fourth month, on the fifth day of the month, as I was among the exiles by the river Chebar, the heavens were opened, and I saw *visions of God* ... the word of the Lord came to Ezekiel the priest, the son of Buzi, in the land of the

Chaldeans by the river Chebar; and *the hand of the Lord was upon him* there. (1:1, 3)

And he said to me, 'Son of man, I send you to the people of Israel, to a nation of rebels, who have rebelled against me; they and their fathers have transgressed against me to *this very day.*' (2:3)

Moreover, in 40:3 we find the use of appearance (*mar'eh*),[1] a term that is a staple of chapter 1. So, the section of the book announcing the new city on a very high mountain (40:2) brings to mind the earlier content of the book and prepares the hearers for the ending of the book's odyssey that culminates with only one city in the new order whose name is "the Lord is there" (48:35b).

As in the case of the divine chariot in chapter 1 where Ezekiel alone was privy to the "visions" he was asked to communicate to his "hearers" through uttered words, also here in the matter of the description of God's new temple he is told: "Son of man, look with your eyes, and hear with your ears, and set your mind (*leb*; heart, core) upon all that I shall show you, for you were brought here in order that I might show it to you; *declare* (*higgid*; retell [in detail]) all that you see to the house of Israel." (40:4) To ensure that Ezekiel would not give his own take on those "visions," he is commanded not only to "look with your eyes" but also to "*hear with your ears.*" Since conveying the divine aural communication entails explaining what is seen, the prophet is

---

[1] In Hebrew the listener actually hears again that same sound *mar'eh* in the following v.4. In this case, *mar'eh* is the active participle of the *hiph'il* form *hir'eh*—of the verb *ra'ah* (see)—whose meaning is "make see" and thus the participle means "one who shows, makes see": "And the man said to me, 'Son of man, look with your eyes, and hear with your ears, and set your mind upon all that I *shall show* (*mar'eh*; am showing; am about to show) you, for you were brought here in order that I might show it to you; declare all that you see to the house of Israel."

The New Jerusalem 331

not simply to hear with his ears, but also and more importantly, to understand with his "mind," the Hebrew *leb* (heart, core). Such is corroborated from the previous two occurrences of the verb *higgid* in the book: "And the people said to me, 'Will you not tell (*higgid*) us what these things mean for us, that you are acting thus?'" (24:19); "And when your people say to you, 'Will you not show (*higgid*) us what you mean by these?'" (37:18) The meaning of the verb *higgid* in Ezekiel is sealed in that its two other instances refer to "abominations" (23:36 where the verb is translated as "declare") and "iniquities" (43:10 where the verb is rendered as "describe") since these two "sins" need to be explained, or at least documented, to the hearers.

This aural communication of prophetic "visions" accounts for the tediously detailed description of God's new abode (40:5-42:20; 43:13-27) and of its function (44:1-47:12). The people do not have the luxury of "seeing" the structure as Ezekiel does; they can only "hear" it described to them. Thus the "reality" of that which is communicated in scripture—including God himself who always remains *unseen* for the hearer of scripture—is never "out there" but always a reality circum*scribed* in and within *scripture*. This will be stated without ambivalence at the closing of canonical scripture:

> I warn (*martyrō*; witness, bear testimony to) every one who hears the words of the prophecy of this book: if any one adds to them, God will add to him *the plagues described* (*gegrammenas*; written, *inscribed*, from the verb *graphō* of the same root as *graphē* [scripture]) *in this book*, and if any one takes away from the words of the book of this prophecy, God will take away his share in *the tree of life and in the holy city, which are described* (*gegrammenōn*; written, *inscribed*) *in this book*. (Rev 22:18-19)

This passage actually forms an *inclusio* with the book's introduction, corroborating the fact that the view imparted in it is not a passing whim on the author's part but rather an essential thought:

> The revelation of Jesus Christ, which God gave him to show to his servants what must soon take place; and he made it known by sending his angel to his servant John, who *bore witness* (*emartyrēsen*; from the verb *martyrō*) to the word of God and to the *testimony* (*martyria*; from the same root as *martyrō*) of Jesus Christ, even to *all that he saw*. Blessed is he who *reads aloud the words of the prophecy*, and blessed are those who *hear*, and who keep what is *written* (*gegrammena*; inscribed) therein; for the time is near. (1:1-3)

In Ezekiel, what is seen only by the seer is communicated through *written* (scripturalized) words to be read aloud so that the recipients can *hear* them. The importance of Revelation for our discussion of Ezekiel lies in that the Book of Revelation is systematically and conspicuously permeated with Ezekelian phraseology as well as metaphors. Consequently, the temple, just as God himself, is communicated exclusively through the prophetic words read aloud and thus perceived exclusively aurally.

This being the case, one cannot miss that it is specifically the "sons of Zadok" (40:46) who are to be the chief priests of the divine altar where God-pleasing sacrifices are to be offered. The mention of Zadok runs as a crimson thread throughout the entire last part of the book (43:19; 44:15; 48:11), culminating with the statement: "This [allotment] shall be for the consecrated priests, the sons of Zadok (*ṣadoq*), who kept my charge, who did not go astray when the people of Israel went astray, as the Levites did." (48:11) The importance of the name *ṣadoq* is that its root *ṣedeq* means "righteousness," and thus denotes someone who does what is righteous in God's eyes. Since the ultimate scope of Ezekiel's mission as a watchman for Israel is to call each and every one to be righteous (3:16-21; 14:12-23; 18:1-32; 33:1-20), the "sons of Zadok" function as the prototypes of those who abide by the prophetic summons and thus are the "closest" to God; they can be in his presence on his "seat of jealousy" without having to worry about being struck by the "jealous" God. Thus, one can still feel the purge that was initiated at the divine intervention in Babylon (20:38) reverberating on God's "holy mountain" (20:40) where there will be a differentiation within the rank of the "Levites," the temple servers, themselves:

> But the *Levites* (*lewiyyim*) who went far from me, going astray from me after their idols when Israel went astray, shall bear their punishment *('awon*; guilt) ... They shall not come near to me, to serve me as priest, nor come near any of my sacred things and the things that are most sacred; but they shall bear their shame, because of the abominations which they have committed. Yet I will appoint them to keep charge of the temple, to do all its service (*'abodah*) and all that is to be done in it. But the *Levitical* (*lewiyyim*) *priests*, the sons of Zadok, who kept the charge of my sanctuary when the people of Israel went astray from me, shall come near to me to minister to me; and they shall attend on me to offer me the fat and the blood, says the Lord God; they shall enter my sanctuary, and they shall approach my table, to minister to me, and they shall keep my charge. (44:10, 13-16)

The "punishment" of the Levites is reflected in the noun *'abodah* used to speak of their "service," which noun and its cognate verb *'abad* occur frequently in scripture in reference to the slavery in Egypt or Babylon. Earlier in Ezekiel we heard God saying "and they shall know that I am the Lord, when I break the bars of their yoke, and deliver them from the hand of those who enslaved (*'obedim*) them" (34:27b).

The Temple Building and Its Law

In scripture, the temple building is referred to either as *bayt* (house) or as *hekal* (structure). This latter term is used also to speak of a palace. RSV, like many other translations, renders both terms as "temple" in Ezekiel and thus blurs the distinction and, by the same token, the intentional choice of one over the other. *hekal* is restricted to 8:16 (twice) and chapters 41 (seven times) and 42 (once). In 8:16 we hear: "And he brought me into the inner court of the house (*bayt*) of the Lord; and behold, at the door of the temple (*hekal*) of the Lord, between the porch and the altar, were about twenty-five men, with their backs to the temple (*hekal*) of the Lord, and their faces *toward the east* (*qedmah*), worshiping the sun *toward the east* (*qedmah*)." The following instance of *hekal* does not occur until 41:1: "Then he brought me to the temple (*hekal*), and measured the jambs: six cubits was the breadth [of the jambs] on one side and six cubits was the breadth [of the jambs] on the other side, the breadth of the tent."[2] Later we hear the following:

> Afterward he brought me to the gate, the gate facing east (*haqqadim*; from the same root as *qedmah*). And behold, the glory of the God of Israel came from the east (*haqqadim*); and the sound of his coming was like the sound of many waters; and the earth shone with his glory. And the vision I saw was like the vision

---

[2] This is the literal translation of the Hebrew. RSV has "Then he brought me to the nave, and measured the jambs; on each side six cubits was the breadth of the jambs." RSV insists, unwarrantedly, to translate all instances of *hekal* into "nave," which is the main central open area inside the temple. By translating once *bayt* as "nave" (41:17) RSV seals its bias toward full equivalence between *bayt* and *hekal*, which I discuss in detail below.

The New Jerusalem

which I had seen when he came to destroy the city, and like the vision which I had seen by the river Chebar; and I fell upon my face. As the glory of the Lord entered the temple (*bayt*; house) by the gate facing east (*haqqadim*), the Spirit lifted me up, and brought me into the inner court; and behold, the glory of the Lord filled the temple (*bayt*). (43:1-5)

It is apparent that the repetition of "toward the east" in 8:16 is intended to underscore the sin of the twenty-five men who were turning their back to God in his temple in order to worship the sun that "comes from the east." This was done in view of 43:1-5 when God will fool everybody by coming himself from the east in order to reside in his new temple that will replace the one he destroyed as punishment for the abominations of the Jerusalemites (8:15). One can then see the functionality of the repeated and thus intended use of *hekal* in 8:16. Such was done in view of 41:1 where one hears of the description of the temple into which the glory of the God of Israel is about to enter (43:4).

Only then will one understand the strange and apparently superfluous phrase "the breadth of the tent (*'ohel*)" at the end of 41:1. This phrase is actually dropped in the LXX and in both RSV and JB. We have here the only instance of *'ohel* in Ezekiel; however, that root is found in combination in the names Oholah and Oholibah in chapter 23. There the names were coined to remind Samaria and Jerusalem that they should have remained cognizant of their humble origin and should not have been impressed with the beauty of the mighty Assyrians and Babylonians and their deities. Put otherwise, the kings of Israel and Judah should have acted as shepherds and tent dwellers, rather than as possessive kings (ch.34:2-10). That is why the new face of the God who is coming to the new temple is that of a shepherd (34:12, 15). Consequently his new temple will look like a "humble" tent in its breadth (41:1).[3]

In spite of the fact that in 8:16 we hear of both "the house (*bayt*) of the Lord" and "the temple (*hekal*) of the Lord" to speak of the same "abode," these two Hebrew nouns have quite different trajectories in Ezekiel. The understanding of their dissimilar odysseys is essential in order to capture the movement of the Ezekelian story. Unfortunately this reality is not only concealed, but actually completely distorted in RSV, which insists, without any textual basis, on reflecting the premise of contemporary Judeo-Christian socio-political "Zionism." RSV does not differentiate between the "ground" (*'adamah*) and the "earth" (*'ereṣ*), thus making of both real estate, that is, a piece of "land property." More so, it systematically eschews the matter of God's abode by the translation of *bayt* into "temple" in chapters 40-48, with the exception of "the house of Israel"[4] and in the unique instance of an individual's "house(hold)" (44:30). Even the Jerusalem Bible that is usually a closer and more accurate translation falls prey to this same presupposition. Throughout Ezekiel we find repeatedly that God's plan aims at transforming the *'ereṣ* into an *'adamah*, and the cities with their stone structures into a pasture where his "flock" would be preserved solely under his protection. Since the temple as *hekal* is the main structure of any city, it stands to reason to expect that, after its destruction under God's express command, a *bayt* (house[hold]) would be raised or, rather, that *be(y)t*[5] *yisrael* (the house[hold] of Israel) would be made *truly* into a "house(hold)," a "family" of

---

[3] In RSV the phrase "the breadth of the tent" is omitted after "the breadth of the jambs."
[4] 40:4; 43:7, 10; 44:6, 12, 22; 45:6, 8, 17.
[5] This is the form *bayt* takes when followed by a noun complement.

"sons and daughters" to God their "father." Such corresponds fully to the imagery of pasture that includes *one* flock of many sheep as well as *one* shepherd whose abode is a tent, as in Ezekiel 34. We find the same metaphor of a shepherd's family in Isaiah:

> Sing, O barren one, who did not bear; break forth into singing and cry aloud, you who have not been in travail! For the *children* of the desolate one will be more than the *children* of her that is *married*, says the Lord. Enlarge the place of your *tent*, and let the *curtains* of your habitations be stretched out; hold not back, lengthen your *cords* and strengthen your *stakes*. For you will spread abroad to the right and to the left, and your *descendants* (*zera'*; seed, progeny) will possess the nations and will people the desolate cities. Fear not, for you will not be ashamed; be not confounded, for you will not be put to shame; for you will forget the shame of your youth, and the reproach of your widowhood you will remember no more.[6] For your Maker is your *husband*, the Lord of hosts is his name; and the Holy One of Israel is your Redeemer, the God of the whole earth he is called. For the Lord has called you like a *wife* forsaken and grieved in spirit, like a *wife* of youth when she is cast off, says your God. For a brief moment I forsook you, but with great compassion I will gather you. In overflowing wrath for a moment I hid my face from you, but with everlasting love I will have compassion on you, says the Lord, your Redeemer. (54:1-8)

In order for me to make my point I need to ask my readers' indulgence to follow my argument on the basis of the original where the count of the instances of *bayt* and *hekal* is a far cry from their count in RSV; I should invite any reader that has an edition of the original KJV—and not the NKJV (the New King

---

[6] Notice the Ezekelian terminology of "shame" and "reproach."

James Version)[7]—to use it in order to follow more closely my presentation. Let me first remind my readers of the radical difference between the two terms. Technically speaking, *hekal* is a structure, something erected out of similar smaller or larger pieces of comparatively hard material (usually brick or stone); that is why it describes perfectly the two central structures of any major city: the temple and the palace; in Hebrew the same noun *hekal* refers to either.[8] Thus it necessarily implies an edifice that is *built* "by the hand of man." A household is, scripturally speaking, a gift from God since it is his express blessing that is behind procreation through "seed" (Gen 1:22, 28). Listen to the following conversation between David and the Lord though Nathan:

> Now when the king dwelt in his house, and the Lord had given him rest from all his enemies round about, the king said to Nathan the prophet, "See now, I dwell in a house of cedar, but the ark of God dwells in a *tent*." And Nathan said to the king, "Go, do all that is in your heart; for the Lord is with you." But that same night the word of the Lord came to Nathan, "Go and tell my servant David, 'Thus says the Lord: Would you build me a house to dwell in? I have not dwelt in a house since the day I brought up the people of Israel from Egypt to this day, but I have been moving about in a *tent* for my dwelling. In all places where I have moved with all the people of Israel, did I speak a word with any of the judges of Israel, whom I commanded to *shepherd* my people

---

[7] Since this revised translation was done in the United States of America at the end of the 1970's and beginning of the 80's, it fully reflects socio-political Zionism by following the path of RSV in translating all the occurrences of *bayt*, when referring to the divine abode, into "temple" instead of "house" in Ezek 40-48. In so doing it betrays the original "spirit" of its predecessor the KJV.

[8] In Arabic *haykal* (of the exact same consonantal root *hykl* as the Hebrew *he[y]kal*) is used to speak of the basic (cement or steel) structure of a building before it is "finished." That is also why the skeleton is known as *haykal 'aṭhmiy* (bony [bone] structure).

Israel, saying, Why have you not built me a house of cedar?' Now therefore thus you shall say to my servant David, 'Thus says the Lord of hosts, I took you from the pasture (*naweh*), from following the *sheep* (*ṣo'n*; flock), that you should be *prince* (*nagid*) over my people Israel; and I have been with you wherever you went, and have cut off all your enemies from before you; and I will make for you a great name, like the name of the great ones of the earth. And I will appoint a place for my people Israel, and will plant them, that they may dwell in their own place, and be disturbed no more; and violent men shall afflict them no more, as formerly, from the time that I appointed judges over my people Israel; and I will give you rest from all your enemies. Moreover the Lord declares to you that the Lord will make you a house. When your days are fulfilled and you lie down with your fathers, I will raise up your offspring after you, who shall come forth from your body, and I will establish his kingdom. He shall build a house for my name, and I will establish the throne of his kingdom for ever.'" (2 Sam 7:1-13)[9]

This phraseology is strikingly similar to that found in Ezekiel. So, if God conceded that Solomon, David's offspring, would build him a temple, it did not mean that he wanted, let alone needed, such. Consequently, after having himself destroyed the temple (Ezek 4) and having taken over as King and Shepherd (ch.34), he would not possibly consider building a temple himself. Notice how, in Ezekiel, there is no mention at all of any erection of the "house" that the glory of the Lord entered (43:4) in spite of the express mention of the earlier destruction of the city (v.3).[10]

---

[9] Notice how David wants to "build" (*banah*) a house for the Lord whereas the Lord vouches to "make" (*'aśah*) a house for David, the verb that occurs frequently in Genesis 1-2 (1:28, 31; 2:2 [twice],

[10] Supplying information from other books, such as Ezra and Nehemiah, as is done in classical exegesis and theology, is a complete disregard to the message of a book that is

Keeping all that in mind, then one can see the logic behind Ezekiel's handling of *bayt* and *hekal* in his story. The very short odyssey of *hekal* is so to speak squeezed into the much more extensive odyssey of *bayt* and is done in such a way that ultimately *hekal* is eliminated from the picture, thus reflecting literally its "destruction" into total oblivion. The occurrences of *hekal* are confined to 8:16 and chapters 41-42 (41:1, 4, 15, 21, 23, 25; 42:8). Although *hekal* is mentioned twice in 8:16, still it appears in the verse secondarily to *bayt* which therefore "steals the show," especially in view of the fact that it appeared two verses earlier:

> Then he brought me to the entrance of the north gate of the house (*bayt*) of the Lord; and behold, there sat women weeping for Tammuz. Then he said to me, "Have you seen this, O son of man? You will see still greater abominations than these." And he brought me into the inner court of the house (*bayt*) of the Lord; and behold, at the door of the temple (*hekal*) of the Lord, between the porch and the altar, were about twenty-five men, with their backs to the temple (*hekal*) of the Lord, and their faces toward the east, worshiping the sun toward the east. (8:14-16)

Not only that, but the way these verses are crafted, *bayt* reflects a positive connotation, whereas *hekal* suggests something negative: *bayt* is used in conjunction with the introduction of God's prophet as witness on his behalf, whereas *hekal* is linked to the blasphemous actions of the elders. Put otherwise, it is their "abominations" that were transforming the Lord's "house" into a mere stone structure the like of the "temples" of Tammuz and

---

embedded in the text itself of that book. If Ezekiel *chose* to look at Babylon in a unique way, then he should be granted to do the same with any other subject matter and be understood on its own grounds.

the sun. It is this *hekal* that the Lord will leave to its own demise. The literary counterpart to this demise can be seen in that *hekal* appears twice in 8:16 only to be relegated to oblivion until chapter 41 where it reappears profusely (41:1, 4, 15, 21, 23, 25; 42:8). However, this impressive epiphany is misleading. Indeed, not only are the seven instances of *hekal* in chapters 41-42 "overrun" by the seventeen occurrences of *bayt*,[11] but also *hekal* vanishes completely after 42:8. Moreover, just as was the case in 8:14-16, *bayt* steals the show in Ezekiel 40-48 since it is found seven times in chapter 40 (vv.5, 8, 9, 43,[12] 45, 47, 48) before *hekal* occurs for the first time in 41:1. Notice also the high frequency of *bayt* (40:43, 45, 47, 48) just before 41:1 which is only two verses removed from 40:48, thus making sure that the hearer is already programmed to view God's new abode as a "house" rather than a stone structure built by man.

The ultimate corroboration for this reading can be found in the passage concerning the coming of the divine glory into the "house" and its consequences, which is worth quoting in its entirety:

> Afterward he brought me to the gate, the gate facing east. And behold, the glory of the God of Israel came from the east; and the sound of his coming was like the sound of many waters; and the earth shone with his glory. And the vision I saw was like the vision which I had seen when he came to destroy the city, and like the vision which I had seen by the river Chebar; and I fell upon my face. As the glory of the Lord entered the *bayt* by the gate facing east, the Spirit lifted me up, and brought me into the inner court; and behold, the glory of the Lord filled the *bayt*. While the man was standing beside me, I heard one speaking to me out of the

---

[11] 41:5 (twice), 6 (twice), 7 (thrice), 8, 9 (twice), 10, 13, 14, 17, 19, 26; 42:15.
[12] RSV translates *babbayt* (in the house) as "within."

bayt; and he said to me, "Son of man, this is the place of my throne and the place of the soles of my feet, where I will *dwell* (*'eškon*) *there* (*šam*)[13] *in the midst* of the people of Israel *for ever*. And the house of Israel shall no more defile my holy name, neither they, nor their kings, by their harlotry, and by the dead bodies of their kings, by setting their threshold by my threshold and their doorposts beside my doorposts, with only a wall between me and them. They have defiled my holy name by their abominations which they have committed, so I have consumed them in my anger. Now let them put away their idolatry and the dead bodies of their kings far from me, and I will *dwell in their midst for ever*. And you, son of man, *relay in words* (*hagged*)[14] to the *bayt* of Israel the *bayt* and its appearance and plan, that they may be ashamed of their iniquities. And if they are ashamed of all that they have done, *make known*[15] to them the *bayt*, its arrangement, its exits and its entrances, and its whole form, and all its statutes (*ḥuqqot*)[16] and *all its forms*[17] and all its laws; and write it down in their sight, so that they may observe *its whole form*[18] and all statutes (*ḥuqqot*)[19] and do[20] them. This is the law of the *bayt*: the whole territory round about upon the top of the mountain shall be most holy. Behold, this is the law of the *bayt*. (43:1-12)

The glory of the Lord comes from Babylon, which lies in the east, to enter into the *bayt*, not the *hekal* (v.4), in order to "dwell *there* in the midst of the people forever" (v.7a; see also v.9b). This phrase brings to mind both the ends of chapter 37 and 48.

---

[13] Omitted by RSV.
[14] RSV has "describe."
[15] RSV supplies the verb "portray" and thus doubles up the verb *hodaʿ* (make known) into "portray" and "make known."
[16] RSV has "ordinances."
[17] Omitted in RSV.
[18] RSV has "all its laws."
[19] RSV has "ordinances."
[20] RSV has "perform."

In spite of the fact that the Lord's sanctuary (*miqdaš*) will be "in the midst of them," nevertheless this abode is actually a dwelling place (*miškan*; from the same root *škn* as *'eškon*)[21] similar to a tent as we hear in 41:1.[22] On the other hand, the adverb "there" (*šam*) looks ahead to the end of the book where, in the midst of the "ground of Israel" as pasture, there will be only one city whose name is "the Lord is there (*šammah*)" (48:35b). A few verses before this we hear of the "sanctuary (*miqdaš*) of the house (*bayt*)" (v.21). A necessary corollary of such is that no other stone building (*hekal*) will be tolerated, including the kingly palace, the other *hekal* besides the temple, let alone majestic kingly mausoleums: "And the house of Israel shall no more defile my holy name, neither they, nor their kings, by their harlotry, and by the dead bodies of their kings, by setting their threshold by my threshold and their doorposts beside my doorposts, with only a wall between me and them." (43:7b-8a)

More importantly, though, given that this reality is metaphoric, and thus neither visible nor palpable, it could not but be "relayed verbally" by Ezekiel (*hagged*). Furthermore this "telling" of the Lord's *bayt* is specifically addressed to the *bayt* of Israel "that they may be ashamed of their iniquities" (43:10) and "abominations" with which "they defiled my holy name" (v.8b). Put otherwise, being a "tent," the Lord's dwelling place (*bayt*) will prove to be a "household" (*bayt*) for Israel where the children will be bound by the "rules of the house." This in turn explains the vocabulary, strange at first hearing, of vv.11-12.

The overlapping between "forms" and "statutes," both equally to *be done*, bears out that what Ezekiel is conveying is not so

---

[21] See my discussion of 37:26-28 on pp.311-2.
[22] See my discussion of this verse above.

much architectural "measures," but rather household "measures,"[23] which are nothing other than the Lord's "law." The centrality of the Law can be seen in that it is mentioned (1) as the conclusion of the passage, and (2) twice for underscoring, the second instance being introduced with "behold" in order to inescapably draw the hearer's attention to the seriousness of the matter. In other words, Ezekiel was "building" God's "house(hold)" not so much "with his hands" but through the utterance of the written words that lay in his stomach (3:3). That is precisely why he was ordered by God himself, the author of the original scroll (2:9-10) to *write down* his *oral* words so that they become *aural* throughout the ages through the reading aloud of the Book of Ezekiel during the gatherings at the divine "tent." It is Ezekiel's lead that ends as the blue print for the Mosaic story. Indeed, upon his decent from the mountain where he beheld the divine "abode," Moses did not bring down architectural measures, but rather the "measures" of the "tent of meeting" (*'ohel mo'ed*) that housed the divine "law" (*torah*).[24]

The Water of Life

Deuteronomy 8:3 casts the Law as the "bread of life." Ezekiel 47:1-12 casts "the law of the house" (43:12) as the "water of life." The water that flows out of the house (47:1-2) slowly expands (vv.3-5a) into "a river that could not be passed through" (v.5b). That river is so mighty that its waters push into the sea and render fresh the sea water (vv.8-9), leaving however swamps and marshes untouched to secure the production of salt, essential for life (v.11). Indeed, that river's main purpose is to sustain all kinds of life on earth. Trees grow on its banks (v.7), fish fill both

---

[23] See earlier my comments on 20:37.
[24] All the apostle to the Gentiles had to do was to implement this same approach among his churches.

its waters and the sea water (vv.9-10). Fishermen are spread between Engedi and Eneglaim (v.10a). Given that the Hebrew *'en gedi* means "the fountain of the kid" and *'en 'eglaym* "the fountain of the two calves," these two nouns ostensibly stand for a region where there is enough water to support plenty of flock and cattle. The passage concludes with the following statement: "And on the banks, on both sides of the river, there will grow all kinds of trees for food. Their leaves will not wither nor their fruit fail, but they will bear fresh fruit every month, because the water for them flows from the sanctuary. Their fruit will be for food, and their leaves for healing." (v.12) What is striking is that it revisits an earlier statement concerning the trees on both banks in v.7. The importance of the trees is that they represent vegetative life that supports animal life (Gen 1:29-30). There are two extra features of Ezekiel 47:12 that are functional within the Book of Ezekiel. First, the reason behind such fruitfulness is that "the water for them flows from the sanctuary" that is the place of God's residence among his people (37:26, 28). Secondly, not only "the fruit of the trees will be for food" but also "their leaves for healing." The idea of healing is very important since it was previously found in 34:4: "The weak [sheep] you have not strengthened, the sick you have not healed, the crippled you have not bound up, the strayed you have not brought back, the lost you have not sought, and with force and harshness you have ruled them." The closeness between 47:12 and 34:4 is sealed in the fact that the root *rapha'* (heal) is encountered in Ezekiel only in 34:4 and 47:8, 9, 11, 12.[25] The connection is even closer than meets the ear since "the land for inheritance among the twelve tribes of Israel" (47:13) is going to be an open pasture with no

---

[25] In 47:8, 9, 11 RSV translates the original Hebrew *niph'al* (passive) form of the verb *rapha'*, literally "be healed," into "become fresh."

cities (47:13-48:29) except for the metaphorical city "the Lord is there" (48:30-35). Its inhabitants will be the sheep of chapter 34.

Just as Ezekiel 34 was a reversal of the story of David and his dynasty—the first David was a shepherd who sought kingship while the new David shall reign as shepherd (34:23-24; see also 37:24-25)—the new land and its allotment among the tribes will be a reversal of what happened in the Book of Joshua. Joshua conquered the land by destroying cities, conquering others, and building new ones, which was the beginning of a sad odyssey that ended with the destruction of the capital cities of Samaria (2 Kg 17) and Jerusalem (ch.25) due to the disobedience of the Law by the king and the people (ch.22). The new land announced by Ezekiel will be an open pasture, without cities, around the Lord who will rule through his law, "the law of the (new) house" (Ezek 43:12) that will be upheld by the priests. Indeed, whereas Jerusalem was punished because "the law perishes from the priest" (7:26), in the Ezekelian Jerusalem "They [the Levitical priests, the sons of Zadok, who kept the charge of my sanctuary when the people of Israel went astray from me][26] shall teach my people the difference between the holy and the common, and show them how to distinguish between the unclean and the clean. In a controversy they shall act as judges, and they shall judge it according to my judgments. They shall keep my laws and my statutes in all my appointed feasts, and they shall keep my sabbaths holy" (44:23-24). That is why (1) the "healing" will flow ultimately from God's new sanctuary: "And on the banks, on both sides of the river, there will grow all kinds of trees for food. Their leaves will not wither nor their fruit fail, but they will bear fresh fruit every month, because the water for them flows from the sanctuary. Their fruit will be for food, and their

---

[26] 44:15.

leaves for healing" (47:12); and (2) God's sanctuary will actually be a "dwelling place" resembling a shepherd's abode (37:26-28).[27] In the Book of Revelation, the Ezekiel-like seer John, who is the disciple of the eschatological "son of man" Jesus, will use both metaphors of dwelling place and of healing river to include the nations:

> And they [those who had conquered the beast and its image and the number of its] sing the song of Moses, the servant of God, and the song of the Lamb, saying, "Great and wonderful are thy deeds, O Lord God the Almighty! Just and true are thy ways, O King of the ages! Who shall not fear and glorify thy name, O Lord? For thou alone art holy. All *nations* (*ethnē*) shall come and worship thee, for thy judgments have been revealed." After this I looked, and the temple of the *tent* (*skēnē*)[28] of witness in heaven was opened, (15:3-5)

> And I saw the holy city, new Jerusalem, coming down out of heaven from God, prepared as a bride adorned for her husband; and I heard a loud voice from the throne saying, "Behold, the dwelling (*skēnē*; tent) of God is with men. He will dwell (*skēnōsei*; will dwell as in a tent) with them, and they shall be his *peoples*[29] (*laoi*), and God himself will be with them." (21:2-3)

> Then he showed me the river of the water of life, bright as crystal, flowing from the throne of God and of the Lamb through the middle of the street of the city; also, on either side of the river, the tree of life with its twelve kinds of fruit, yielding its fruit each month; and the leaves of the tree were for the healing of the *nations* (*ethnē*). (22:1-2)

---

[27] See my comments on those verses on pp.311-2.
[28] From the same root as the Hebrew *miškan* (dwelling place).
[29] RSV has "people."

Further Reading

Commentaries and Studies

Allen, L. C. *Ezekiel 1-19*. Word Biblical Commentary 28. Dallas: Word Books, 1994.

Allen, L. C. *Ezekiel 20-48*. Word Biblical Commentary 29. Dallas: Word Books, 1990.

Betts, T. J. *Ezekiel the Priest: A Custodian of Tôrâ*. Studies in Biblical Literature, 74. New York/Washington: P. Lang, 2005.

Block, D. I. *The Book of Ezekiel: Chapters 1-24*. Grand Rapids MI/ Cambridge UK: Eerdmanns, 1997.

Block, D. I. *The Book of Ezekiel: Chapters 25-48*. Grand Rapids MI/ Cambridge UK: Eerdmanns, 1997.

Clements, R. E. *Ezekiel*. Westminster Bible Companion. Louisville, KY: Westminster John Knox, 1996.

Corral, M. A. *Ezekiel's Oracles against Tyre: Historical Reality and Motivations*. Bibliotheca Orientalia 46. Rome: Biblical Institute, 2002.

Crane, A. S. *Israel's Restoration: A Textual-Comparative Exploration of Ezekiel 36-39*. Vetus Testamentum Supplementary Series 122. Leiden/Boston: Brill, 2008.

Duguid, I. M. *Ezekiel & the Leaders of Israel*. Vetus Testamentum Supplementary Series 56. Leiden/Boston: Brill, 1994.

Greenberg, M. *Ezekiel 1-20*. A New Translation with Introduction and Commentary. Anchor Bible. New York: Doubleday, 1983.

Greenberg, M. *Ezekiel 21-37*. A New Translation with Introduction and Commentary. Anchor Bible. New York: Doubleday, 1995.

Hummel, H. D. *Ezekiel 1-20*. Concordia Commentary. Saint Louis: Concordia Publishing House, 2006.

Hummel, H. D. *Ezekiel 21-48*. Concordia Commentary. Saint Louis: Concordia Publishing House, 2007.

Joyce, P. *Ezekiel: A Commentary*. Library of Old Testament Studies, 482. New York/London: T & T Clark, 2007.

Lyons, M. A. *From Law to Prophecy: Ezekiel's Use of the Holiness Code*. Library of Studies, 507. New York/London: T & T Clark, 2009.

Odell, M. S. and Strong, J. T. (eds.) *The Book of Ezekiel. Theological and Anthropological Perspectives*. Atlanta: Society of Biblical Literature, 2000.

Olley, J. W. *Ezekiel: A Commentary Based on Iezekiēl in Codex Vaticanus*. Septuagint Commentary Series. Leiden-Boston: Brill, 2009.

Stevenson, K. R. *Vision of Transformation: The Territorial Rhetoric of Ezekiel 40-48*. Atlanta: Scholars, 1996.

Tooman, W.-A. and Lyons M. A. (eds.) *Transforming Visions. Transformations of Text, Tradition and Theology in Ezekiel*. Princeton Theological Monograph Series 127. Eugene, OR: Wipf & Stock, 2010.

Tuell, S. *Ezekiel*. New International Biblical Commentary: Old Testament Series. Peabody, MA: Hendrickson, 2009.

Wong K. L. *The Idea of Retribution in the Book of Ezekiel*. Vetus Testamentum Supplementary Series 87. Leiden/Boston: Brill, 2000.

Zimmerli, W. *Ezekiel 1: A Commentary on the Book of the Prophet Ezekiel, Chapters 1-24*. Hermeneia. Philadelphia: Fortress Press, 1979.

Zimmerli, W. *Ezekiel 2: A Commentary on the Book of the Prophet Ezekiel, Chapters 25-48*. Hermeneia. Philadelphia: Fortress Press, 1983.

Further Reading 351

Articles

Adams, S. L. "Ezekiel 34:11-19." *Interpretation* 62 (2008) 304-6.

Barriocanal Gómez J. L. "Ez 20: Una historia distinta de Israel." *Burgense* 44 (20037) 9-43.

Boyle, B. "The Figure of the *Nasi'* in Ezekiel's Vision of the New Temple (*Ezekiel* 40-48)." *Australian Biblical Review* 58 (2010) 1-16.

Bogaert, P.-M. "Le Lieu de la Gloire dans le livre d'Ezechiel et dans les Chroniques. De l'arche au char." *Revue Theologique de Louvain* 26 (1995) 281-98.

Davidson, R. M. "The Chiastic Literary Structure of the Book of Ezekiel" in Merling D. (ed.) *To Understand the Scriptures: Essays in Honor of William H. Shea.* Berrien Springs, MI (1997)

Day, P. L "Adulterous Jerusalem's imagined demise: death of a metaphor in Ezekiel xvi." *Vetus Testamentum* 50 (2000) 285-309.

Ganzel, T. "The Defilement and Desecration of the Temple in Ezekiel." *Biblica* 89 (2008) 369-79.

Hahn, S. W. and Bergsma J. S. "What Laws Were 'Not Good'? A Canonical Approach to the Theological Problem of Ezekiel 20:25-26." *Journal of Biblical Literature* 123 (2004) 201-18.

Harland, P. J. "What Kind of 'Violence' in Ezekiel 22?" *Expository Times* 108 (1996) 111-14.

Holladay, W. L. "Has Ezekiel Known Jeremiah Personally?" *Catholic Biblical Quarterly* 63 (2001) 31-34.

Hossfeld, F-L. "Ezechiel und sein Buch." *Bibel und Kirche* 60 (2005) 148-52.

Kelle, B. E. "Dealing with the Trauma of Defeat: The Rhetoric of the Devastation and Rejuvenation of Nature in Ezekiel." *Journal of Biblical Literature* 128 (2009) 469-90.

Lang, B. "Ezechiel: Ort, Zeit und Botschaft der Propheten." *Bibel und Kirche* 60 (2005) 130-35.

Launderville, D. "Ezekiel's Cherub: A Promising Symbol or a Dangerous Idol." *Catholic Biblical Quarterly* 65 (2003) 165-83.

Launderville, D. "Ezekiel's Throne-Chariot Vision: Spiritualizing the Model of Divine Royal Rule." *Catholic Biblical Quarterly* 66 (2004) 361-77.

Leicht, B. "Ich bin ein Mannzeichen für euch. Priester, Prophet, Performance Künstler." *Bibel und Kirche* 60 (2005) 145-47.

Lyons M. A. "Marking Innerbiblical Allusion in the Book of Ezekiel." *Biblica* 88 (2007) 245-50.

McKeating, H. "Ezekiel the 'Prophet like Moses'?" *Journal for the Study of the Old Testament* 61 (1994) 97-109.

Nielsen, K. "Ezekiel's Visionary Call as Prologue: From Complexity and Changeability to Order and Stability." *Journal for the Study of the Old Testament* 33 (2008) 99-114.

Odell, M. S. "You Are What You Eat: Ezekiel and the Scroll." *Journal of Biblical Literature* 117 (1998) 229-48.

Odell, M. S. "The City of Hamonah in Ezekiel 39:11-16: The Tumultuous City of Jerusalem." *Catholic Biblical Quarterly* 56 (1994) 479-89.

Phinney D. N. "The Prophetic Objection in Ezekiel IV 14 and Its Relation to Ezekiel's Call." *Vetus Testamentum* 55 (2005) 75-88.

Poser, R. "'In der ruach liegt die Kraft.' Zur Bedeutung der Geisteskraft im Buch Ezechiel." *Bibel und Kirche* 60 (2005) 162-66.

Prinsloo, G. T. M. "Lions and Vines: The Imagery of Ezekiel 19 in the Light of Ancient Near-Eastern Descriptions and Depictions." *Old Testament Essays* 12 (1999) 339-69.

Railton, N. M. "God and Magog: the History of a Symbol." *The Evangelical Quarterly* 75 (2003) 23-43.

Schöfflin, K. "The Composition of Metaphorical Oracles in the Book of Ezekiel." *Vetus Testamentum* 55 (2005) 101-20.

Tuell S. "Ezekiel 40-42 as Verbal Icon." *Catholic Biblical Quarterly* 58 (1996) 649-64.

Tuell, S. "Should Ezekiel go to Rehab? The Method of Ezekiel's Madness 5." *Perspectives in Religious Studies* 36 (2009) 289-302.

Wendland, E. R. "Scattred Bones But a Single Stick: A Rhetorical-Stylistic Overview of the Gospel in Ezekiel 37." *Old Testament Essays* 12 (1999) 149-72.

Wendland, E. R. "'Can These Bones Live Again?' A Rhetoric of the Gospel in Ezekiel 33-37, Part I." *Andrews University Seminary Studies* 39 (2001) 85-100.

Wendland, E. R. "'Can These Bones Live Again?' A Rhetoric of the Gospel in Ezekiel 33-37, Part II." *Andrews University Seminary Studies* 39 (2001) 241-72.

Wendland, E. "Translating Ezekiel's Vision of the Dry Bones--Visually." *The Bible Translator* 56 (2005) 76-87.

Wong K. L. "Profanation/Sanctification and the Past, Present and Future of Israel in the Book of Ezekiel." *Journal for the Study of the Old Testament* 28 (2003) 210-39.

www.ingramcontent.com/pod-product-compliance
Lightning Source LLC
Chambersburg PA
CBHW022102150426
43195CB00008B/232